→ Contemporary Art

↓

from Studio to Situation

edited by Claire Doherty

Edited by Claire Doherty
Produced by Catherine Grant
Designed by John and Orna Designs
Biographical assistance by Lucy Steeds
Transcription by DeeWP and Audiosec;
Donald Ekins, Arnolfini; Jaqui Sutton
Translation by Helen Bubb, UWE

Black Dog Publishing Limited
Unit 4.4 Tea Building
56 Shoreditch High Street
London E1 6JJ

Tel: +44 (0)20 7613 1922
Fax: +44 (0)20 7613 1944
Email: info@bdp.demon.co.uk

www.bdpworld.com

British Library Cataloguing-in-
Publication Data.

A catalogue record for this book is
available from the British Library.

ISBN 1 904772 06 4

Cover image: Jimmie Durham, *A Tragic
Story of the Little Mouse Girl in Yakutia*

→ Contemporary Art

Preface

Critical context

In conversation

Case studies

↓

from Studio to Situation

edited by Claire Doherty

Black Dog Publishing

Acknowledgements

I am extremely grateful to the artists, curators and academics who contributed to the success of the first *Situations* lecture series, and who have subsequently given valuable time and thought to this publication. I would also like to extend my thanks to the following individuals and organisations for their considerable support for the *Situations* programme: The Bristol School of Fine Art, Media and Design, University of the West of England (in particular Professor Paul Gough, Mark Dunhill, the Fine Arts staff, Angela Cooper and Sue Matheron at the Projects Office); Arnolfini; Carolyn Black, Projects Assistant; Carina Lopes and Ruth Harvey; Picture This; Sandie Macrae, R O O M; Jonathan Banks and Jon Brett, Bristol City Council; Mariam Sharp, Arts Council of England South West; Mary Jane Jacob and Ruby.

Claire Doherty

This publication was supported financially through the generous support of the following organisations: University of the West of England, Bristol; Arnolfini; the Arts Council of England, the Arts and Humanities Research Board (AHRB) and the Institut français du Royaume-Uni.

situations · UWE BRISTOL University of the West of England · ARNOLFINI · ARTS COUNCIL ENGLAND · A · H · R · B arts and humanities research board · institut français

Preface

Situations is a programme of activity devised to investigate the significance of context in the commissioning and production of contemporary art works. The project began in 2001 when Arnolfini invited Claire Doherty to research opportunities for a scattered-site art project in Bristol. Appointed Research Fellow in Fine Art at the University of the West of England in 2003, Claire has developed the resulting programme as one of the primary components of the University's research into contextual fine art practices, forming a unique alliance between UWE and Arnolfini.

Situations seeks to create a distinctive network of debates and projects, radiating from its Bristol base across the south-west region, nationally and internationally, informing the ways in which art is commissioned and made. It is led by the University of the West of England in association with Arnolfini and other partners including Bristol City Council and Picture This. By autumn 2005, the programme will have included public lectures, a two-day conference, publications, artists' laboratory and informal workshops as well as the commissioning of eight new artists' projects in Bristol.

This publication emerges from the lecture series that took place between October 2003 and March 2004. Attracting some 2000 audience members and 17 international speakers, this series formed part of Arnolfini's *Interlude* programme of events while its building was closed to the public for major refurbishment. The lectures offered a broad public, including students and staff at the University, artists, arts practitioners and commissioners, the opportunity to meet and hear from an extraordinary range of speakers, underpinned by a wider research project. This book is derived from transcripts of those lectures and includes additional existing and newly commissioned material and an introduction to the field of enquiry.

The University of the West of England and Arnolfini are pleased to be able to work together on this initiative and would like to thank those who have supported the first lecture series and who continue to support the on-going research programme that constitutes *Situations*.

Caroline Collier
Director, Arnolfini

Professor Paul Gough
Dean of the Bristol School of Art, Media and Design
University of the West of England, Bristol

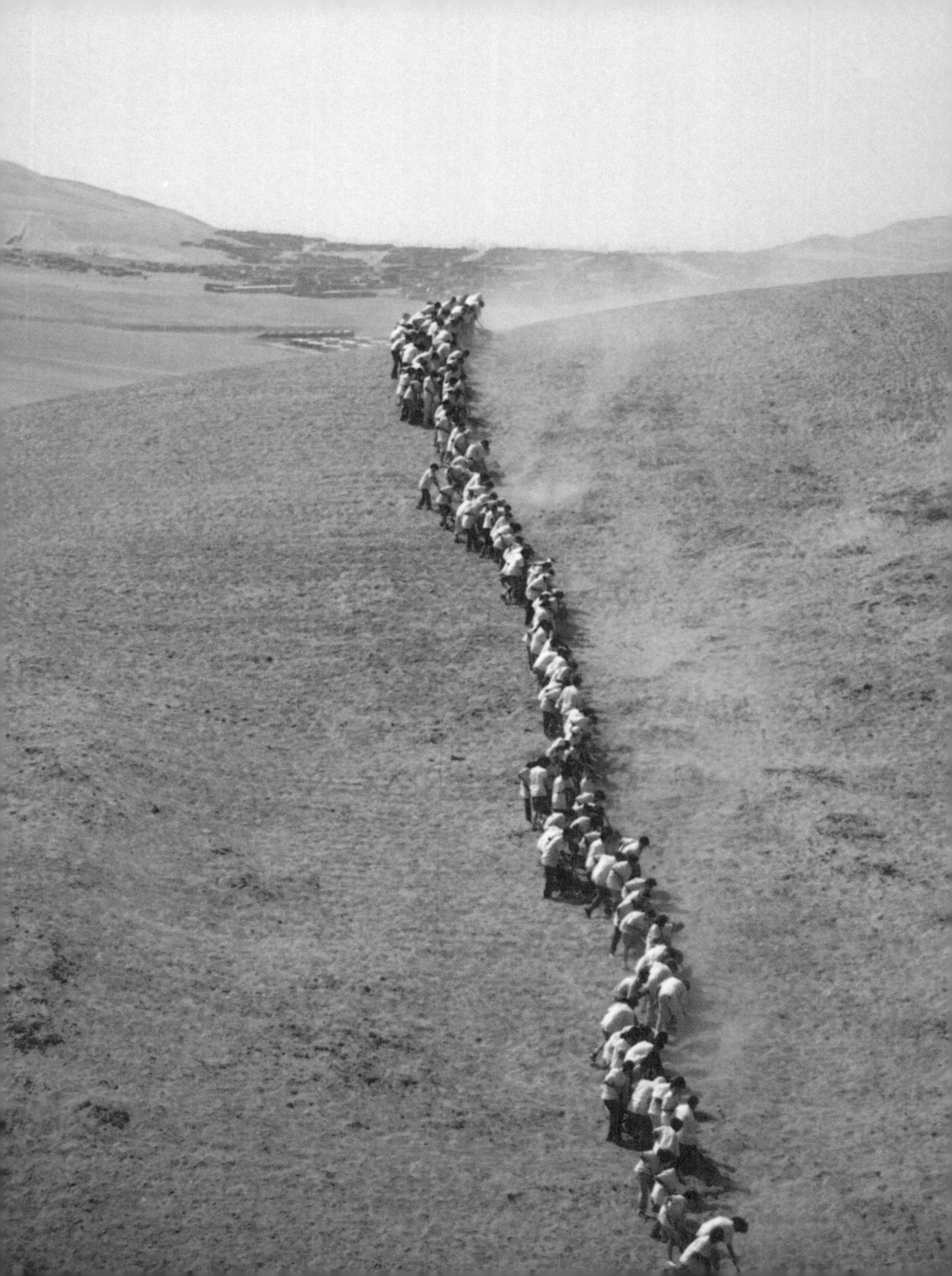

Claire Doherty

The New Situationists

Situations describes the conditions under which many contemporary artworks now come into being. By 'situated', we refer to those artistic practices for which the 'situation' or 'context' is often the starting point. This book does not approach 'context' as purely a discreet category of public art discourse, nor is it concerned with 'contextual practice' as an artistic genre. Rather, it is concerned with 'context' as an impetus, hindrance, inspiration and research subject for the process of making art, whether specified by a curator or commissioner or proposed by the artist. By way of an introduction, this text reflects on the analytical, dialogic and anecdotal evidence in this publication to draw out some of the tendencies and implications of the shift from studio to situation.

On 11 April 2002, 500 volunteers were supplied with shovels and asked to form a single line at the foot of a giant sand dune in Ventanilla, an area outside Lima in Peru. This 'human comb' pushed a quantity of sand a small distance, thereby moving a 16,00 foot long sand dune about four inches from its original position. The act constituted *When Faith Moves Mountains*, a project by artist Francis Alÿs, in collaboration with Rafael Ortega and Cuauhtémoc Medina. It was acclaimed in the international art press as a "biblical performance" and "one of the artistic highlights of 2002".[1] Subsequently the film of the event became an editioned artwork–a 34 minute long, three-channel video installation which was purchased for the Guggenheim Collection in New York later that year.

How do we come to judge such an event, and its documentation, as art? Where does the work start and end? Where does meaning reside–in its execution and/or documentation, in the fledgling idea or in the posthumous circulation of the anecdote? How does such a work operate in, what might be termed, its 'originating' context (Ventanilla) and subsequently its 'displaced' context (an American art collection or curated exhibition)?[2] And what is the difference between the experience of the work's first and second audiences–from the participants in the desert outside Lima to the museum visitors on Fifth Avenue? Furthermore, if this work is not exactly 'site-specific', why not? Though it can be removed from its original context or functional site, unlike Robert Smithson's *Spiral Jetty*, 1970–one of its antecedents–it is, nevertheless, a work made in context, the product of a 'situated', rather than studio-based, artistic practice.[3]

Francis Alÿs describes *When Faith Moves Mountains* as "my attempt to de-romanticise Land art".

> Here, we have attempted to create a kind of Land art for the land-less, and, with the help of hundreds of people and shovels, we created a social allegory. This story is not validated by any physical trace or addition to the landscape. We shall now leave the care of our story to oral tradition.... Only in its repetition and transmission is the work actualised.[4]

When Faith Moves Mountains was Alÿs' contribution to the third *Bienal Iberoamericana de Lima* (Ibero-American Biennale of Lima). Visiting the city for the first time in 2000 with curator Cuauhtémoc Medina, Alÿs was confronted with the turmoil and instability that preceded the collapse of the Fujimori dictatorship:[5]

> I felt that it called for an 'epic response', a '*beau geste*' at once futile and heroic, absurd and urgent. Insinuating a social allegory into those circumstances seemed to me more fitting than engaging in some sculptural exercise.[6]

Alÿs was called upon to make a work that would resonate in a highly charged local context and translate to a global biennale culture. He neither professed to reveal something new to the local inhabitants (his practice as a whole is 'complicit' rather than 'investigative'). Nor did he position his experience as outsider or tourist at the centre of the work.[7] The performance simply effected a near imperceptible "linear geological displacement". Yet, by establishing a shift in the status-quo, by creating a memorable and metaphorical act for (one hopes and imagines) the participants and certainly us, the secondary audience, Alÿs made a work that is embedded in the context of Ventanilla, but which is not simply about Ventanilla, Lima or Peru.

Alÿs is what Miwon Kwon, in her significant study *One Place After Another: Site-Specific Art and Locational Identity*, has identified as one of a burgeoning number of nomadic artists:

> The increasing institutional interest in current site-orientated practices that mobilise the site as a discursive narrative is demanding an intensive physical mobilisation of the artist to create works in various cities throughout the cosmopolitan art world.[8]

And nowhere is this more evident than at the biennale. There are currently over 50 biennales of visual art world-wide including those in Lima, Berlin, Havana, Istanbul, Johannesburg, Gwangju, Liverpool, Lyon, Sydney and Venice, as well as *Manifesta*, the nomadic European biennale, not to mention *Documenta* and *Skulptur Projekte Münster*. This broad biennale culture has emerged from the integration of the festival model and scattered-site international exhibition over the past ten years, through which cultural activity has become allied with economic growth. The public's experience of the biennale phenomenon has developed from viewing to participation, giving rise to a marked shift, in some instances, in the role of the artist from object-maker to service provider.[9] The creative and operational workforce, within or outside existing art institutions in biennale cities, which initiates, produces and sustains this considerable level of artistic public output, have developed a diverse range of curatorial strategies to support the visiting artist, particularly in relation to the creation of new work. Concurrently, off-site commissioning and artist residency programmes have responded to the discernable emphasis on engagement in current artistic practice, by drawing upon the complex discourse of the relationship between artist and place, re-imagining place as a situation, a set of circumstances, geographical location, historical narrative, group of people or social agenda.

When Daniel Buren commented, in the winter of 1970-1971, that, "it is impossible... by definition, to see a work in its place", he was referring to the conventional appreciation of the studio as primary site of meaning, in isolation from the real world.[10] Since Buren first proposed to work *in situ*, we have witnessed the convergence of site-specific, installation, community and public

Previous page:
Francis Alÿs, *Cuando la fé mueve montañas (When faith movesmountains)*, 2002, in collaboration with Cuauhtémoc Medina and Rafael Ortega. Performance view, Lima. Peru, 11 April 2002. Courtesy the artist and Lisson Gallery, London

art, institutional critique and political activism. Miwon Kwon suggests, as artists and cultural theorists have become informed by a broader range of disciplines (including anthropology, sociology, literary criticism, psychology, natural and cultural histories, architecture and urbanism, political theory and philosophy), "so our understanding of site has shifted from a fixed, physical location to somewhere or something constituted through social, economic, cultural and political processes".[11] Given this new mutable notion of site, practitioners, commissioners and critics have become dissatisfied with the expression 'site-specific', submitting a gamut of new terms to describe artworks and projects which deal with the complexities of context–amongst them context-specific, site-oriented, site-responsive and socially engaged.

What distinguishes the situated practices in this publication from the historical premise of site-specificity is the convergence of three key factors: firstly, if as Kwon suggests, "feeling out of place is the cultural symptom of late capitalism's political and social reality", then to be 'situated' is effectively to be displaced.[12] Hence, what emerges through the artworks discussed here is an emphasis on experience as a state of flux which acknowledges place as a shifting and fragmented entity; secondly, as Nicolas Bourriaud suggests in his "Berlin Letter about Relational Aesthetics", a new vocabulary has emerged, "one analogous to Minimal Art and that takes the *socius* as its base".[13] Bourriaud suggests that relational aesthetics operates to elude alienation, the division of labour and the commodification of space which characterises our new "network society". And finally, as cultural experience has become recognised as a primary component of urban regeneration, so the roles of artists have become redefined as mediators, creative thinkers and agitators, leading to increased opportunities for longer-term engagement between an artist and a given group of people, design process or situation.

Despite increasingly sophisticated curatorial appraisals of what place might mean to artists and participants in projects which profess to 'engage', there is still considerable debate about whether projects can or should respond directly to a place, considering the itinerancy of most international artists and the consequential lack of sustained contact with the host city or context.[14] In his essay, "The Artist as Ethnographer", Hal Foster warns that participants are often defined by their habitation of 'elsewhere', acting as the 'other' to the 'ideological patron' of the artist.[15] Furthermore, even if the ethnographic mode of 'rapport' is to be avoided through either a process of complicity or genuine collective decision-making and shared responsibility, how does an artist begin such a process and what are the pitfalls? Given the social and cultural experience of being 'out of place', how is this state of being reflected in the process and final form(s) of works or curatorial activity which respond to given situations?

This publication presents a number of strategies set within a critical context, which by no means comprehensive, are representative of the broad tendencies of situated practice–from the spectacular re-enactment, to the quiet intervention, from remedial collaboration to dialogic, open-ended process.

The groundwork Where to start? What emerges through the interviews and conversations here is a common process of resistance. Though this may not always reveal itself as a process of *dérive,* described by Guy Debord of the Situationist International as, "playful-constructive behaviour and awareness of psycho-geographical effects" in which persons "drop their usual motives for movement and action... and let themselves be drawn by the attractions of the terrain and the encounters that they find there", all artists and collectives here maintain that their status as artists allows them to circumnavigate predictability.[16] Kathrin Böhm states, "As an artist you're non-threatening, because no one expects you to have power". Jeremy Deller suggests, "your role is far more fluid", whilst Jimmie Durham proposes, "I'm not an outsider or an insider and I still have the great privilege to talk." Contrary to Hal Foster's cautionary note, many of these artists resist ethnographic processes of mapping, but rather, introduce themselves through a series of conversations (Böhm, Shaw, Deller), or merge into the daily activities of a city (Wentworth, Dant, Mejor Vida Corp.) or become residents themselves (Oda Projesi, Hirschhorn). They resist the ascribed role of witness, often choosing to research or observe the overlooked (Coley, Dickinson).

Irit Rogoff's critical analysis of the distinction between fieldwork that is done "through a mode of *rapport* [of proximity and a sense of having rapport with the place] and fieldwork that is done through an understanding of one's complicity with the work" is crucial to this process of enquiry. It proposes a strategy for preparing the ground.

When projects occur at the artist's instigation within the context of their own practice, the idea–such as *The Battle of Orgreave* or *The Milgran Re-enactment*–is simple, though the period of research can stretch to years, involving the recruitment of participants, experts and skilled practitioners. In contrast, artists such as Minerva Cuevas or Adam Dant work almost virally within their home territory, using the mechanisms of the media to distribute their 'products' for free. Though *FURTHER Up in the Air* proposed a conventional residency relationship for the 18 invited artists, the groundwork, as Paul Domela observes here, was laid by the artist-organisers, Neville Gabie and Leo Fitzmaurice, who built up a relationship with the community over five years, recognising it as "an unstable transitionary context". Like Oda Projesi, Gabie and Fitzmaurice recognise the residents' involvement as significant to the legacy of the project in the long-term.

The engagement process In many of these projects, process and outcome are marked by social engagement.[17] Maria Lind distinguishes the difference between aspects of participatory practice, using Vienna-based critic Christian

Kravagna's four models: 'working with others', interactive activities, collective action, and participatory practice. What seems to distinguish the types of engagement evident here is whether a dialogical relationship is established. In a significant text on Littoral art, Grant Kester has proposed this as, "that which breaks down the conventional distinction between artist, artwork and audience–a relationship that allows the viewer to 'speak back' to the artist in certain ways, and in which this reply becomes in effect a part of the work itself".[18] It is vital, when reviewing the stated aims and outcomes of such projects, to establish the distinction between those practices which, though they employ a process of complicit engagement, are clearly initiated and ultimately directed by the artist (Hirschhorn, Deller, Coley) and those which, though still often authored by the artist or team, are collaborative–in effect 'social sculpture' (Böhm, Oda Projesi, Shaw).[19] Furthermore, where practices become peripatetic in the social fabric of a city, a distinction should be made between the strategies of the activist (Cuevas) and the trickster (Dant and Durham), though their intentions may be similar–namely to provoke social conscience. It is important to attempt to find a language for engagement, because the gaps between the current rhetoric of engagement and actual experience may lead to confusion about the aims and potential outcomes of a project.[20]

The exhibition and curator Given that these processes of engagement and intervention need interlocutors, as Bourriaud notes, the role of the curator or commissioner as mediator becomes vital. In many cases, such as the partnership between Kunstverein München and Kunstprojekte_Reim for Oda Projesi or Gasworks in the case of Kathrin Böhm and public works, the role of the art institution to initiate, mediate and sustain relationships with participants beyond the project is crucial. Furthermore, as Catherine David explains, new exhibition models are addressing the implications of cross-cultural engagement and representation, many of which are cumulative in process, open-ended and dialogic. The biennale is a natural home for situated practice. It bears a resemblance to a 'circus blowing through town', flouting its propensity for transient encounters, and hence the festival context in which such projects occur lends itself to the situated work as performance, event, screening, re-enactment or workshop. But it is the capacity for the work to morph from one form to another that allows these artists to produce work for the biennale, the art institution and a local context. As practitioners, commissioners, participants and viewers, we need to understand the complex processes of initiation, development and mediation of this work. We need to make the distinctions between the types of engagement that are occurring and the promises that are made. We need to question what levels of support this work needs (information, time, technical resources, distribution mechanisms and personnel). And we need to find a critical language to unravel the implications of this work beyond the specifics of time and place.

[1] See Kate Bush in Lisa Liebmann, "Best of 2002", *Artforum*, December 2002.

[2] *When Faith Moves Mountains* was included in *Somewhere Better Than This Place: Alternative Social Experience in the Spaces of Contemporary Art*, at the Contemporary Art Center, Cincinnati, 31 May-9 November 2003.

[3] See http://www.robertsmithson.com/earthworks/spiral_jetty.htm.

[4] Francis Alÿs, "A thousand words: Francis Alÿs talks about *When Faith Moves Mountains*", *Artforum*, Summer 2002, pp. 108-109.

[5] Alberto Kenyo Fujimori was president of Peru from 1990 to 17 November 2000, when he fled to Japan as allegations of far-reaching corruption in his administration began to emerge. He was subsequently removed from office by the Peruvian Congress.

[6] Alÿs, "A thousand words", p. 108.

[7] Noticeably Alÿs describes the process and performance as collaborative, though he is primarily credited as the author of this work. His work often begins as simple actions performed by him or commissioned volunteers, which are recorded in photographs, film, and other means of documentation such as postcards.

[8] Miwon Kwon, *One Place After Another: Site-Specific Art and Locational Identity*, Cambridge, MA: MIT Press, 2002, p. 46.

[9] Perhaps best exemplified in *Utopia Station* at the 2003 *Venice Biennale*, curated by Molly Nesbit, Hans Ulrich Obrist and Rirkrit Tiravanija. *Utopia Station* was promoted as "nothing more or nothing less than a way station, a place to stop, to look, to talk and refresh the route". See Scott Rothkopf, "Pictures of an exhibition" in *Artforum*, September 2003, p. 240.

[10] See Daniel Buren, "The Function of the Studio" in this publication, pp. 15-28.

[11] Miwon Kwon, p. 10.

[12] Miwon Kwon, "The Wrong Place", in this publication, p. 35.

[13] Nicolas Bourriaud, in this publication, p. 45.

[14] See *Liverpool Biennial* 2002 catalogue essays in particular, *International 2002*, Liverpool: Liverpool Biennial, 2002.

[15] Hal Foster, "The Artist as Ethnographer", *The Return of the Real: The Avant-Garde at the End of the Century*, Cambridge, MA: MIT Press, 1996.

[16] Guy Debord, "Theory of Derive", *Situationist International Anthology*, 1958.

[17] This is a field of artistic practice complex in its manifestations and diverse in its pedagogy. The recent Arts Council of England *Interrupt* symposia began to unpick the nuances between the roles and processes of socially engaged art practice. See www.interrupt-symposia.org.

[18] Grant Kester's paper, "Dialogical Aesthetics: A Critical Framework for Littoral Art", was delivered at the *Critical Sites: Issues in Critical Art Practice and Pedagogy* conference held at the Institute of Art, Design and Technology, Dun Laoghaire, Co. Dublin in September 1998 and now forms the basis of a Socially Engaged Practice Forum on-line and a continuing series of responses in the print and on-line versions of *Variant*.

[19] Beuys proposed a notion of *Soziale Plastik* (social sculpture) as an interdisciplinary and participatory process in which thought, speech and discussion could be core 'materials'. See Social Sculpture Research Unit at Oxford Brookes University at www.brookes.ac.uk/schools/apm/social_sculpture. Other artists groups such as Superflex (Denmark), Oreste (Italy), Wochenklasur (Austria), Ala Plastica (Argentina) and Critical Art Ensemble (US) have used communicative action to develop a series of interventionist projects which allow participants to shape their own agendas.

[20] See my article, "The institution is dead! Long live the institution! Contemporary Art and New Institutionalism", *Engage 15, The art of encounter*, 2004, pp. 6-13.

Daniel Buren
The Function of the Studio

One of the most prominent and influential aspects of Daniel Buren's art and writings since the 1960s has been his deliberate inversion of the relationship artworks maintain with the places where they are exhibited. Throughout his career, Buren has maintained a resolute engagement with working *in situ*, whether in Paris at the Palais-Royal, at the prestigious festival of newly commissioned art *Skulptur Projekte Münster* or at the *Venice Biennale*.
The following text is key in Buren's career-long treatise on the "desertion of the studio and its implications" and was written between December 1970 and January 1971. It was originally published in French in *Ragile*, Paris, vol. III, September 1979 and in English in *October 10*, Autumn 1979.

Daniel Buren
The Function of the Studio

There are frames, envelopes and limits that enclose and 'make' the work of art, such as the awning, the pedestal, the frame, the castle, the church, the gallery, the museum, power, art history, the market economy and so on, but they are usually not perceived and certainly never questioned. Among these factors which determine and condition art, there's one that is never mentioned and even less questioned, although it comes first, it is the artist's studio.

In most cases, the studio is more necessary (crucial) to the artist than the gallery or the museum. As a matter of fact, it precedes both. More importantly, we will see that the studio on one hand, and the gallery and the museum on the other, are completely linked. They form two foundations of the same building and the same system. Questioning one (such as the museum or gallery) without touching the other (the studio) inevitably implies questioning nothing at all. All questioning of the art system will therefore have to re-examine the studio as a unique place where the work originates, just as the museum needs to be re-examined as the unique place where the work is seen. Both need to be questioned again as habits, rigid habits, of art.

But what, then, is the function of the studio?

It is the work's place of origin.
It is most often a private place; it could be an ivory tower.
It is a fixed place where objects are created that must be transportable.
It is an extremely important place, as is already evident.
It is the first frame, the first limit, upon which all the other ones will depend.

How does the studio present itself physically, architecturally? Indeed, the artist's studio isn't just any poor little room?[1] We will distinguish two types:

The European-type studio, as illustrated by the Parisian studio at the end of the nineteenth century is generally a spacious place characterised by its rather high ceiling of at least four metres. Sometimes it even has a loggia, which increases the distance between the viewpoint and the work. The access is such that large works can be brought in and taken out. Sculptors' studios are on the ground floor, painters' on the upper floors. Finally, there is natural light, generally diffused by glass windows or roofs which are oriented to the north to receive the softest and flattest light possible.[2]

The studio of American artists has a more recent origin.[3] Though it hasn't usually been constructed specially or according to certain norms, it is often much more spacious than the European studio, not necessarily higher, but much longer and wider and situated in recuperated, old 'lofts'. Natural light plays a much smaller role, if any at all, than surface and volume. Electric light is on day and night, if possible. Hence a certain similarity between the products originating in these 'lofts' and their 'placement' on the walls or floors of modern museums, which are electrically lit day and night, too. I will add that this type of studio also influences the places that today function as studios in Europe and which can be for those who find them, either an old barn in the countryside, an old garage, or other commercial spaces in the city. In either case, it is possible to see the architectural relationships thus installed between the studio and the museum–whereby one inspires the other, and vice versa–as well as between one type of studio and another.[4] We will mention here neither those who transform part of their studios into exhibition halls, nor curators who dream of museums as permanent studios! After having considered some of the studio's architectural characteristics, let's take a look at what usually happens there.

As a private space, the studio is a place of experiments to be judged only by the artist-resident, nothing will leave the studio unless he decides so. This private place also allows for other manipulations, which are indispensable for museums and galleries to function well. It is, for instance, the place where the art critic, the exhibition organiser, the museum director or curator can come to select quietly among the presented works (presented by the artist) which will take part in which exhibition, gallery or combination. The studio thus becomes a commodity for the organiser. He can 'compose' his exhibition as he pleases (the artist cannot, although he puts up with being gently manipulated in this situation, pleased as he is with the prospect of the exhibition). Hence the organiser runs the least of the risks: not only has he already selected the participating artist, he even selects the works he desires in the studio. Thus the studio is also a boutique, where one finds ready-to-wear art for exhibition.

The studio is also the place where, before a work is publicly shown, whether in a gallery or a museum, the artist can invite critics and other specialists in the hope that their visit will allow some works to leave the private space–a kind of purgatory–to be on some public (museum) or private (collection) walls–a kind of paradise for the works! The studio thus plays the role of production place on one hand, a storage or waiting room on the other hand, and finally–if all goes well–as a distribution centre, becoming a kind of shunting yard.

The studio, the first frame of the work, is in fact a filter which will serve a double selection, first of all the artist's, away from the eyes of others, and second, that of exhibition organisers and art dealers, so as to be seen by others, immediately evident is that the work thus produced passes–in order to exist–from one refuge to another. Therefore, it needs to be at least transportable and, if possible, manipulable without too many restrictions for the person (other than the artist himself) who will adopt the right to remove it from the first (original) place, to allow it to access the second (promotional) place. Therefore as it is produced in the studio, the work can only be conceived as an object to be manipulated indefinitely and by whomever, in order for this to occur, and from the moment it is produced in the studio, the work is isolated from the real world. Meanwhile, it is at that very moment, and only at that moment, that it is closest to its own reality. The work will subsequently not stop to distance itself from this reality, and even sometimes borrow another reality unanticipated by anyone, including the artist by whom it was created. This reality can even be totally contradictory to the work itself, and usually serves mercantile benefits as well as the dominant ideology. Hence it is when the work is in the studio, and only at this moment, that it is in its place. This leads to a moral contradiction for the work of art, which it will never overcome, as its end implies a devitalising displacement as to its own reality, as to its origin. If, on the other hand, the work remains in this reality–the studio–it is the artist who is at risk… of starvation!

The work we can see is thus totally foreign to the place where it is welcomed (museum, gallery, collection): hence the ever-increasing gap between works and their places (and not their placement), a yawning chasm which, if it were seen (and it will be seen sooner or later) would hurt art and its pomp (this is to say, art as we know it today, and in 99% of the cases, art as it is made) into historical oblivion. This gap, however, is partially clogged by the system which causes us–the public, the artist, the historian, the critic, and others–to accept the convention of the museum (of the gallery) as an inescapable neutral frame, the unique and definitive venue of art. Eternal venues in function of arts eternity!

The work thus constitutes itself in a very specific place, which, however, it cannot take into account. Not only does this place command and forge the work in many aspects, it remains the only place in which art takes place. We thus arrive at the following contradiction: it is impossible, on the one hand, and by definition, to see a work in its place. On the other hand it is the place which serves as a refuge and where it can be seen that will mark it, that will influence it, even more than the place in which it was made and from which it has been removed. One can thus say that we find ourselves facing the following short-coming: either the work is in its own place, the studio, and doesn't take place (for the public), or it finds itself in a place which isn't its place, the museum, where it takes place (for the public).

Removed from the ivory tower where it has been produced, the work ends in another place which, although foreign, can only reinforce the impression of comfort the work had already acquired by taking refuge in a citadel, the museum, in order to survive its trajectory. Therefore the work passes–and can only exist this way, as it is pre-destinated by the imprint of its place of origin–from a closed place/frame, the world of the artist, to another place–paradoxically even more closed–the place of the art world. Hence the alignment of works in museums may have a lot in common with a cemetery. Whatever they may say, wherever they may come from, it is there that they end, and it is also there that they become lost. A partial loss, however, compared to the total loss of works that never leave their studios. Hence the undetailed compromise of manipulable works.

Photo-souvenir:
Tel un palimpseste ou la métamorphose d'une image, work *in situ*, June 1997, in *Skulptur Projekte Münster 1997*, Münster (detail)
Courtesy Daniel Buren

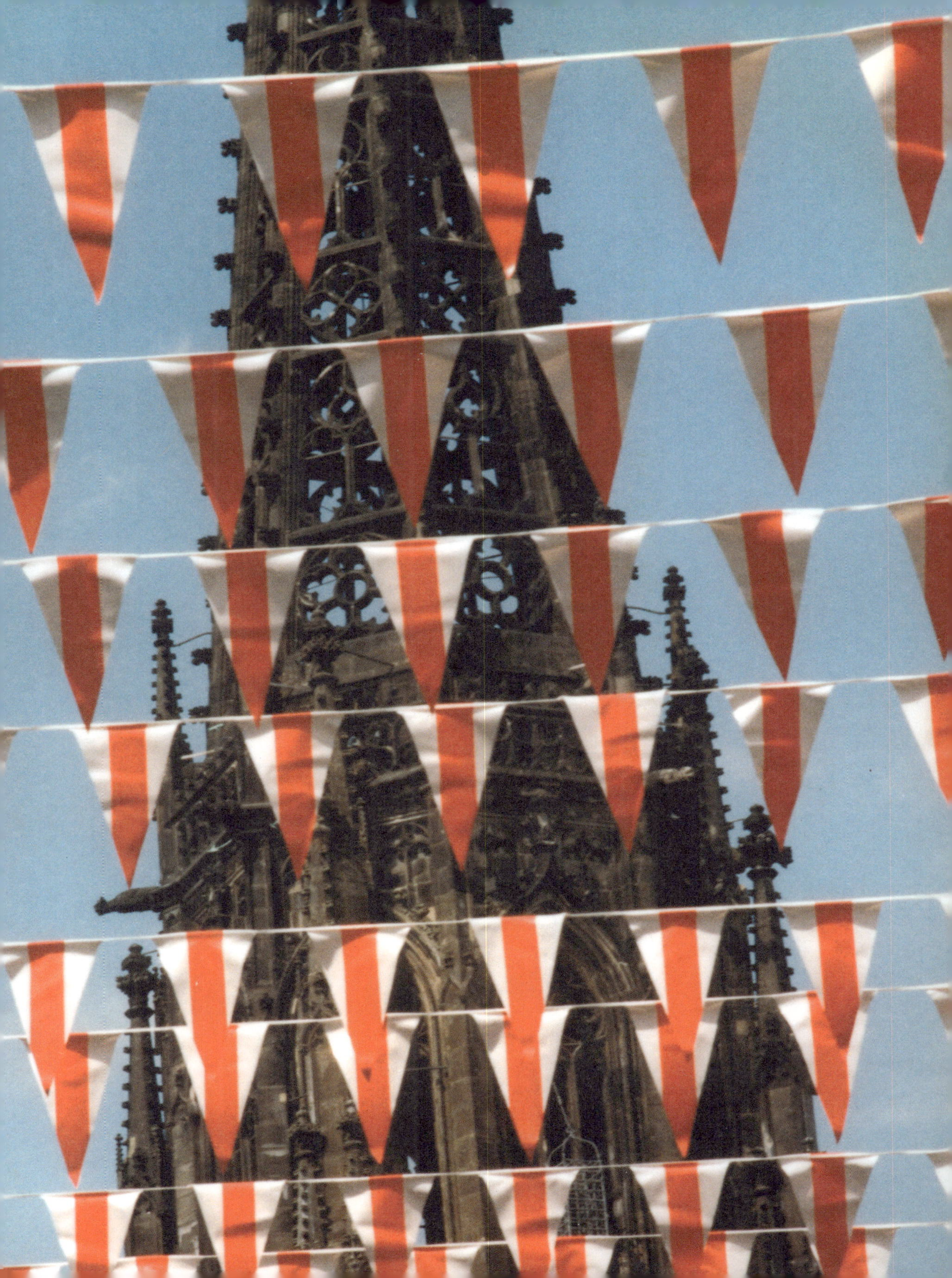

The work that ends in the museum is forever both in its 'place' and at the same time in 'a place' which is never its own. In 'its place' as this was the aspiration when it was made, yet it is never 'its own' as the place has not been defined by the work that is situated there, nor has the work been made exactly as a function of a place that is necessarily, *a priori* concretely and practically unknown to it. For the work to be in place without being specially placed, it needs to be identical to all the other existing works, which are identical among themselves, in which case it passes (and places itself) everywhere and anywhere (as do all the other identical works). Otherwise the frame–which welcomes the original work as well as all other original works, all fundamentally different from one another–must be a *passe-partout* frame which adapts itself perfectly and to the millimetre to each work.

Now if one examines these two extremes separately, one may formulate only extreme and idealising but nevertheless interesting statements. For instance:

a) all works of art are strictly identical, whatever their period, their author, their country, and so on, which explains their identical placement in millions of museums in the entire world, depending on fashion and curators; or

b) all works being absolutely different from one another, their differences respected and therefore readable, both explicitly and implicitly, each museum, and each room in each museum, each square metre on every wall is perfectly adapted to each work, in every place and at every moment.

What one notices in these two statements is the asymmetry beneath their apparent symmetry. If one can't logically accept that all works of art, whatever they are, are identical among themselves, one is forced to state that they are (depending on the period) installed the same way, whatever they may be. On the contrary, if one can accept that each work has its uniqueness, one is forced to note that no museum is adapted to this, and acts–paradoxically, as it pretends to defend the uniqueness of the work–as if this assertion of the work, its uniqueness, doesn't exist and manipulates it as it pleases.

To bring to mind two examples among thousands, those in charge of the Jeu de Paume in Paris present impressionist works encased in the walls, which therefore frame them directly, the walls themselves even painted a certain colour. At the same time, other works of the same period and by the same artists are presented eight thousand kilometres away in the Art Institute of Chicago under enormous sculpted frames. Does this mean, to return to our two examples, that the works in question are absolutely identical, and that they acquire their won and differentiated expression by grace of the intelligence of those who present them? Exactly to have them state in a different way what they hid, by definition the same aspect, the absolute neutrality of identical works, waiting for their 'frame' in order to express themselves!

Or, according to the second example, does it mean that each museum adapts itself as closely as possible to the specific statement of the works in question? But who could explain to us, then, where in Claude Monet's works it is explicit that 70 years after they were made certain canvases needed to be walled in and surrounded by a mild salmon colour, as in Paris, and others framed in enormous moulds and juxtaposed with other works of impressionist artists, as in Chicago? If we exclude both extreme statements (a) and (b) above, we find ourselves facing a third, which is evidently the most current, and which implies, as we know today, a *sine qua non* relationship from the studio in the museum. Indeed, as it is hardly probable that the work made in the studio will remain there. This is inherent to the work, and it will wind up in another place (museum, gallery, collection): it is necessary not only for the work to be made, but also to be seen in another place, and subsequently in any place. In order for this transfer to take place, two conditions are needed, either:

1) The definitive place of the work has to be the work itself. This is a widely held belief or philosophy in artistic circles, as far as this opinion regarding the work allows one to escape all questioning of its physical place of visibility as a consequence of the system, and thus of the dominant ideology reflected in the specific ideology of art. It is a reactionary theory, as it allows the entire system, under the pretext of escaping, or rather, of not being concerned, to reinforce itself without having to be justified, as per definition (the definition of the supporters of this theory) the place of the museum is without any connection to the place of the work: or

2) The creator 'imagines' the place where his work will end up, which leads him to try to imagine either all the situations possible for each work (which is simply impossible) or (which is the case) a possible average place. We then get the banal cubic space, neutralised to the extreme, with a flat and uniform light, one which we know, that is, the space of the museums and galleries, as they exist today. This obliges the producer in the studio, consciously or not, to produce for a type of banalised space, and consequently to banalise his own work in order to conform.

By producing for a stereotype, one evidently winds oneself up fabricating a stereotype; hence the bewildering academic character of today's artworks, even if they are camouflaged by the most diverse forms. I would like, by the way of ending, to support my 'suspicions' about the studio and both its idealising and its sclerotic functions with two examples which have conditioned me. One is personal, the other historic.

Personal When I was very young (17) I began a study on painting in Provence from Cezanne to Picasso (specifically: on the influences of the geographical place on the works). To bring this work to a satisfactory conclusion, I not only scoured southwest France, I also visited a large number of artists in their studios. My visits took me from the youngest artists to the oldest, from total unknowns to the most well-known. What struck me, first, was the diversity of work, followed by its quality, richness and particular reality, that is to say 'sincerity', independent of who the artist was or what his reputation was. I mean 'reality/sincerity' not only in regard to the author and his workplace, but also in relation to the environment, the landscape.

A bit later, I visited the exhibitions of the artists I had met, one after the other, and there my amazement blurred, even sometimes totally disappeared, as if the works I had seen in the studios were no longer the same or even made by the same person. Torn from their context, one could say from their environment, they lost their sense, their life. It was as if they became 'frauds'. I didn't immediately understand very well (far from it) what was happening or the reason for my disillusion. One single thing became certain, and that was deception. Several of the artists I saw several times, and each time the gap between their studios and the walls in Paris became more accentuated for me, up to the point that it became impossible for me to continue visiting their studios and their exhibitions. From that time on, something irreparable was shattered, although the reasons for this were confused. Later I repeated the same disastrous experience with friends of my generation, even though the profound 'reality/sincerity' of the work was close to me. This 'loss' of the object, this degradation of the interest for a work out of its context–as if an energy essential to its existence disappeared as soon as the threshold of the studio was crossed–was starting to preoccupy me enormously. The sensation that the essence of the work gets lost somewhere between the place where it is produced (the studio) and the place where it is consumed (the exhibition) pushed me extremely early on to pose the problem under the signification of the place of the work for myself. A little later, I understand that what got lost, what most surely got lost was the work's reality, its 'sincerity', that is its connection to its place of creation, the studio–a place where finished works intermingle with works in the process of being made, works that will never be finished, sketches, etc.. All these traces, visible at the same time, allow the comprehension of the work underway, which the museum definitely extinguishes in its desire to 'install'. Doesn't one speak, by the way, more and more of an 'installation' instead of an 'exhibition'? And isn't that which is installed closer to establishing itself?

Historical In my opinion, Constantin Brancusi was the only artist who proved to have real intelligence when it comes to the museum system and its consequences. Moreover, he tried to conquer it, that is, tried to avoid that his work became rooted there, to make it impossible to settle it according to the whim of the current curator. Indeed, by bequeathing a major part of his work under the reservation that it was to be kept as it was in the studio where it originated, Brancusi cut short once and for all its dispersion, as well as any speculation. Furthermore, this offered any visitor exactly the same viewpoint as his own at the time of production. Thus Brancusi was the only artist, who, even if he worked in the studio and was aware of the fact that his work was closest to its 'sincerity' there, took the risk–preserving the relationship between the work and the place where it was made–of 'confirming' *ad vitam* his production in the spot that saw its origin. Among other things, he thus shortcut the museum and its desire to classify, beautify, select and so on. The work remains visible the way it was produced, for better and for worse, work, which the museum is anxious to take away from all that it exhibits.

One could also say–but this would necessitate a longer study–that the fixing of the work in the sense that it is to be seen in the place where it was made has nothing to do with the 'fixing' as practiced by the museum on everything that is shown in it. Brancusi also proved that the so-called purity of his works is neither less beautiful nor less interesting within the four walls of the artist's studio, surrounded by various utensils, other works, some unfinished, others finished, than between the immaculate walls of the aseptic museums. Whereby the entire production of art, both yesterday and today, is not only marked but preceded by the use of the studio as an essential, even sometimes unique place of creation, all my work derives from its abolition.

[1] A bit further on, I describe the studio as an archetype, knowing very well that all artists 'starting out' (and some even their entire lives) have to be content with the squalid shack or a ridiculously small room. I would like to add that those who keep to sordid places of work in spite of all the difficulties are evidently those for whom the idea of possessing a studio for their work is a necessity, and who, as a consequence, dream of premises which, if they had them, would most probably approach the archetype we speak of.

[2] To control the display of works once they have left the studio, the exhibition of the artist's studio requires much more care from architects when it comes to lighting, orientation, and so on, than an artist himself often would take!

[3] I am talking here about the New York-type studio. In its desire to annihilate *L'Ecole de Paris* by supplanting it with a badly remembered version, the United States managed to reproduce all its defaults, including the principal one, that is, a forced centralisation that was already the ridicule of France and even Europe.

[4] To the usually electrically-lit American museums, one might contrast the European ones, usually lit by daylight thanks to the profusion of glass roofs. One may also note what is to some an antagonism, which is but a difference in style produced by the environments of European and American production.

Photo-souvenir: *Criss-crossing*, work *in situ*, *Göteborgs International Konstbiennal*, Göteborg, June-September 2001 (detail)
Courtesy Daniel Buren

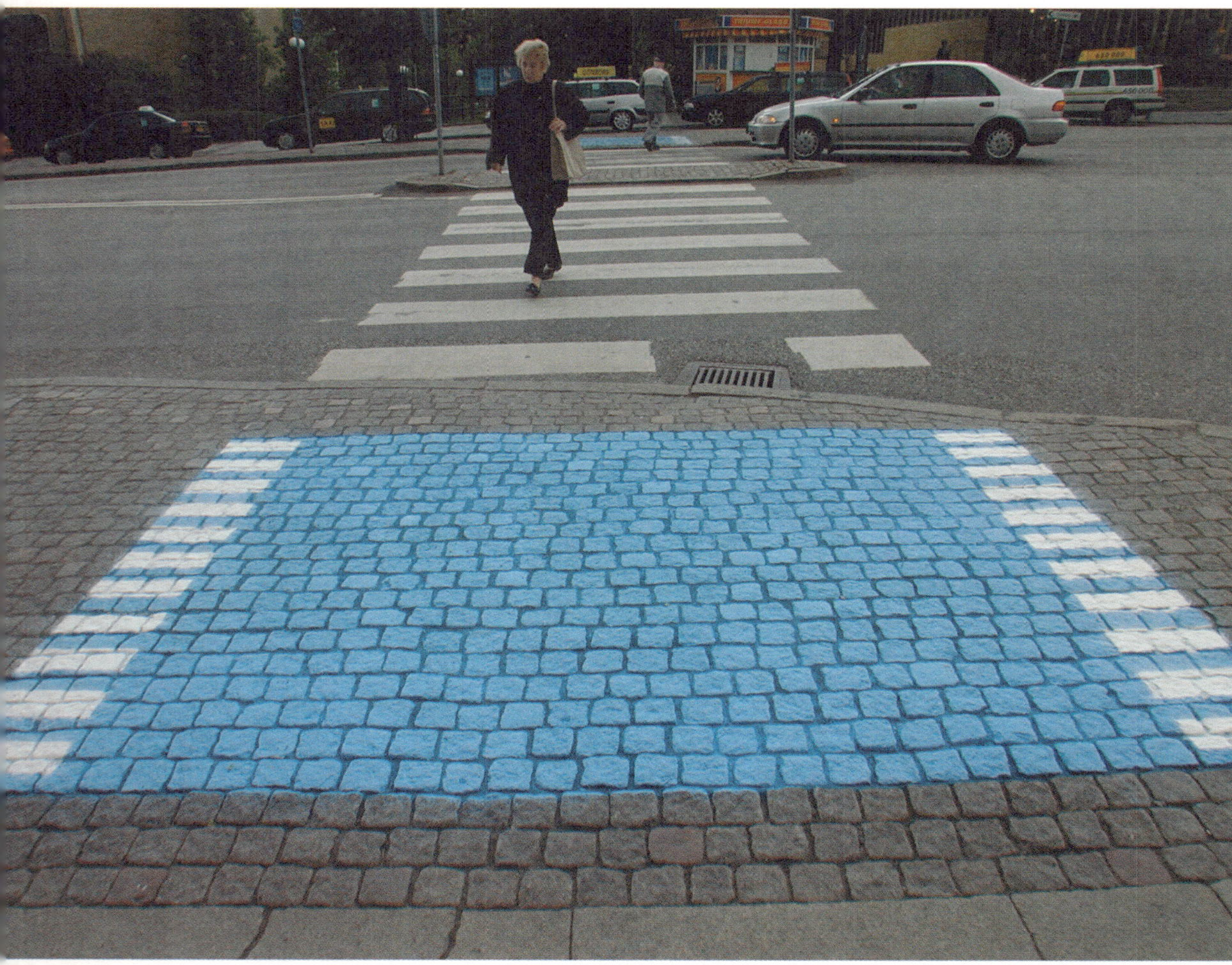

Photo-souvenir: *Les Deux Plateaux*, sculpture *in situ*, Royal Court, Palais-Royal, Paris, 1985-1986 (detail)
Courtesy Daniel Buren

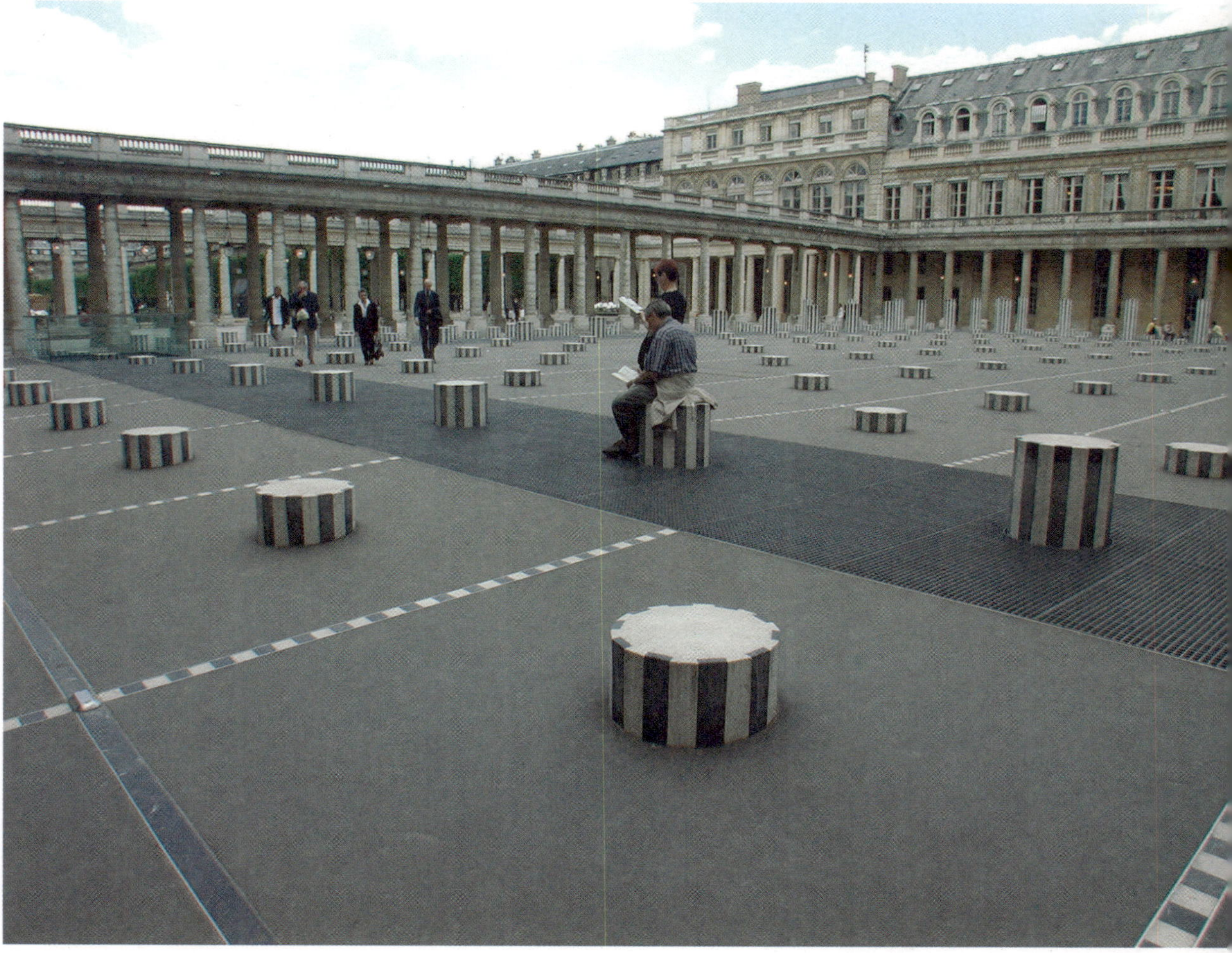

Photo-souvenir: *Tel un palimpseste ou la métamorphose d'une image*, work *in situ*, in *Skulptur Projekte Münster*, 1997, Münster (detail)
Courtesy Daniel Buren

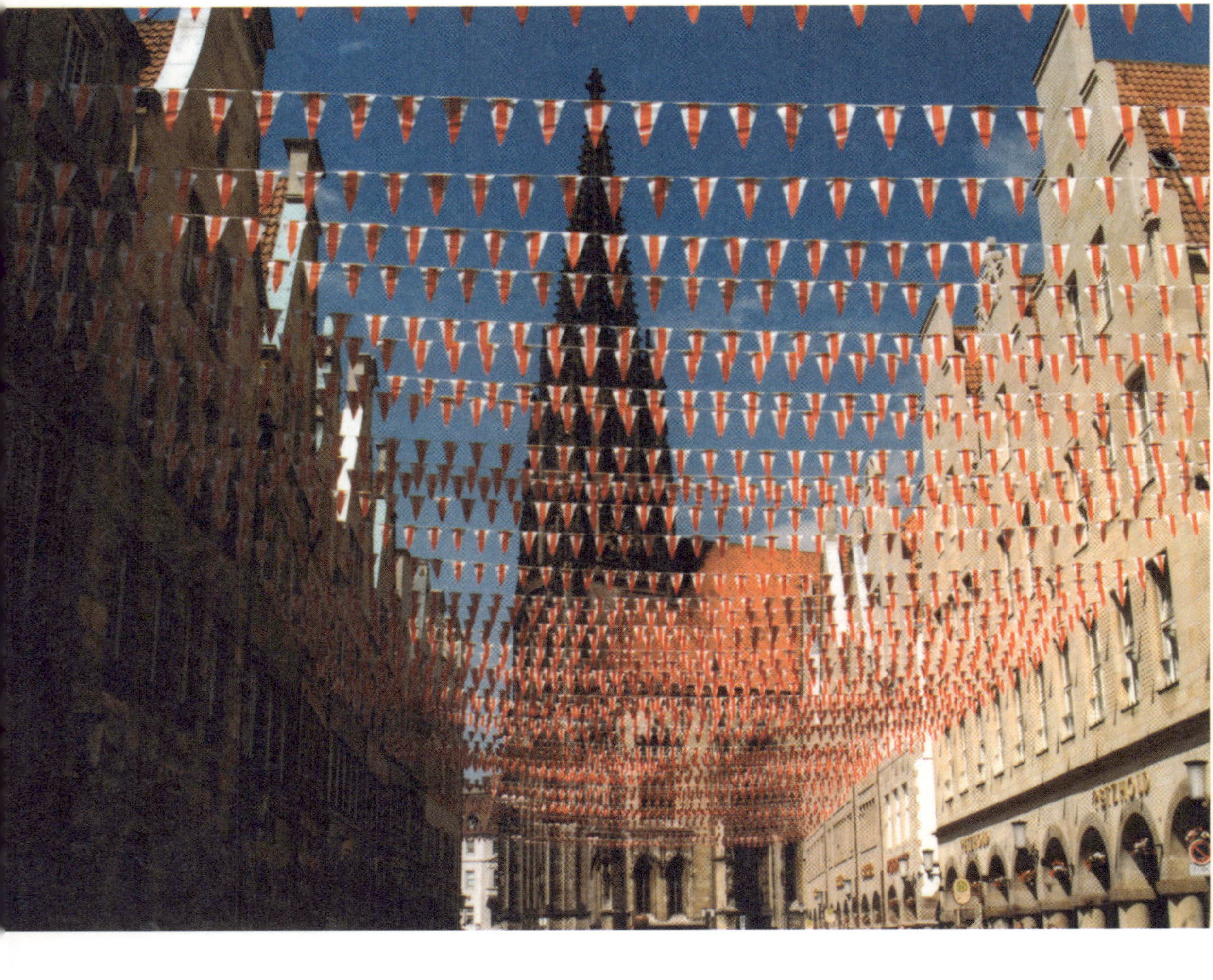

Photo-souvenir: *D'une cercle à l'autre: le paysage emprunté*, work *in situ*, Casino Luxembourg, July-August 2001 (detail)
Courtesy Daniel Buren

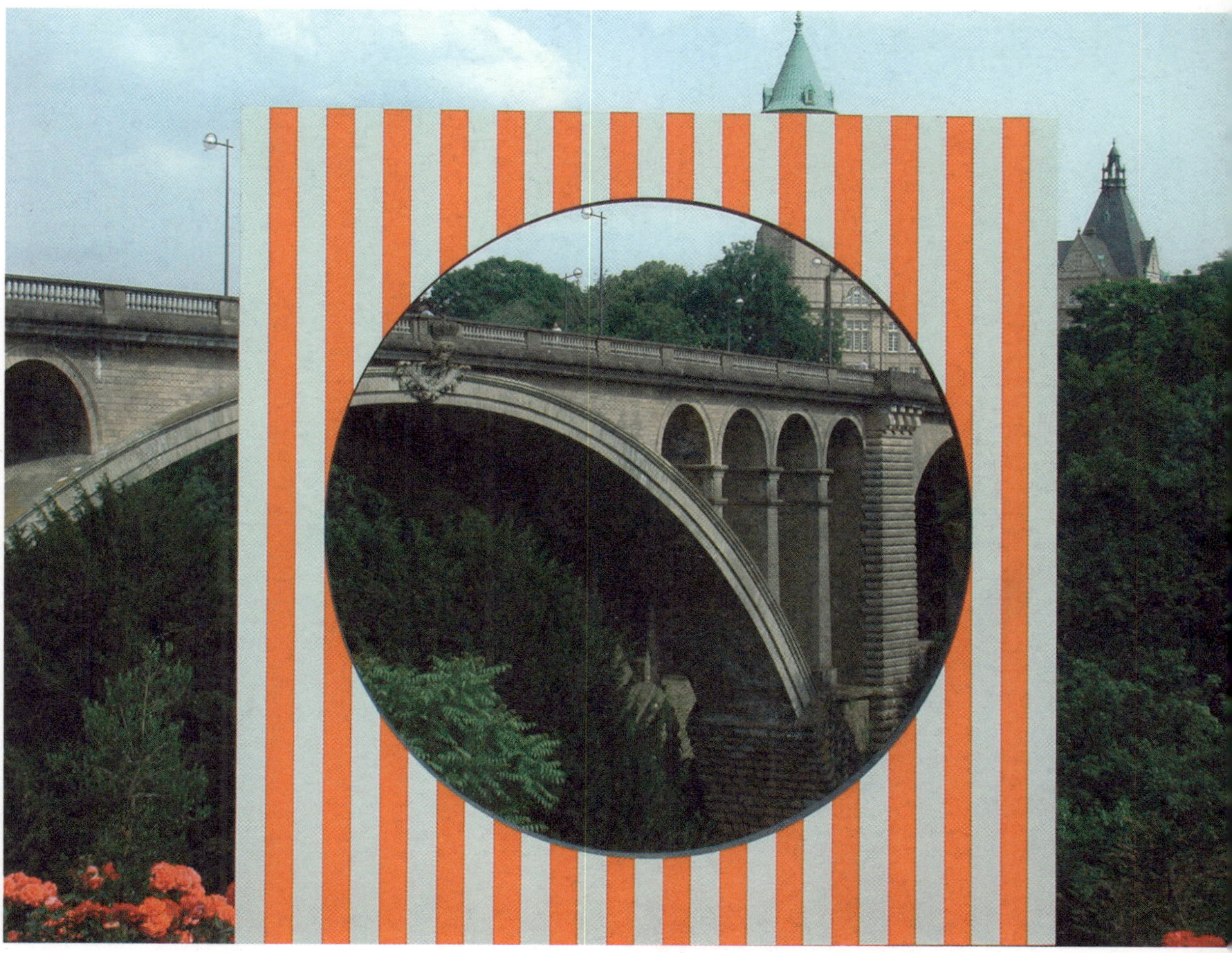

Miwon Kwon
The Wrong Place

This essay was originally prepared for the International Lecture Series developed as an integral part of *In All the Wrong Places*, a project presented by The Ottawa Art Gallery. Curated by Sylvie Fortin, *In All the Wrong Places* took place over a six-month period (May-November 1999) featuring new works by 11 local, national and international artists. Foregrounding practices that exceed the physical confines of the gallery, *In All the Wrong Places* activated many off-site locations throughout the city and generated alternative spatial and temporal relations between the artist, site, work, and audience. It was originally published in *Art Journal*, Spring 2000 and modified for Kwon's book *One Place After Another: Site-Specific Art and Locational Identity*, MIT Press, 2002.

Miwon Kwon
The Wrong Place

It occurred to me some time ago that among many of my art and academic friends, success and viability of one's work is now measured in proportion to the accumulation of frequent flyer miles. The more we travel for work, the more that we are called upon to provide institutions in other parts of the country and world with our presence and services, the more that we give into the logic of nomadism, one could say, as pressured by a mobilised capitalist economy, the more we are made to feel wanted, needed, validated, and relevant. It seems our very sense of self-worth is predicated more and more on our suffering through the inconveniences and psychic destabilisations of ungrounded transience, of not being at home (or not having a home), of always traversing through elsewheres. Whether we enjoy it or not, we are culturally and economically rewarded for enduring the 'wrong' place. It seems we're out of place all too often.

But what is a 'wrong' place? How does one recognise it as such, as opposed to a 'right' place? What do we really mean by these qualifying adjectives? Is being in the wrong place the same thing as being out of place? And what are the effects of such mis/displacements for art, subjectivity, and locational identities? In light of the intensified mobilisation of bodies, information, images, and commodities on the one hand, and the greater and greater homogenisation and standardisation of places on the other (which, by the way, facilitates the smooth, unimpeded mobilisation and circulation of these bodies, information, images, and commodities), I continue to wonder about the impact, both positive and negative, of the spatial and temporal experiences that such conditions engender not only in terms of cultural practice but more basically for our psyches, our sense of self, our sense of well-being, our sense of belonging to a place and a culture.

Within the limited critical discussions concerning present-day, site-oriented art, one tendency has been to valorise the nomadic condition. Referencing the writings of Gilles Deleuze and Félix Guattari as theoretical support, some critics have championed the work of artists such as Andrea Fraser, Mark Dion, Renée Green, and Christian Philipp Müller, among many others, for having abandoned the phenomenologically-oriented mode of site-specific art (best exemplified by Richard Serra's sculptures). This is a mode that is seen to be outdated now. Moving beyond the inherited conception of site-specific art as a grounded, fixed (even if ephemeral), singular event, the work of these younger artists are seen to advance an altogether different notion of a site as predominantly an 'intertextually' coordinated, multiply-located, discursive field of operation.[1]

This is the reading, for example, of art historian and critic James Meyer, who has coined the term 'functional site' to distinguish recent site-oriented practices from those of the past.[2] This conceptual shift has embraced the idea of meaning as an open, unfixed constellation, porous to contingencies–an idea that most of us accept and welcome. But in the process, the idea of the fluidity of meaning has tended to get conflated/confused with the idea of fluidity of identities and subjectivities, even physical bodies, to such an extent that a certain romanticism has accrued around the image of a cultural worker on the go. It is not only the artwork that is not bound to the physical conditions of a place anymore; it is the artist-subject who is 'liberated' from any enduring ties to local circumstances. Qualities of permanence, continuity, certainty and groundedness (physical and otherwise) are thought to be artistically retrograde, thus politically suspect, in this context. By contrast, qualities of uncertainty, instability, ambiguity and impermanence are taken as desired attributes of a vanguard, politically progressive, artistic practice. But I remain unconvinced of the ways in which a model of meaning and interpretation is called forth to validate, even romanticise, the material and socioeconomic realities of an itinerant lifestyle. I am suspicious of this analogical transposition and the seductive allure of nomadism it supports if for no other reason than for the fact of my own personal ambivalence toward the physical and psychical experiences of mobilisation and destabilisation that such nomadism demands.

At the same time, however, I remain wary of the more prevalent position, the anti-nomadic and anti-technology argument, like that proposed by art historian Lucy Lippard. In her book *The Lure of the Local: Senses of Place in a Multi-Centred Society*, she presents a holistic vision of place as a kind of text of humanity, "the intersections of nature, culture, history, and ideology" that is understood as such from a position of being an 'insider'. Place is, according to Lippard, "a portion of land/town/cityscape seen from the inside, the resonance of a specific location that is known and familiar.... the external world mediated through human subjective experience".[3]

It is Lippard's contention that despite the fact that our sense of identity is fundamentally tied to our relationship to places and the histories that they embody, the uprooting of our lives from specific local cultures and places–through voluntary migrations or forced displacements–has contributed to the waning of our abilities to locate ourselves. Consequently, a sense of place remains remote to most of us. And this deficiency can be seen as a primary cause in our loss of touch with nature, disconnection from history, spiritual vacancy, and estrangement from our own sense of self. Her argument is not only that we need to pay closer attention to the role that places have in the formation of our identities and cultural values, it is to encourage a particular type of relationship to places so as to divert or turn around the trends of the dominant culture. Vaguely recalling Martin Heidegger's phenomenological philosophy on dwelling and place, which diagnosed the modern condition as one of an existential "homelessness" (according to the philosopher, the world hasn't been the 'right place' for humankind for a very long time), Lippard presents the notion of a sense of place as therapeutic remedy: sense of place is "the geographical component of the psychological need to belong somewhere, one antidote to a prevailing alienation".[4]

In this regard, even as she recalls the conservatism of Heidegger, or more accurately the conservatism of his subsequent interpreters such as Yi-Tu Fuan and Christian Norberg-Schulz, Lippard seems to incorporate aspects of the Marxist analysis of the "production of space" as well. She begins, for instance, from the basic premise that space is not a neutral container or void within which social interactions take place but rather an ideological product *and* instrument in itself. More specifically, she believes that the rapacious growth and transformation of capitalism has subsumed the distinctions of local differences and cultures, and that the particularity of places are continually being homogenised, genericised, and commodified to better accommodate the expansion of capitalism via abstraction of space (or 'non-places' as some sociologists prefer). These processes, in turn, exasperate the conditions of alienation and placelessness in contemporary life.

Much of this I agree with, but unlike Henri Lefebvre, who provides the deepest dialectical consideration of the "production of space" (his phrase); Lippard seems unable to resist the nostalgic impulse. In the end, the task of a progressive oppositional cultural practice is conceived as a retrieval and resuscitation of a sense of place, a sense that ostensibly once was but now is lost. Her project implicitly calls for a slower, more sedentary mode of existence. Despite her disclaimers, hers is a vision that favours the 'return' to a vernacular, non-urban sociality of small-scale spaces and face-to-face exchanges. Not that such a vision isn't appealing: the problem is that perhaps it is all too appealing, not only to us individually but to the machinations of capitalism itself.

What is lost in Lippard's thinking are Lefebvre's important insights on the dialectical rather than oppositional relationship between the processes of expanding abstraction of space and the 'production' of particularities of place, local specificity, and authenticity of cultures (a concern that informs many site-oriented art practices today). Production of difference, to say it in more general terms, is itself a fundamental activity of capitalism, necessary for its continuous expansion. One might go so far as to say that this desire for difference, authenticity, and our willingness to pay high prices for it (literally), only highlights the degree to which they are already lost to us, thus the power they have over us.

Yet it is not a matter of choosing sides–between models of nomadism and sedentariness, between space and place, between digital interfaces and the handshake, between the 'wrong' and 'right' places. Rather, we need to be able to think the range of these seeming contradictions and our contradictory desires for them together, at once. To understand seeming oppositions as sustaining relations, how do we account for, for instance, the sense of soaring exhilaration *and* the anxious dread engendered by, on the one hand, the new fluidities and continuities of space and time, and on the other hand, the ruptures and disconnections of space and time? And what could this doubleness of experience mean, in our lives, in our work, within ourselves?

I want to remember the lessons of two scenes–or 'wrong places'–in this context. One is Fredric Jameson's by-now famous telling of a deliriously confounding spatial experience at the Westin Bonaventure Hotel in downtown Los Angeles. It is an historically unprecedented experience of hyperspace that, for Jameson, serves as an emblematic instance of "the originality of post-modernist space".[5] The second scene is one described by novelist Don DeLillo in his two-act play *Valparaiso*, 1999, in which the protagonist, Michael Majeski, an average middle-class businessman (assumed white), on an ordinary business trip to Valparaiso, Indiana, ends up in the other part of the world in Valparaiso, Chile, presumably by mistake, to then have to confront himself as a minor media celebrity on his return home. Majeski's extra-ordinary misadventure of falling off the track of his set itinerary, ending up in the wrong place (which isn't to say that he gets lost), is the starting point for DeLillo's fictional critique of the postmodern condition. In both Jameson's and DeLillo's work the disruption of a subject's habitual spatio-temporal experience propels the breakdown of its traditional sense of self.

First to the Bonaventure Hotel: for Jameson, the building is like an alien ship, a space capsule. It is "a total space, a complete world, a kind of miniature city", which turns its back on the city fabric to create an isolated zone (not unlike a shopping mall) that might as well be floating in outer space. Indeed the view from one common approach to the hotel off of Third Street is of a building that seems to be hovering above the ground, a mirage-like vision of a shiny dirigible. This physical hermeticism and disjuncture is accentuated by the building's glass skin, which "repels the city outside". The glass skin exterior "achieves a peculiar and placeless dissociation of the Bonaventure from its neighbourhood: it is not even an exterior, inasmuch as when you seek to look at the hotel's outer walls you cannot see the hotel itself but only the distorted images of everything that surrounds it".[6]

If the glass skin presents a dissimulating perceptual experience of the building as a whole, the sense of disorientation is furthered by the dis-coordination between exterior and interior spaces. Jameson highlights the experience of entering the building: the building has three entrances, yet none of them are recognisable as such not only because they lack the familiar fanfare of architectural symbols (marquees, banners, oversized doorways, etc.) but because all three land you in a kind of no-man's land–either a second-storey shopping balcony or the sixth floor of one of the four interiorised towers.

Once admitted into the building in such an unceremonious fashion, one must further negotiate elevators, stairs, or escalators in order to get to the lobby's front desk. Which is to say, the traditional hierarchies of spatial organisation (of front and back, outside and inside, centre and periphery) or choreography of spatial experience (designing of an entry with a sense of arrival, for instance) are forgotten at the Bonaventure Hotel. Jameson continues with descriptions of the "milling confusion" and the "bewildering immersion" of one's eyes and body once inside the hyperspace of the lobby atrium,

> with its great central column surrounded by a miniature lake, the whole positioned between the four symmetrical residential towers with their elevators, and surrounded by rising balconies capped by a kind of greenhouse roof at the sixth level.... Hanging streamers indeed suffuse this empty space in such a way as to distract systematically and deliberately from whatever form it might be supposed to have, while a constant sense of busyness gives the feeling that emptiness is here absolutely packed, that it is an element within which you yourself are immersed, without any distance that formerly enabled the perception of perspective or volume.[7]

In describing the intensity and destabilising aspects of the Bonaventure Hotel lobby in vivid detail, Jameson throws into relief the disparity between the spatial organisation (or disorganisation) of such new postmodernist hyperspaces and a subject's capacity to comprehend and mentally 'map' these spaces. The heightened visual and sensorial stimulation in the Bonaventure lobby, as vacant as it may be in one sense, functions well to obscure the proper perception of one's surroundings. According to Jameson, there remains no vantage from which to take in a perspective, no possibility of depth perception, only readings of surfaces upon surfaces. And movement through such spaces becomes exaggerated and totally controlled, directed and restricted by transportation machines functioning, in Jameson's view, like "allegorical signifiers of that older promenade [which] we are no longer allowed to conduct on our own".[8] So that rather than our being able to make sense of the space, the space makes sense of us, acts upon us, with "something like a vengeance". This "mutation in space" simultaneously thrills us and incapacitates us (or incapacitates us through the intensity of sensorial thrills). "[P]ostmodern hyperspace finally succeed[s] in transcending the capacities of the individual human body to locate itself, to organise its immediate surroundings perceptually, and cognitively to map its position in a mapable external world".[9]

If Jameson does not celebrate places/buildings like the Bonaventure Hotel, he remarkably does not condemn it either. He is more intent on analysing the nature of an altogether different order of spatial experience as a means to access the logic of a larger field of the late capitalist political economy. He sees "this alarming disjunction point between the body and its built environment... as the symbol and analogue of that even sharper dilemma which is the incapacity of our minds, at least at present, to map the great global multinational and decentred communicational network in which we find ourselves caught as individual subjects".[10] In other words, the breakdown of spatial experience in both perceptual and cognitive registers–being lost, disoriented, alienated, feeling out of place, and consequently unable to make coherent meaning of our relation to our physical surroundings–is the cultural symptom of late capitalism's political and social reality.

As various critics have pointed out, there are many elements in Jameson's thesis to contend and argue against: his economic determinism, his dismissive attitude towards poststructuralism, his use of the concept of "cognitive mapping" as a sly stand-in for class consciousness. But a point of particular interest in the context of this essay is the idea that a new spatial paradigm has developed at a faster rate than our capacity to perceive and understand it. It is implied that economic changes have a more direct bearing and quicker impact on cultural forms, like architecture, and that our bodies, with their physical habits, and our consciousness, locked into received knowledge, trail along belatedly. So places can feel wrong not because it does not correspond to our self-perception and world view but rather because our self-perception and world view are out of synch, too outmoded, to make sense of the new spatial and economic organisation that confronts us.

I implied toward the beginning of the essay that a place that instigates a sense of instability and uncertainty, lacking in comfort, a place unfamiliar and foreign, might be deemed 'wrong'. And by extension, a place that feels like 'home' might be deemed 'right'. But *this* is wrong. The determination of right and wrong is never derived from an innate quality of the object in question, even if some moral absolutes might seem to preside over the object. Rather, right and wrong are qualities that an object has *in relation* to something outside itself. In the case of a place, it indicates a subject's relation to it and does not indicate an autonomous, objective condition of the place itself. So it is not so much that the Bonaventure Hotel is a 'wrong' place (although critics like Lucy Lippard would think it so, and to some degree, as with most Marxist geographers and cultural critics, Jameson too is likely to deem such spaces as politically and ethically problematic). The more important point here is that it is *we* who are wrong for this kind of 'new' space. We fall far short of being able to understand the organisation of its logic, which means we are subjected by it without even recognising our own subjection.

So under such circumstances, what do we do? For Lippard and many others, the goal is clear: retrieve the older model of spatial experience so that we can feel comforted, secure, empowered, and 'whole' again in relation to our surroundings. Conditions of groundedness and connectedness are themselves imagined as resistant to the forces of the dominant culture. But to my mind, this kind of old-school oppositional politics seems unproductive, limited at best, since, as noted earlier, it fails to recognise the extent to which such opposition *sustains* dominant cultural trends. Instead, it seems it is only from the position of being out of place that we can attempt to develop new skills–perceptual and cognitive–to map the new hyperspaces wherein we have to survive. But I don't want to celebrate, as some critics might, the conditions of disjuncture,

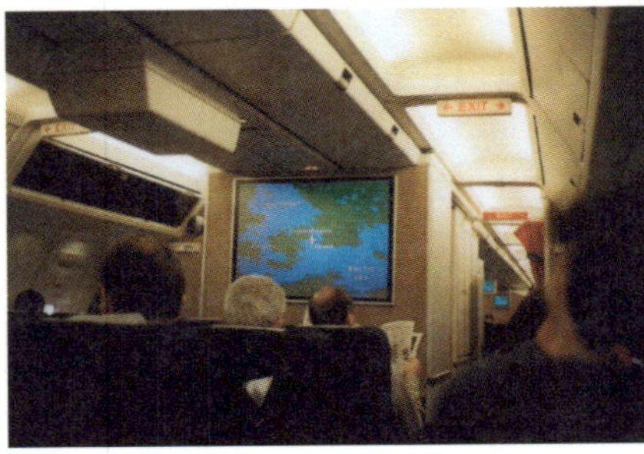

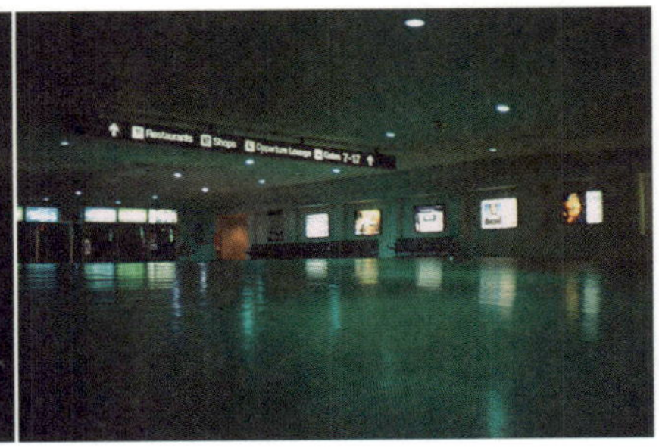

instability, uncertainty, and estrangement as a basis for self-knowledge or as the basis of a critical cultural practice either. Because to embrace such conditions is to leave oneself vulnerable to new terrors and dangers. At the very least, we have to acknowledge this vulnerability. In one sense, Don DeLillo's play *Valparaiso* can be interpreted as a darkly cast study on the toll that such exposure takes on the integrity of a sense of self.

The play begins with the character Michael Majeski's having recently returned from the unintended destination of his trip, the wrong Valparaiso in Chile (there are four Valparaisos in the world as far as I'm aware). Upon his return, he is confronted with numerous demands from the media–radio, television, newspapers, magazines, documentary filmmakers–to recount his experience. It is a great human interest story, after all... we all want to know what happened. How could anyone make such a big mistake? Didn't he notice that he was headed for the wrong city? When did he notice? Why was he going to Valparaiso in the first place? What happened exactly? Who is Michael Majeski? What was he like as a child? What are his dreams? Does he love his wife? Submitting to such questions, he performs 67 interviews in 4½ days in 3½ cities (at least we are told so by the wife character), being forced to repeat his narrative over and over again in front of microphones and cameras, simultaneously constructing and confessing his identity, his life history, including his struggles with alcoholism and the drunken car accident that debilitated his only son.

It is quite clear, with most of the scenes set in talk show 'living rooms', that DeLillo's primary concern is not so much the originality of the postmodernist space as confirmed by its architecture but the omnipresence of broadcast technology as an organising force in our lives and minds. Indeed the collapse of traditional spatial and temporal modalities, and the fragmentation, discontinuity, and intensities presented by new modalities, is not so much described in terms of physical forms (as is in Jameson's narrative) but performed by the characters through language. The dialogue is full of truncated hesitations, random misfires, incomplete thoughts, and broken repetitions, as if the characters aren't really speaking to one another but through and past each other. Their disjunctive conversations sound more like each has his or her own uncoordinated soundtrack. Their words do not constitute even a monologue in that there are no real

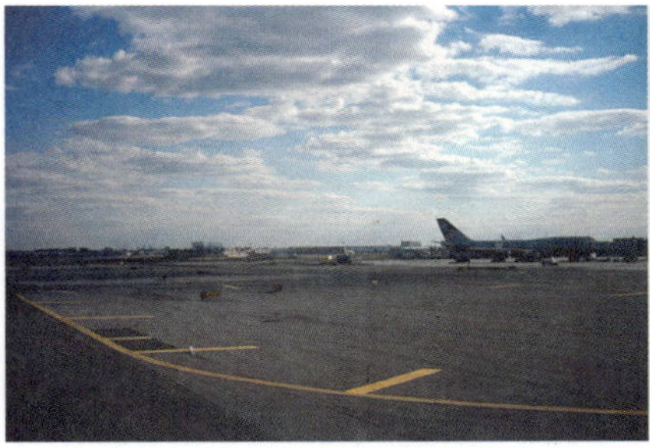
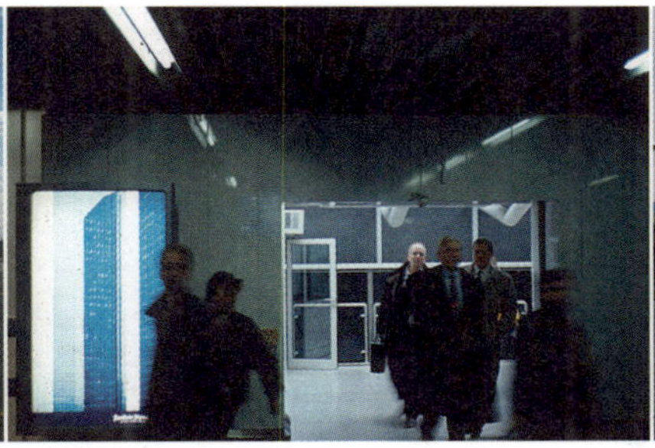
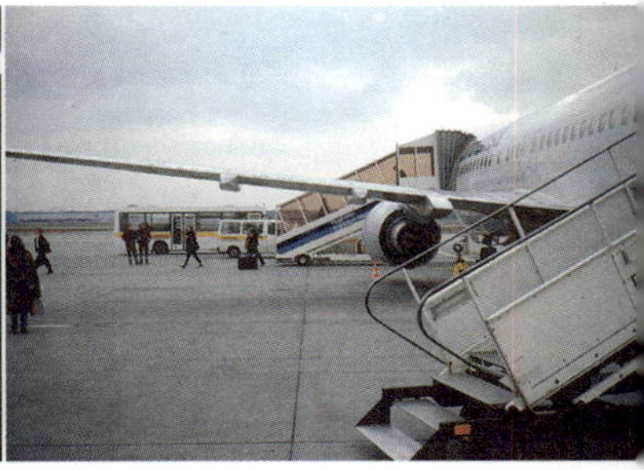

listeners, not even an inner self. Everyone speaks to, and answers to, an invisible ear, one that belongs to a phantom body of a televisual public.

The fractured nature of DeLillo's language is not unlike the one that might be spoken by Jameson's schizophrenic postmodern subjects, who, in the throes of an overwhelmingly intense, even traumatic, present is unable to make coherent sense in any recognisable, conventional manner due to an utter breakdown of the basic temporality of narrative continuity. But DeLillo's play also has much to say on spatial issues too, even if only implicitly. First, the space of our public conversations is now fully circumscribed by the camera or rather the media: life is footage waiting to be shot. Experience is not real unless it is recorded and validated through the media. It is in this mediated virtual space (rather than an architectural hyperspace) that we talk to each other today. This is the way we tell each other things, in public, before listening millions that we don't dare to say privately. Secondly, spatial experience, like the broken temporality of language, is discontinuous and creepily disembodied. The words do not reach deep, they collage fleeting surface impressions. And vision does not (cannot) distinguish between what is seen and the mediation of that scene. Majeski describes the beginning of his journey to an interviewer:

> I'm watching the take-off on live video. I'm on the plane, I'm in my seat. There's a monitor on the bulkhead. I look at the monitor and the plane is taking off. I look out the window and the plane is taking off. Then what. The plane is taking off outside the cabin and the plane is taking off inside the cabin. I look at the monitor, I look at the earth.[11]

Thirdly, it is important to remember that the plot of the play is premised on an instance of a locational misrecognition, on a character temporarily losing his way in the world. How does this happen? Majeski leaves his house early in the morning to board a plane to Chicago. From there, he is to be picked up and driven to Valparaiso, Indiana, some 40 miles away. But at the airport, the ticket counter attendant notices a discrepancy between his ticket (for Chicago) and his printed itinerary (for Miami). She tries to be helpful and finds him a seat on the Miami flight, about to take off; and even though he was fully prepared for the Chicago trip, Majeski, not wanting to be discourteous makes a quick non-decision to head for Valparaiso, Florida, via Miami. Once in Miami, instead of

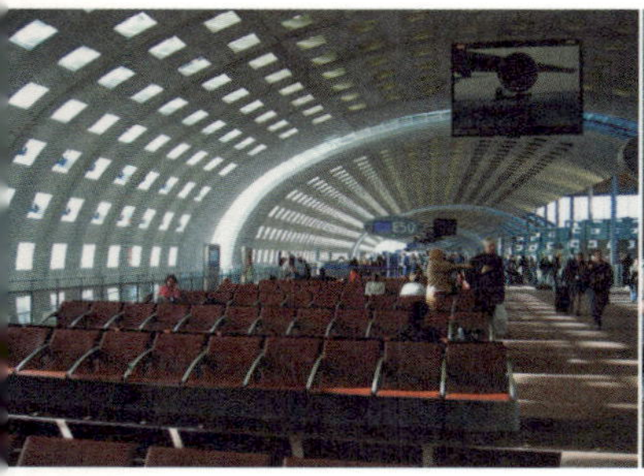
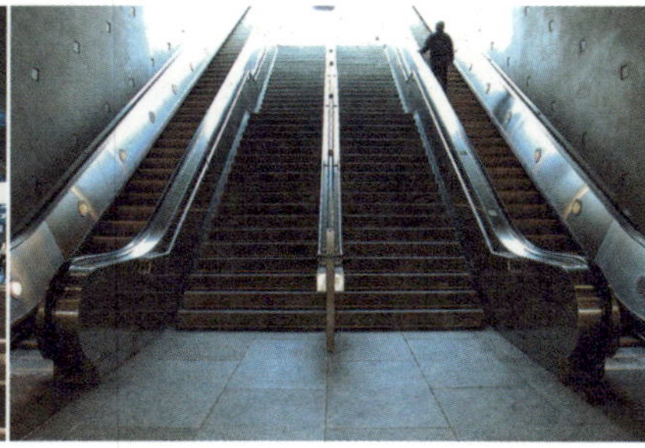
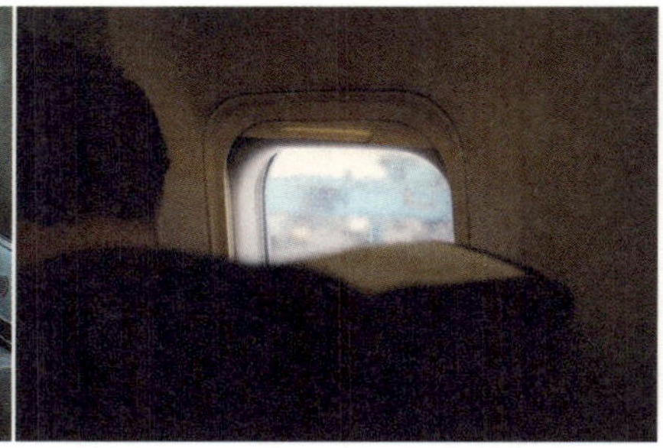

boarding a charter plane, he somehow ends up on an international flight to Santiago, headed for Valparaiso, Chile. Details remain vague. Majeski recalls the experience on a television talk show:

> Yes. It was strange. The aircraft seemed too big, too wide-bodied for an intrastate flight [....] And I said nothing. I was intimidated by the systems. The enormous sense of power all around me. Heaving and breathing. How could I impose myself against this force? The electrical systems. The revving engines [....] The sense of life support. The oxygen in the oxygen masks [....] I felt submissive. I had to submit to the systems. They were all powerful and all-knowing. If I was sitting in this assigned seat. Think about it. If the computers and metal detectors and uniformed personnel and bomb-sniffing dogs had allowed me to reach this assigned seat and given me this airline blanket that I could not rip out of its plastic shroud, then I must belong here. That's how I was thinking at the time.[12]

Majeski ends up in Chile not out of absent-mindedness, but because he recognises a hitherto unknown logic of belonging. A sense of belonging that is not bound to any specific location but to a 'system of movement'. Majeski does not resist the ways in which bodies are channelled through the sky along the prescribed trajectories of commercial air travel. He believes in its intimidating logic, has faith in its procedures, and respects its timetables. He attributes almost mystical powers to the system. He might have ended up in the wrong city, but, in a sense, he was in the right place all along. So that when he reaches Santiago, fully aware of his mistake, it no longer matters how far he has strayed. He is calm. Instead of turning back, he is convinced to complete his mistake, to go all the way to Chile's Valparaiso. "For the beauty and balance. The formal resolution."[13] (Indeed if Michael Majeski had been an artist and his trip had been a project for an exhibition, I would have been moved to think it a brilliant critique of site-specificity.)

Often we are comforted by the thought that a place is ours, that we belong to it, perhaps even come from it, and therefore are tied to it in some fundamental way. Such places ('right' places) are thought to reaffirm our sense of self, reflecting back to us an unthreatening picture of a grounded identity. This kind of continuous relationship between a place and a person is what is deemed

All photos:
Miwon Kwon
Except above centre:
Seong Hyeok Kwon

lost, and needed, in contemporary society. In contrast, the wrong place is generally thought of as a place where one feels one does not belong–unfamiliar, disorienting, destabilising, even threatening. This kind of stressful relationship to a place is, in turn, thought to be detrimental to a subject's capacity to constitute a coherent sense of self and the world.

But thanks to the perfection and formal beauty of Majeski's mistake, we can think about the 'wrong place' in altogether new ways. Rather than 'losing himself' because he ends up in the wrong place, quite the opposite seems to happen in *Valparaiso*. It is from the instance of being in an airplane headed for the wrong city that Majeski begins to recognise himself, or rather his own estrangement, and is set on a journey to account for his identity. And it is in the telling and retelling of the tale that his rather tragic and fractured sense of self is revealed not only to us, the audience, but to the character himself. Which is to say, it is the wrongness rather than rightness of place that brings Majeski into focus. Furthermore, as the play progresses, it become less and less clear as to whether Majeski was trapped in a journey headed for the wrong place or if the trip was in fact an attempt to escape *from* a wrong place–his home, his job, his marriage, his family, his life, 'himself'. A lesson to be drawn here is that an encounter with a 'wrong place' is likely to expose the instability of the 'right place', and by extension the instability of the self.

The price of such awakening is steep, however, as is revealed in the concluding scenes of DeLillo's play (not to be divulged here). Suffice to say that the psychological unmooring of Majeski as a result of his trip both liberates *and* shatters him. In light of DeLillo's inconclusive conclusion, how should we characterise Michael Majeski's perfect mistake? Was he in the right place at the right time or in the wrong place at the wrong time? We often use these phrases, 'in the right place at the right time', or so-and-so was 'in the wrong place at the wrong time', to describe degrees of fortune and misfortune, to indicate in shorthand someone's good luck or bad luck, and to concede casually (but definitively) the presence of chance or fate, or perhaps even God, as a force in directing the great and terrible things that happen in our lives. It is a moment when we acknowledge that things are beyond our will, as Majeski does himself when he concedes the power of the 'system of movement'.

But if we return to a consideration of art at this point, it is clear that the idea of the right place or the wrong place for art has less to do with chance or luck and more to do with the distinctions of propriety and impropriety as set by social conventions, ideological regimes, religious dictates, or habitual familiarity. Thought in these terms, one could argue that throughout the twentieth century, the history of avant-garde, or 'advanced', or 'critical' art practices (however one might want to characterise those practices that have pressured the status quo of dominant art and social institutions) can be described as the persistence of a desire to situate art in 'improper' or 'wrong' places. That is, the avant-garde

struggle has in part been a kind of spatial politics, to pressure the definition and legitimation of art by locating it elsewhere, in places other than where it 'belongs'. But in breaking with its traditional grounding, I wonder if such artistic endeavours haven't unknowingly acquiesced to a different order of belonging: to a system of movement and ungrounding somewhat analogous to the one that Don DeLillo's Michael Majeski confronts.

In the past, the avant-garde was extolled for its improprieties, for its acts of transgression against fixed, grounded order of traditional art categories and institutions. In recent years, the very idea of the avant-garde and its program of 'improper' behaviour has come to be viewed as historically exhausted in as much as such programmes have been co-opted or, in the least, the social conditions within or against which such behaviour was perpetrated no longer exist in tact. Once heroic improprieties are now seen as pathetic improprieties. But critical artistic practice is neither heroic nor pathetic. There are no other options than to confront an ongoing predicament *as* a predicament. It bears the burden of the necessity and impossibility of modelling new forms of being in-place, new forms of belonging. This precarious and risky position may not be the right place to be, but it is the only place from which to face the challenges of the new orders of space and time.

[1] See Miwon Kwon, "One Place After Another: Notes on Site Specificity", *October* 80, Spring 1997, pp. 20-30.

[2] See James Meyer, "The Functional Site", *Documents*, no. 7, Autumn 1996, pp. 20-29.

[3] Lucy Lippard, *The Lure of the Local: Sense of Place in a Multicultural Society*, New York: New Press, 1997, p. 11.

[4] Lippard, *The Lure of the Local*, p. 12.

[5] Fredric Jameson, "Postmodernism, or, The Cultural Logic of Late Capitalism", *Postmodernism, or, The Cultural Logic of Late Capitalism*, Durham: Duke University Press, 1991.

[6] Jameson, "Postmodernism", p. 42.

[7] Jameson, "Postmodernism", p. 43.

[8] Jameson, "Postmodernism", p. 42.

[9] Jameson, "Postmodernism", p. 44.

[10] Jameson, "Postmodernism", p. 44.

[11] Don DeLillo, *Valparaiso*, New York: Scribner, 1999, p. 32.

[12] DeLillo, *Valparaiso*, pp. 86-87.

[13] DeLillo, *Valparaiso*, pp. 86-87.

Nicolas Bourriaud
Berlin Letter about Relational Aesthetics

Nicolas Bourriaud is co-director, with Jerome Sans, of the newly created Palais de Tokyo Contemporary Art Centre in Paris. As a young critic in the 1990s, Bourriaud offered one of the earliest readings of the emergent new forms of artistic production, which he termed 'relational aesthetics', also the title of his first book of criticism in 1998 and one of the more frequently heard catchphrases when it came to the practices of artists like Rirkrit Tiravanija, Philippe Parreno, Liam Gillick and Vanessa Beecroft. This text, looking back at the social and cultural context in which such artists emerged, was commissioned for and published in the exhibition catalogue for the second *Berlin Biennale* in 2001, curated by Saskia Bos, published by the Berlin Biennale für Zeitgenössiche Kunst E. V., 2001.

Nicolas Bourriaud

Berlin Letter about Relational Aesthetics

Since the first article in the corpus that I have built up under the generic title of 'relational aesthetics' and published in the journal *Documents sur l'art* in 1995, a lot of things have changed, and much faster than I thought they would. My thesis arose from the observation of a group of artists whom I frequently visited at the time with great assiduity (from Rirkrit Tiravanija to Pierre Huyghe, from Douglas Gordon to Vanessa Beecroft, including Liam Gillick and Maurizio Cattelan, and not forgetting all those featured at the time in the exhibition *Traffic*), and did no more than display the common denominator between their highly diverse bodies of work.[1] This inter-human sphere and the service industries constitutes the universe to which this generation of artists refers, just as the worlds of consumption and industrial infrastructure did for Pop Art and Minimalism. It is no doubt time to look more closely at the relations between these artworks and the social and economic configuration that allowed them to emerge.

The work of the sociologist Michel Maffesoli asserts that nowadays, "style, the image, no longer has anything to do with the individualism of modernity".[2] He attempts to decipher the new forms of sociality in postmodern society, with their hedonistic and tactile orientation. "The image", writes Maffesoli, "is a bonding-agent; it creates community, it welds together".[3] In his book *Société en reseaux*, Manuel Castells describes the birth of a network-based society in which the fluxes of communication and the technological revolution are radically overturning the structures of work and everyday life.[4] The incredible growth of the World Wide Web, but also a growing need for bonds and contact, frustrated as this is by an abstract, individualistic society, have prompted artists to explore the field of the inter-human. They are thus inventing models of sociality or modes of communication, drawing, more or less, immateriality on the fluxes that tie us to one another. These relational practices are rooted in the appearance of these new interactive technologies that are threatening to commodify human relations within 'spaces of encounter', but also in the emergence of the tertiary sector and the service industries.

The question I would like to ask today is this: now that the ideology of internet links and continuous contact has come to pervade the globalised economy (Nokia: 'Connecting people'), how much critical radicality is left to work based on sociality and conviviality? Or to mimetic approaches?

At the beginning of the 1990s, a number of artists showed very clearly what society was heading towards. Today, now that they are surrounded by the tide whose rise they predicted, can we still see their works in the same way? The aquatic metaphor is important here: postmodern society is fluid, flexible and enveloping. Those who claim to describe it from the outside are taking themselves for God, not for artists. An artist invents new ways of swimming, he or she does not spend time sitting on the shore deconstructing the wakes of the boats, as if it were somehow possible to step outside human society.

As it happens, at the 1993 *Venice Biennale*, Rirkrit Tiravanija presented a metal gondola full of boiling water, which visitors could take for mixing with their powdered soup before sitting down to eat in the middle of the installation. I can remember the critics wondering if the piece were not a 'performance'. Even though that same year, Christine Hill polished the shoes of visitors to the *Unfair* in Cologne and then gave them a massage. She spoke of art as a socially useful activity. Since the first wave of artists working on the relational sphere (which, let me say this once and for all, is not synonymous with interactivity or conviviality); a new generation has appeared. Though hardly distinct in terms of time frame, it confirms the perception that there is a new worldview which is radically different from that of preceding generations.

In 2000 Surasi Kusolwong took part in the *Kwangju Biennale* with an environment made up of monochrome mattresses (*Happy Kwangju*), on which candidates for a massage were kindly asked to lie down. In 2001 Alicia Framis exhibited a minimal structure in dark wood, inside which only women were allowed to entrust their bodies to a masseur.

Copies? No, massage is used here rather like a colour, as a tool that underlines rather than attenuates the difference between these works that all emerged from the relational sphere. The world of work offers artists a reservoir of forms, forms that are as flexible and manipulative as the elements used by Felix Gonzalez-Torres or the 'Arte Povera' materials that serve as supports for pieces by Maurizio Cattelan. A hurried observer would see only repetition. One needs to look more closely to realise what is emerging here is a new vocabulary, one analogous to Minimal Art and that takes the *socius* as its base.

When invited to the *Venice Biennale*, Maurizio Cattelan hired out his space to a cosmetics company (*Lavorare e un brutto mestiere*, 1993). Business is a material. Fabrice Hybert is campaigning for an 'artistic use of the economy'. In 1995 Pierre Huyghe set up the *Association des Temps libérés* (*Freed Time Society*), and Svetlana Heger and Plamen Dejanov rented out their labour to BMW for the year 1999. Is this mimicry? A fascination with the absolute power now represented by the economy, which is as invisible, abstract and holistic as God Himself? There is only one question that can help us decide: What is it for? What is the purpose of using the forms of business, of taking human relations as a model? Art is not merely a trade dedicated to producing forms; it is an activity whereby these forms come to articulate a project. Liam Gillick blends modernist abstractions with corporate scenography, reconstituting the invisible links between the avant-garde and the transformations of the global economy, between Sony and contemporary video art. His *Negotiation Plaform* is not a pretext, an object for producing conviviality, but a cognitive tool. Because it included objects to be handled, actors and extras, the type of exhibition that emerged in the 90s generated a new problematic, that of the coexistence of humans, objects and forms, which generates a specific meaning.

The exhibition becomes one big film set (a "film without a camera", as Philippe Parreno put it), a set in which we can mount our own sequences of meanings. In the titles of his works, Rirkrit Tiravanija always includes the words "lots of people", indicating that they are an integral part of it all. The forms that he presents to the public do not constitute an artwork until they are actually used and occupied by the people who thus become both the walk-ons and passengers of the exhibition. "I am not a customer", wrote Liam Gillick.

The private view is the crucial moment in the exhibition's emergence as scenario. Felix Gonzalez-Torres installed a go-go dancer on the sculpture at *Post Human*, 1993; with *Jenny Happy*, Carsten Holler exhibited a young girl wearing red contact lenses; Pierre Joseph scatters "living characters to be reactivated", around his exhibitions, later replacing these with a photograph of the same people in action; Vanessa Beecroft presents groups of young women, motionless amidst the visitors-cum-voyeurs. Criterion of coexistence: how do we cohabit with forms? And with the characters delegated by the artist to inhabit them? Kendell Geers, for example, proposes ways of using contemporary images, thereby confronting us with their utter strangeness, our incapacity to live with them.

The interview has become an artistic form. Countless works are the result of an encounter or a questionnaire. The videos of Rebecca Bournigault, the photos of Tracey Moffat, the works of Gitte Villesen, Monica Bonvicini or Christian Jankowksi, all work on the basis of the encounter with others. Joseph Grigely's materials are the tools that enable him to communicate with other people. When Dominique Gonzalez-Foerster produces her works in collaboration with the 'memory' of her respondents (*Daughter of a Taoist*, at the Esther Schipper Gallery) or invites visitors to draw their childhood memories at her little consultancy booths, the role that she assigns to the public is not that of beholder but of analyser.

Artists seek interlocutors. Since the public is a somewhat unreal entity within the economy of contemporary art this interlocutor is usually brought into the production process itself as a result of a phone call, an advertisement or a chance encounter. The meaning of the work emerges from the movement linking the signs put out by the artist (Tiravanija), but also from the collaboration of individuals within the exhibition space. As Karl Marx wrote, "reality is none other than the result of what we do together". The relational aesthetic integrates this reality.

What for? (art after the homepage).

The criticism commonly levelled at these relational practices generally concerns just this transposition: if the idea is to produce alternative forms of social bonds, why confine yourself to galleries and art centres? The aesthetic content of

Michael Lin, *Le Salon*, 2003. Courtesy Palais de Tokyo, Paris

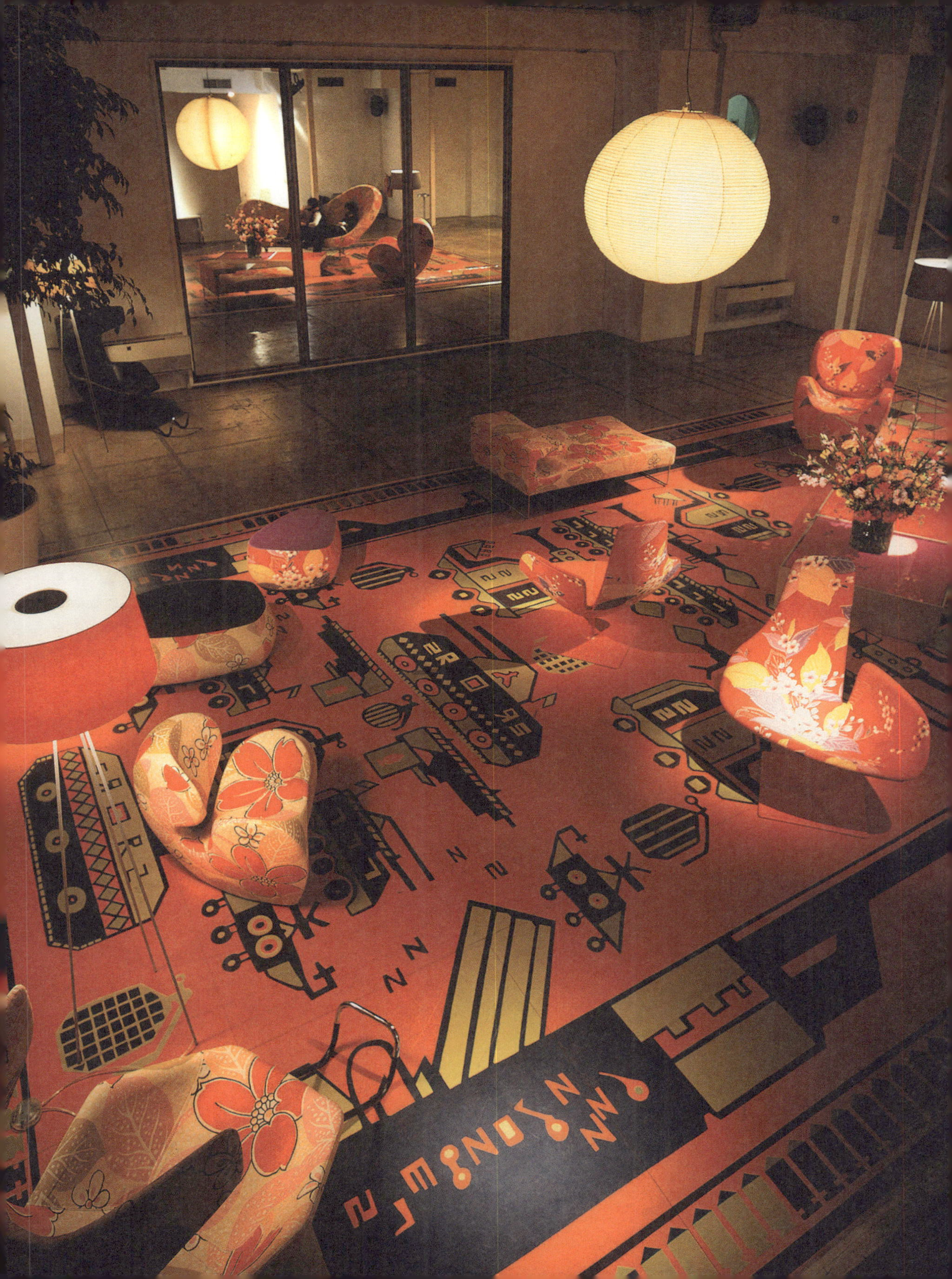

these artistic propositions must be judged formally, by translating into lived experience, the space modelled or imagined by the artist. It would be absurd to judge the social and political content of a work while stripping it of its aesthetic value, as if forms were neutral. Relational practices are not a kind of 'social' or 'sociological art'. Rather, they aim at the formal construction of space-time entities that may be able to elude alienation, the division of labour, the commodification of space and the reification of life. We could thus say that the exhibition constitutes an interstice, which sometimes reproduces or uses the very forms of our alienation. Philippe Parreno's exhibition, *Werktische*, 1994, produced on Sunday 1 May in Cologne, thus gathered leisure activities around the image of their diametrical opposite, the factory assembly line.[5] The artist didn't deny the dominant form of social relations, but put them into perspective using the specific means of art, which is neither more nor less alienated than what surrounds it. It is important to understand, therefore, that the convivial environments, encountered here and there, do not, if the artists are aware of what they are doing, represent an end in themselves. They bring into play this great, "What's it for?" which marks the true dividing line between entertainment and artistic praxis. For Tiravanija or Parreno, the use value of conviviality is combined with its exhibition value within the framework of an artistic project.

The enemy clearly designated by the important artists of the present period is the generalisation of supplier-customer relations to all levels of human existence, from work to living space and taking in all the tacit contracts that determine our private life. The failure of the modernist project can be seen in the commodification of human relations in the poverty of political alternatives and in the devaluation of work as a factor for the improvement of daily life.

As both Guy Debord and Henri Lefebvre remarked, we are experiencing an irremediable pauperisation, that of lived experience. How can you expect anyone to believe that it would be beneficial to go back to aesthetic values based on tradition, technical mastery, respect for historical conventions and the petty individual ownership of 'creation'? When you want to kill democracy, you start out by muzzling experimentation and you end up accusing freedom of having rabies. The political value of the relational aesthetic lies in two very simple observations: social reality is the product of negotiation and democracy is a montage of forms. Whatever the artist's degree of awareness, every artistic practice secretes and transposes social values, bringing them to bear on the individual or the collective. The role of the art critic is to take these forms apart, to clarify their content.

Psychiatrist, David Cooper, explained that 'madness' is not 'inside' a person (as if it were a foreign body), but inside the system of relations in which that person participates.[6] Art must work to expose these systems and to produce machines for subjectivity in opposition to 'mass-media machine processing' and its levelling instruments. What has been ground down by the machine of community must be re-singularised. And this work implies the constitution of temporary subject groups, or micro-communities, the modelling of alternative modes of sociality and the appropriation of industrial production and economic structures.

That is what the relational aesthetic is about, the emphasis on a parallel engineering, on open forms based on the affirmation of the trans-individual.

[1] *Traffic* at CAPC Musée d'Art Contemporain, Bordeaux, 1995.

[2] See Michel Maffesoli, *The Time of Tribes: The Decline of Individualism in Mass Society*, London: Sage Publications Ltd., 1996.

[3] Maffesoli, *The Time of Tribes*.

[4] Manuel Castells, *The Information Age: Economy, Society and Culture: First Volume, The Rise of the Network Society*, London: Blackwell, 1996, revised edition 2000.

[5] Philippe Parreno, *Werktische* at Schipper & Krome, Cologne, 1994.

[6] See Dr. David Cooper, *The Language of Madness*, London: Penguin Books, 1980.

In conversation
Rod Dickinson and Charlie Gere

Rod Dickinson is interested in the peculiarities of human behaviour and exploring the mechanism of belief systems. He is best known for his covert creation of crop circles during the 1990s. More recently his work has included a reconstruction of Stanley Milgram's 1961 *Obedience to Authority* experiment and the building of the *Air Loom*. Here he discusses his investigations and experiments with Charlie Gere, historian of cybernetic and computer art. A different, longer version of this interview was published as Charlie Gere, "The technologies and politics of delusion: an interview with artist Rod Dickinson", in Cathy Gere and Charlie Gere, eds., *Studies in History and Philosophy of Science Part C: Studies in History and Philosophy of Biological and Biomedical Sciences* (special issue on "The Brain in a Vat"), vol. 35, issue 2, June 2004.

In conversation

Rod Dickinson and Charlie Gere

'The Brain in a Vat' is a modern expression for the long standing philosophical problem of scepticism. How do we know what we know and perceive is actually true in a world dominated by information and communication technologies and in which much of what we receive as knowledge is heavily mediated by the (aptly named) mass media? Indeed, in such a situation, is it possible to believe in the existence of objective and transcendent truth altogether? Such issues have long been the concern of certain strands of philosophical investigation, most famously those pursued by thinkers such as Jean Baudrillard. His famous (or rather infamous) piece "The Gulf War Did Not Take Place"[1] *is in fact a brilliant dissection of our current vat-brain condition, in which our experience of a highly destructive war is entirely mediated and pre conditioned.*

Such concerns are central to the work of Rod Dickinson. Over the last 15 years, Dickinson has used his art to pursue questions of truth, delusion and mediation. He first came to public attention through his work with the Circlemakers organisation. This was a collaborative venture, involving a number of partners, most consistently John Lundberg, dedicated to making elaborate crop circles anonymously and covertly as a form of art practice. Of particular interest was the rage provoked by their practice in the self-proclaimed experts, many of who were looking to construct elaborate pseudo-scientific justifications for their extraterrestrial theories.[2]

Following the crop circle work, Dickinson then started to develop a number of works involving the re-enactment of historical events. In 2000, at the ICA, he re-enacted one of Jim Jones' sermons from the Peoples' Temple in Guyana, later the scene of the notorious mass suicide. After this piece he made the work for which he is probably most well known; his re-enactment of psychologist Stanley Milgram's notorious Obedience to Authority *experiment.*[3] *In the* Obedience *experiments volunteers were asked to give apparently real electric shocks to other individuals they could only hear. Though under the impression that they were assisting the experiment, they were in fact its subjects, while the apparent victims of the shocks were in fact acting. The aim was to see how far an individual would obey an order from a figure of authority, even if it meant subjecting another human to pain. The fact that two-thirds of the subjects would go on doing so until asked to desist is well known. Less well known is the drama of the event, and it was this that Dickinson intended to capture in his re-enactment, which rigorously followed the transcripts to present a four-hour live event. and subsequent film.*[4]

Dickinson's next work looked more closely at questions of mental delusion. In 2002, as part of a group show at the Laing Gallery in Newcastle, Dickinson built a full-scale model of the Air Loom, an imaginary device described and drawn in the early nineteenth century by James Tilly Matthews, an inmate at the Bethlem Royal Hospital, popularly known as 'Bedlam'. Matthews, who was possibly schizophrenic, was convinced that machines, of the sort he described, were being used by the French to brainwash the British government. This extraordinary delusion has survived owing to its inclusion in one of the first works of psychiatry, a treatise on Matthews by his keeper at Bedlam, John Haslam, Illustrations of Madness.[5] *Dickinson's realisation of the Air Loom was meticulous and was accompanied by actors in early nineteenth century dress, playing some of the characters involved.*[6] *This piece both continues and presages Dickinson's long term concern with brainwashing and with questions of social control, truth and knowledge.*

Charlie Gere Your work seems to me to be relevant to the state of generalised and institutionalised paranoia in which we live now. It reflects extremely well the mechanics of how this situation operates.

Rod Dickinson One of the things I am always keen to do is try to deflect the absolutely specific reading of the pieces of work, because I think, whether we are talking about the *Air Loom* or the Milgram piece, they themselves refer to very specific events, and they can be read in exactly the way you are talking about. I am really keen to distance them from any specific reading because in many ways those kinds of ideas and narratives are actually running more or less the whole time through culture and it's very easy to map them at any place or any time. I chose those particular events that are almost like templates and can then be mapped onto other places and times.

CG It's a question of exploring the apparatus of knowledge and of paranoia–false knowledge in a general sense, rather than being a specific reaction to events?

RD Exactly. I do see the pieces of work as very hypothetical and very abstract. In the case of *The Milgram Re-enactment,* its subject is an experiment that itself was a piece of deception and was in fact a coded re-enactment of another event, the Holocaust. There is an idea of hypothesis and deferral that runs right the way through it, and in some senses the original is a fiction. Though my piece was a painstaking accurate piece of history, the history is founded upon an experiment that is based around or uses the apparatus of fiction. The *Air Loom* operates in a very similar way, but from a slightly different perspective, where again it's a very accurate historical representation in some senses, but only from the perspective of one person's mind. In a way I'm disassembling the beliefs of one individual and then representing them as if they were orthodox history. This seems to me to be quite an abstract approach.

CG This seems similar to what you were doing with the crop circle work, which involves layer upon layer of fictional discourse, which reflect back onto each other, especially through the medium of the web.

RD In 1995 or 1996 the web emerged into mainstream culture and it was really apparent that all those marginal micro social groups that were formed around crop circles, that were primarily belief-led, adopted the web as their primary source of dissemination and exchange, which is completely logical and in many ways a fantastic working example of how the web functioned, especially in those early days. Consequently I got introduced to those possibilities very early. I was also interested in moving my work away from institutionalised art contexts and trying to construct another context that could operate independently, and that as practitioner would give me more control.

CG So the web represented a particular ambivalent space, in which issues about authorship and authenticity are mixed up with questions about knowledge and ownership. It seems an ideal space for complicating those kinds of questions.

RD Absolutely. It is the primary or even the best model for generating folklore. It does it better than any other medium I can think of. One of our aims was to create a kind of mythology not just around other people's beliefs of what crop circles were but also around the idea of what it might mean for people to be making them, so we were actually interested in propagating the kinds of conspiracy theories that were being applied to us. The early exhibitions I did in the mid to late 90s of crop circle work were basically documentation. Making a crop circle is a live event but arguably the art resides in the reaction people have to it and the folklore it generates. Not in the object itself. So the documentation of the circles was very important, inevitably, beautiful aerial photos, but also texts and writing by believers. The gallery walls resembled low tech information centres, full of texts which denied my authorship in making the circles. So the paradox at the heart of one of these exhibitions is that the moment you walk into the gallery you are presented with information that is emphatically telling you that you are not looking at an artist's work.

CG None of your work resembles any other artwork that I can think of, in that it is not self-consciously art, it is self-consciously something else. *The Milgram Re-enactment*, the work for which you are most well known so far, could equally well be a very serious sociological or social science experiment. It is presented absolutely deadpan with no attempt to impose any notion of the artist or the art world. What particularly attracted you to that piece?

RD I think the thing that really drew me towards the Milgram experiment went beyond the statistics and beyond the questions: "Will you or won't you press the electric shock switch?", "Will you or won't you shock the learner with a fatal dose of electricity?" What really interested me was the drama that took place in front of the electric shock machine. I only really realised this when I saw footage from the original experiment, which very few people have seen. It shows people in acute distress, facing a terrible dilemma. Rather than showing those who obeyed the scientists administering the maximum amount of shocks as sadistic, or even as unprotesting, institutional and zombie-like, the footage actually shows them in acute distress, in this terrible moral dilemma, not sure what they should do. They believe in the moral worth of the experiment which they think they are taking part in which of course is not the experiment they are taking part in at all, and at the same time try to empathise with the person who is screaming in (apparently) terrible pain and begging them to stop. It was that drama that was so condensed and so spare, almost Beckett-like in its density. That is the thing that really compelled me.

CG So the real value of doing the re-enactment was that it involved a completely opposite response to that which you expected.

RD Yes–and the only way to represent it was experientially, so that's why the resulting film I produced from the live piece is four hours long and that's why the re-enactment was four hours long. Basically you have to sit there, you have to be there with that person the whole time they are going through the experiment, to understand

Rod Dickinson in collaboration with Graeme Edler and Steve Rushton, *The Electro Shock Machine: The Milgran Reenactment* (detail), 2002

Rod Dickinson in collaboration with Graeme Edler and Steve Rushton, *The Laboratory: The Milgran Reenactment* (detail), 2002

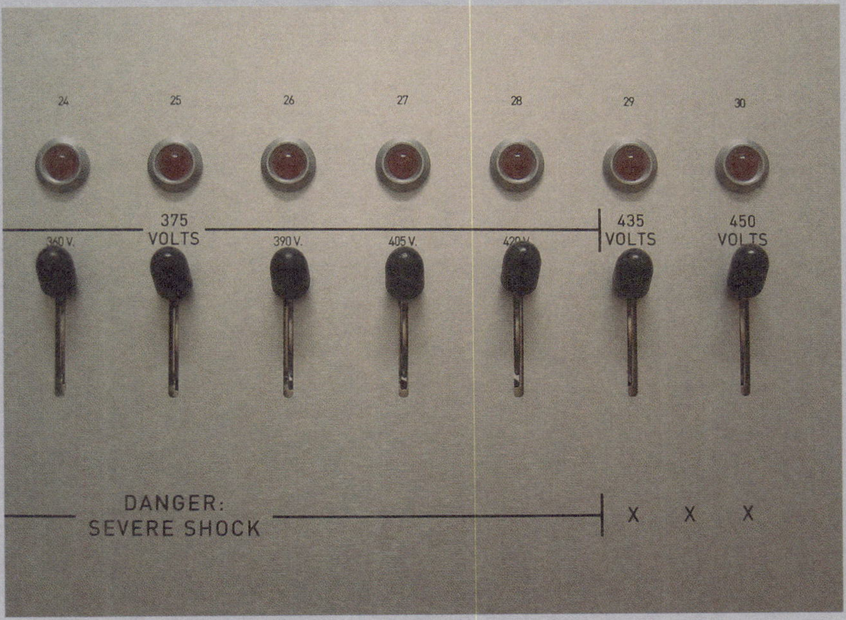

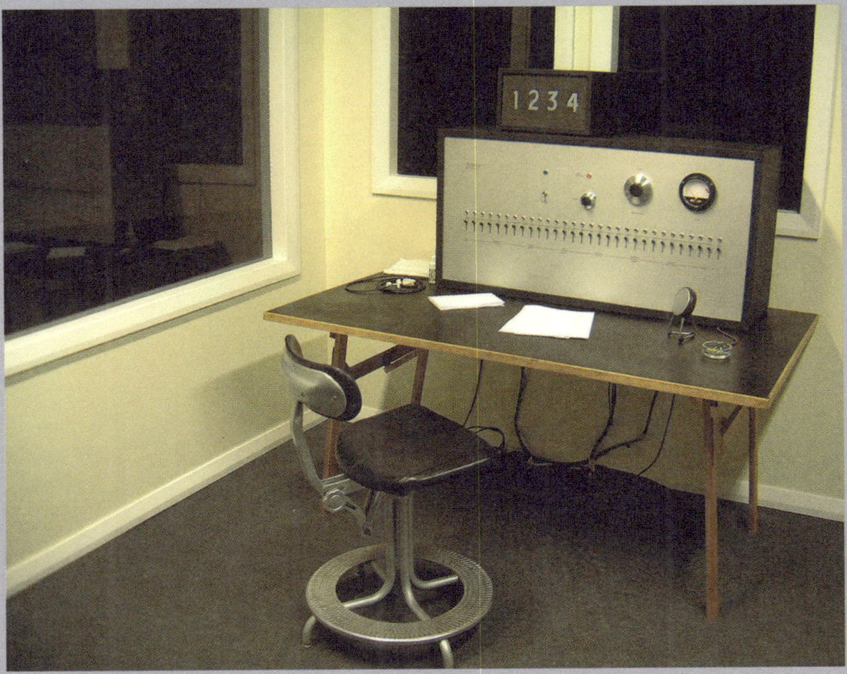

what it is they're going through and to be able to put yourself in their position and figure out what your own response might have been. Though I like to think of my work as very information based, even if it is done through experiential means, there really isn't any way of conveying that experience as pure information and pure data. It's actually a dramatic structure that is durational. This is for me what was really interesting, and the re-enactment involved repeating the same procedures again and again. There is a sort of nihilism to that endless repetition. I think Milgram always wanted people to disobey, but people so persistently obeyed.

CG Finding results with which I suppose he was pleased but appalled him at the same time. What I really like on your website is a quote from Orwell from his essay *England Your England*: "As I write, highly civilised human beings are flying overhead, trying to kill me. They do not feel any enmity against me as an individual, nor I against them. They are 'only doing their duty', as the saying goes." I know you don't want to map these things onto specific things, but it is a very good allegory of the whole apparatus of the 'technologised' modern world.

RD That's one of the things that was important to the re-enactment. I think Milgram was a brilliant dramatist and he makes the relationship between humans and technology become increasingly visible.

CG Clearly the apparatus is at the heart of this.

RD It is, because Milgram in his endless and intricate variants of the experiment places victim and punisher both further away and closer to each other. Those separations were achieved through technology and physical distance, so the closer he places victim and perpetrator the less they are likely to obey and give the shocks and the further apart they are, the more they are mediated by technology consequently the more likely they are to obey and give the shocks.

CG It makes one wish that Walter Benjamin had been able to comment on this particular experiment. He would have had such a lot to say about questions of technology and distance and even the aura in a bizarre way. When you say Milgram's a dramatist, I think you're right. He's an artist in a sense and in all sorts of ways.

RD I think he was a sort of proto-situationist. He used to conduct lots of impromptu social experiments with his students.

CG I suppose he's working in the context, and this is pure speculation, of somebody like Alan Kaprow, who was doing happenings, which are often about engaging in real life, and which are the American version of Situationism to some extent, involved with that American Pragmatist tradition of a particular engagement with art and life.

RD Yes, though obviously it is scientifically really important; it's one of the most important social psychology experiments ever done, but the thing that really drew me to it is that there are elements that are totally negated and not engaged with. The whole point in my re-enactment was not to make any new data. I wasn't interested in doing that.

CG Well you'd be a social scientist if you did that.

RD And I think that would be a far less interesting thing to do. What was far more important was to try and occupy that moment in history and see it through as closely as we could. It was important that the words that everyone spoke in the re-enactment were the actual transcripts of the real experiment, so it was a word-for-word copy.

CG So your piece has a whole other dimension in relation to the fiction that the piece itself embodied.

RD Absolutely. I am really interested in the role of mediation in certain kinds of representation, and in looking at moments of history that are characterised by their artifice and by being underpinned by layers of fiction. Moments that are always referring to something else, so there's a self-truth to Milgram's experiment, and I suppose to my re-enactment, where the truth is actually embedded in its fiction, in its construction, which is based around a fiction. So you have to engage in the idea that you are witnessing something which is a very heavily constructed piece of artifice.

CG That will take me some time to unpack. *The Milgram Re-enactment*, the James Tilly Matthews *Air Loom* and the work that you are going on to do now, are all concerned with the ways mental responses to the world are constructed in different kinds of contexts, environments and in the ways that truth is constructed. So in the Milgram experiment certain kinds of fictional set-ups are put in place and people have to go along with them. They are led along to play along with these ideas and believe them to be true.

RD Yes. I am making a whole series of pieces about brainwashing. The first piece is the *Air Loom*, which is obviously made from the perspective of someone who is incarcerated in Bedlam and regarded as a lunatic by the authorities, and whose delusion is preserved by a fluke of history.

CG By the Haslam book.

RD Yes that's right. The next piece I am working on looks at brainwashing in a broader sense and from a totally different perspective, from the point of view of state control. This piece looks at how the FBI used a very bizarre psychological warfare programme against the Branch Davidians, a small religious community in Waco, Texas who besieged in 1993. The siege ended in a fire at the Branch Davidians church, where many were killed. What's interesting for me is, rather than taking the Waco community as a subject, is to take the state's actions against the community as a subject, and this bizarre psychological warfare programme that they used against them. This was basically sensory deprivation, playing very strange audio that you couldn't imagine would have any effect on anyone apart from annoying them and making them think how stupid the state was. Statements from witnesses, from survivors from Waco, testify to that kind of thing. So my piece is partially about what belief is it inside the state that allows them to think that somehow this is going to actually make people more malleable and coerce them into a set of predictable actions. It seems as delusional as Matthew's *Air Loom*.

CG They've being doing that for some time, haven't they? They did it with General Noriega and loud rock music. I sort of see that might work (laughter). But I presume it's a legacy of the fairly strange psy-ops tendency within the American military.

RD Actually it's a legacy of MK Ultra and Artichoke, which were the CIA's mind control experiments in the 50s. What's fascinating about the history of those experiments is that they were an unmitigated failure too, and they didn't manage to manifest the perfect mind control assassin the "Manchurian Candidate", but out of it came these other things like the psy-ops programme.

CG All of which are not particularly effective.

RD Exactly. And in a way this series of works is about the impossibility and the irrationality of the idea of trying to brainwash somebody.

CG And how it begs all sorts of questions of what exactly there is to be washed.

RD Exactly.

CG Let me just go back to the James Tilly Matthews piece. Where did you find out about it?

RD I found it in 1995 in an exhibition in the Museum of London, of art from the Bethlem museum archive which included work of patients from Bethlem (Bedlam) throughout the centuries. Matthew's original drawing was one of the exhibits there and it stuck in my mind. It's a very powerful image and I guess it re-emerged as something that had been sitting in the back of my mind for a very long time. This was also prompted by discussion

Original diagram of *The Air Loom*, drawn by James Tilly Matthews from *Illustrations of Madness* by John Haslam, 1810

Rod Dickinson with Headway Community Theatre Group, *The Air Loom: A Human Influencing Machine*, 2002

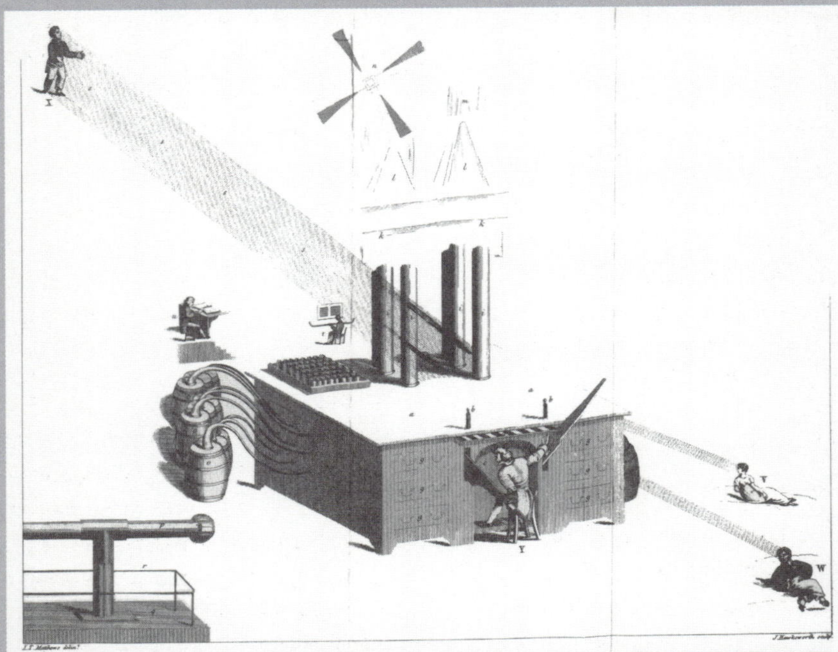

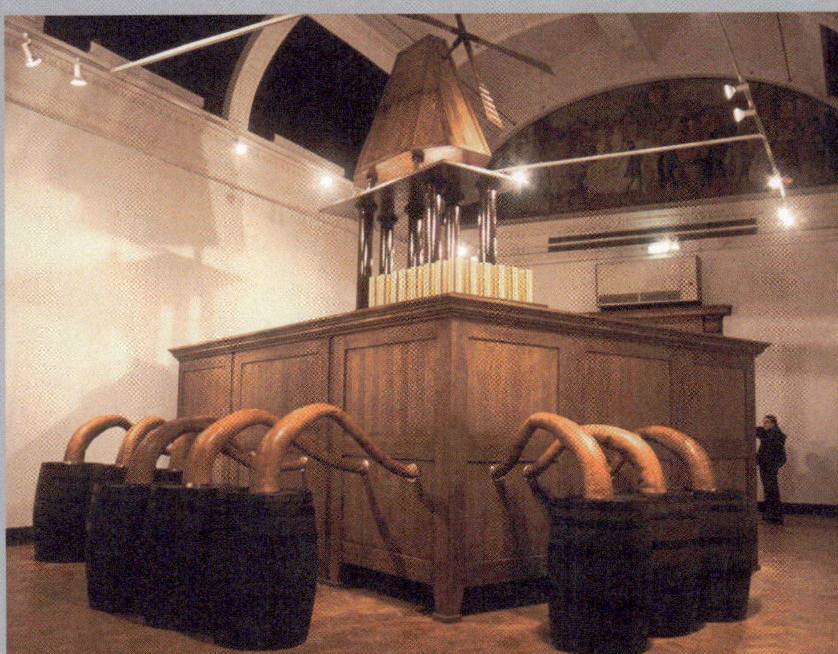

with writer Mike Jay, who's just published *The Air Loom Gang*.[7] The thing for me that rings true and has a very strange parallel to contemporary reports about mind control is that Matthews was definitely involved in political intrigue during the French Revolution. There is evidence that he travelled to France, effectively as a kind of emissary of the British Government in some capacity or another, and negotiated with the French to try and stop what would become the Napoleonic Wars, and failed, obviously. He got back to England, his pleas to meet with the Home Secretary and others in the Government whom he had some relation with before were rejected. He ended up in Bedlam because he went to the public gallery at the Houses of Parliament and accused the Home Secretary of treason, and then was promptly carted off to Bedlam, and locked up. What fascinates me is the parallel with contemporary reports of mind control where political intrigue and real events become confused with delusional ones, and there always seems to be this very strange relationship between mental illness and mind control.

CG: The thing this brings up is the question of knowing what reality is. Trying to negotiate between opposing versions of reality may have made it impossible to negotiate between the truth and whatever might be said to be untrue.

RD Mike Jay talks about the *Air Loom* as being Matthews' way out, his way of almost staying sane. If he can believe that the *Air Loom* is manipulating the British government and therefore stopping the peace treaty and precipitating the war with France, then that in some ways can make his world view whole, and the coherence can come, not through his own failure at peace negotiations or through the other negotiators' failure, but by people being controlled by this machine, which can explain their actions.

CG There's a natural progression from questions of brainwashing, cults and so forth to terrorism and the whole apparatus that does actually surround and also is perceived to surround it, in the way that terrorists are portrayed in the media, which is an issue that begs to be investigated.

RD Yes. It's only relatively recently that terrorism has been so constantly and explicitly linked to religious beliefs. It has a long history, but it's only recently that it is now impossible to think about terrorism without thinking about religious ideas, whereas it was possible before, even though that might have been a misunderstanding of much terrorism, it was possible to do it. It wasn't mediated in that way.

CG It's the question of the totally dedicated fanatic who believes that if he crashes into the World Trade Centre he will go to heaven. The way that these activities are presented in the press seems to me to suffer from exactly the same kinds of problems with the portrayals of the cults. The complexity and depth of the discourse surrounding terrorism from the point of view of the participants is lost in the account.

RD Yes absolutely. One of the really interesting things that emerged for me out of making crop circles was a really clear and good understanding of how the media functions.

CG This is something you found when you were doing that work?

RD Absolutely. Simply because that work was the subject of many media stories and to some extent we were able to control the mediation indirectly and telling different journalists different stories. We had a slightly covert platform that we were able to exploit in order to at least see how those kinds of mechanisms worked and how the media functioned. Actually I am still always surprised at how predictable their reactions are and how prepared they were to print unsubstantiated information. It seems to me that journalism is about making narratives. It's not about information.

CG That becomes more obvious the more one tries to understand what is going on, in the current situation for example, for which such an understanding is needed.

RD Despite the net print journalism hasn't really changed, but journalism that takes place online is radically different, because the Internet is a medium in which information can be disseminated pretty raw, without any kind of narrative being attached to it.

CG It is perhaps the general issue around knowledge in our current world that all your work seems to be about.

RD For me the interesting thing is taking modes of representation that have implicit within them models or ideas about disseminating data. Re-enactments are usually conducted by amateur enthusiasts and amateur historians, people who usually know an awful lot about the subject matter that they are re-enacting, and are keen to disseminate that. But they find a way of disseminating information that is very theatrical and very entertaining, but nevertheless implicit in it is their understanding and knowledge. Their enactment of these things seems to be about going through the routines, demonstrating the knowledge they have acquired about a specific period or event. It's about the demonstration of knowledge. I am interested in using those models.

CG It's about the performative aspect of knowledge. It seems to be a total desire for authenticity in a world where such a thing just isn't possible, but which can only be approached through the inauthentic, through re-enactments or belief systems that create a whole system of knowledge around something

RD And that's why I am interested in historical moments that are so mediated by artifice.

CG It goes way beyond even Baudrillard's notion of simulation. It becomes the last grasp at authenticity through simulation. Perhaps this is the message in your work. All the pieces seem to be about that.

RD I always think the best grasp you can get of reality is when it's at its most artificial.

CG It's like Benjamin's image of the way film does not show the apparatus of filming: "The equipment-free aspect of reality here becomes the height of artifice; the sight of immediate reality has become an orchid in the land of technology". It's a notion of purity that's totally fake but serves to represent itself as pure.

[1] Jean Baudrillard, *The Gulf War Did Not Take Place*, Bloomington, IN: Indiana University Press, 1995.

[2] For an informed and critically acute account of Dickinson's crop circle work, see John Roberts' article "Trickster", originally written for Dickinson's 1998 exhibition *Half Lit World* at Camerawork in London. John Roberts, "Trickster", *Oxford Art Journal* 1999 also at www.circlemakers.org/trick.html.

[3] Milgram is equally famous for his *Small World* research, in which he studied the degree of separation and connection between individuals. His surprising results led to the idea of 'six degrees of separation' being the average number of connections between any two individuals.

[4] See also Steve Rushton, *The Milgram Re-enactment*, Amsterdam: Jan van Eyck Akademie, 2003.

[5] Originally published in 1810, the book was reprinted in 1988, with an introduction by Roy Porter by Routledge in their series *Tavistock Classics in the History of Psychiatry*.

[6] Images of the piece are available at www.theairloom.org.

[7] Mike Jay, *The Air Loom Gang*, London: Bantham Press, 2003.

Diagrams and cuttings from crop circle researchers and enthusiasts' pamphlets, 1999

Crop Formation, Woodborough Hill, Wilts, UK, August 2000. Both courtesy Rod Dickinson

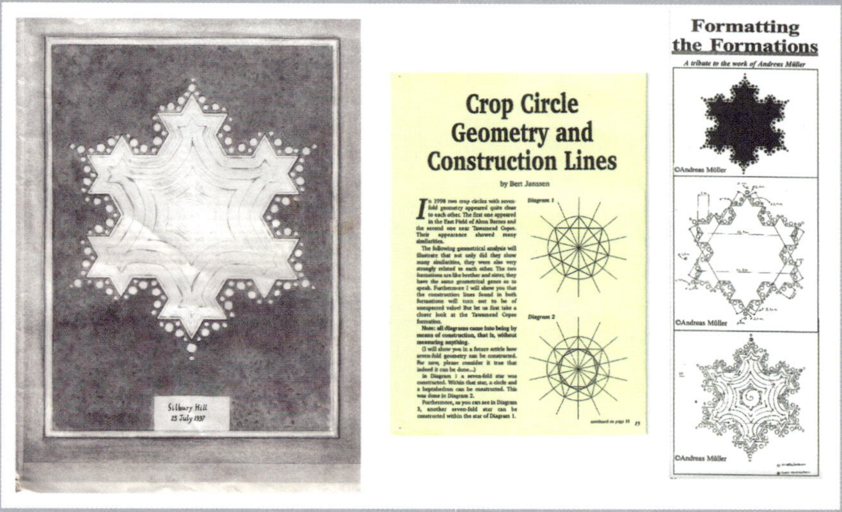

Crop Circle Geometry and Construction Lines

by Bert Janssen

In 1998 two crop circles with seven-fold geometry appeared quite close to each other. The first one appeared in the East Field of Alton Barnes and the second one near Tawsmead Copse. Their appearance showed many similarities.

The following geometrical analysis will illustrate that not only did they show many similarities, they were also very strongly related to each other. The two formations are like brother and sister, they have the same geometrical genes so to speak. Furthermore I will show you that the construction lines found in both formations will turn out to be of unexpected value! But let us first take a closer look at the Tawsmead Copse formation.

Note: all diagrams came into being by means of construction, that is, without measuring anything.

(I will show you in a future article how seven-fold geometry can be constructed. For now, please consider it true that indeed it can be done...)

In Diagram 1 a seven-fold star was constructed. Within that star, a circle and a heptahedron can be constructed. This was done in Diagram 2.

Furthermore, as you can see in Diagram 3, another seven-fold star can be constructed within the star of Diagram 1.

continued on page 16 15

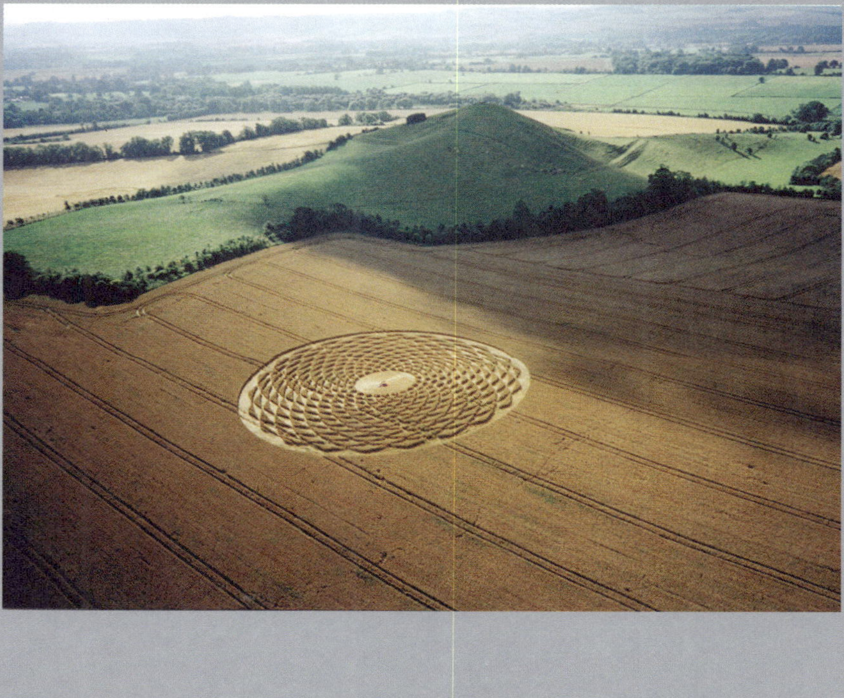

In conversation
Aleksandra Mir

Plane Landing, 2003 and *First Woman on the Moon*, 1999, are projects conceived by artist Aleksandra Mir. Mir's vision for *Plane Landing*, launched in the Capability Brown designed grounds of Compton Verney in summer 2003, centred on the creation of a purpose-designed helium balloon in the shape and size of a passenger jet plane that would 'travel' to picture-postcard locations. *Plane Landing*, like *First Woman on the Moon*, is an event: the production of the balloon, its journey to new destinations, the inflation, its 'landing' and the documentation of all these parts constitutes the artwork. What follows are two interviews with the artist: a transcript of a BBC Radio Bristol interview contemporaneous with the first *Plane Landing* and a conversation with Claire Doherty subsequent to Mir's lecture in Bristol in October 2003.

In conversation
Aleksandra Mir and BBC Radio Bristol

Rachel Burden It's 90 minutes past seven on *Morning West*, BBC Radio Bristol with Rob Salvidge and Rachel Burden. Bristol-based Cameron Balloons have developed a giant inflatable jet plane which, when filled with helium, will float as a sculpture in a permanent state of landing. The plane balloon was dreamt up by the American artist Aleksandra Mir, who was inspired on a visit to Bristol four years ago. The plane took months to build. It weighs as much as a large man. Flo Bailey visited the Cameron Balloons factory and spoke to some of the staff who work there.

Male speaker This one is shaped like an aeroplane. It's a project for an artist, Aleksandra Mir, who has had the concept of making an aeroplane fly, but just hover as a helium-filled balloon. It has a body that is filled with helium and the wings will be air-pressurised. It's very unusual to see an aeroplane that is flying but not moving forward, and is static in the air. Very tricky to get the thin surfaces, the wings and the tail surfaces
to hold their position just from air pressure alone.

Female speaker It took us roughly about four weeks to actually make the jumbo jet. So, it took awhile for designers to design it… but just for the sewing part, I would have said about four weeks.

Flo Bailey Okay Liz, do you enjoy working on these strange balloons?

Liz Yeah, it's quite nice because everything's different jobs all the time. Yeah.

FB And joining me now is Gavin Hales. He's just jumped out of his fork lift truck.

Gavin Hales Well my job primarily was to interface between the design and the production side and to deal with all the patterning of the material, and cutting it and ensuring that all the bits and pieces go together as they should do. And of course with these sorts of things, inevitably there are problems along the way. And it's sort of my job to try and iron them out as best as I can [chuckling].

Plane Landing, 2003
Factory view Cameron Balloons, Bristol, 9 July 2003

Plane Landing is a Compton Verney Commission
All images courtesy Aleksandra Mir

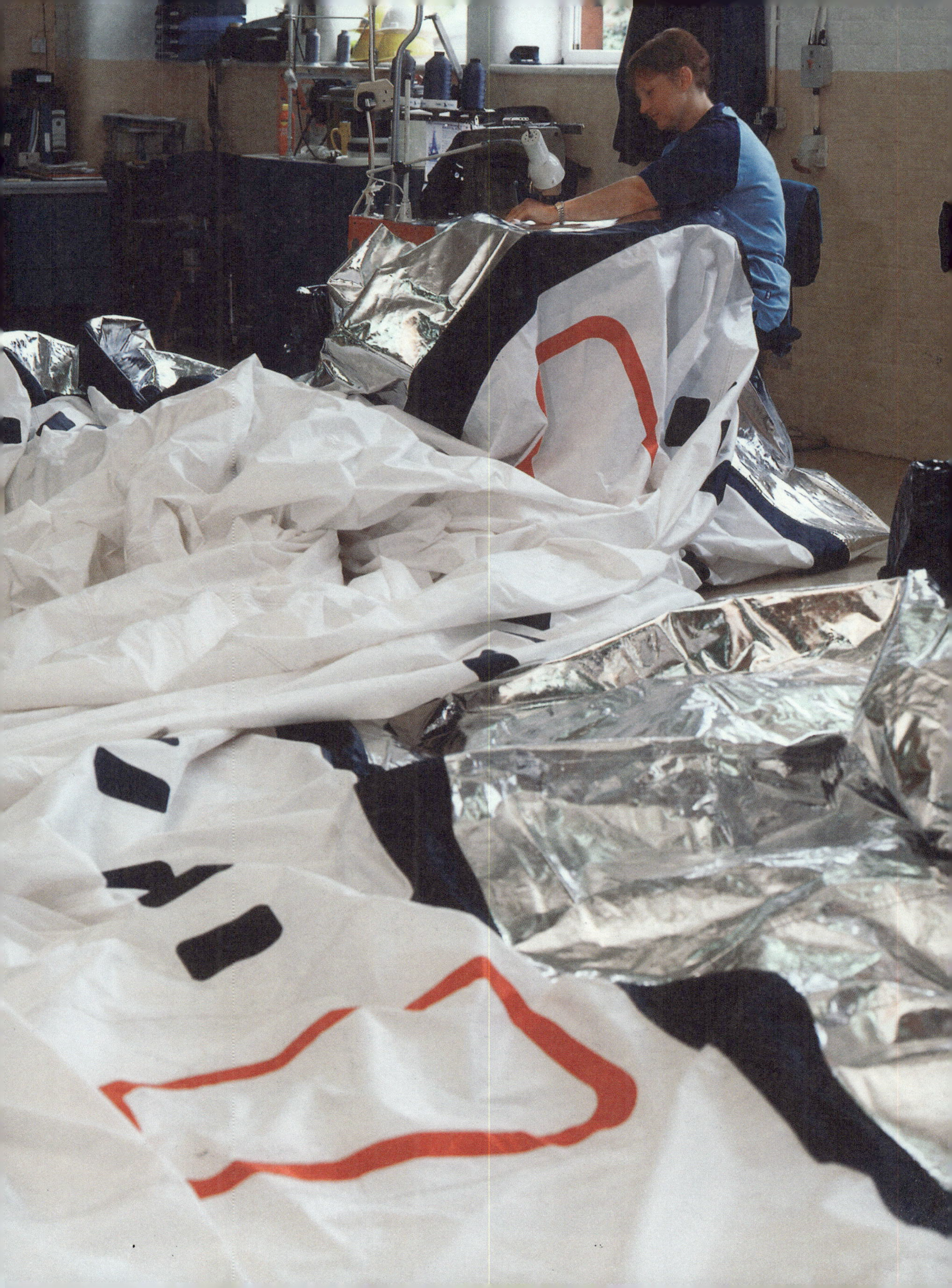

Plane Landing, 2003
Test inflation, Bristol hangar, 13 July 2003

Compton Verney, 6.30am, 20 July 2003

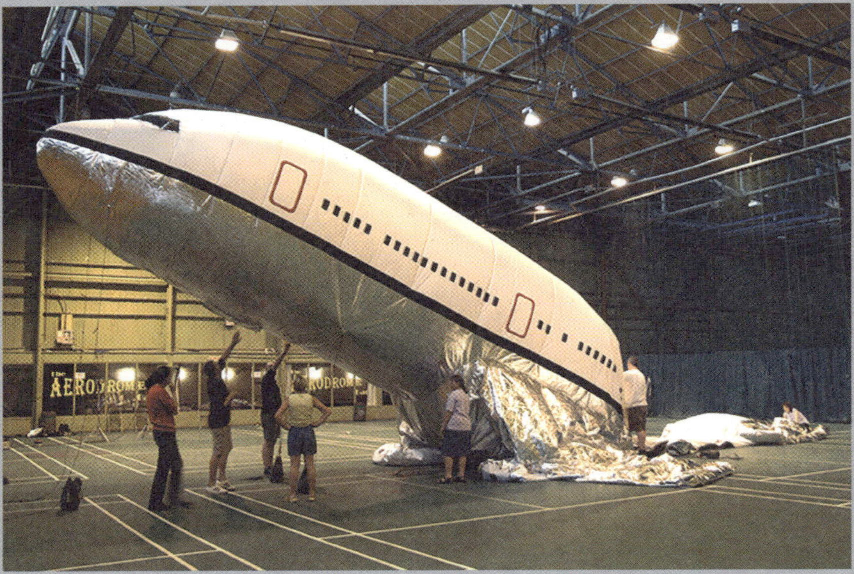

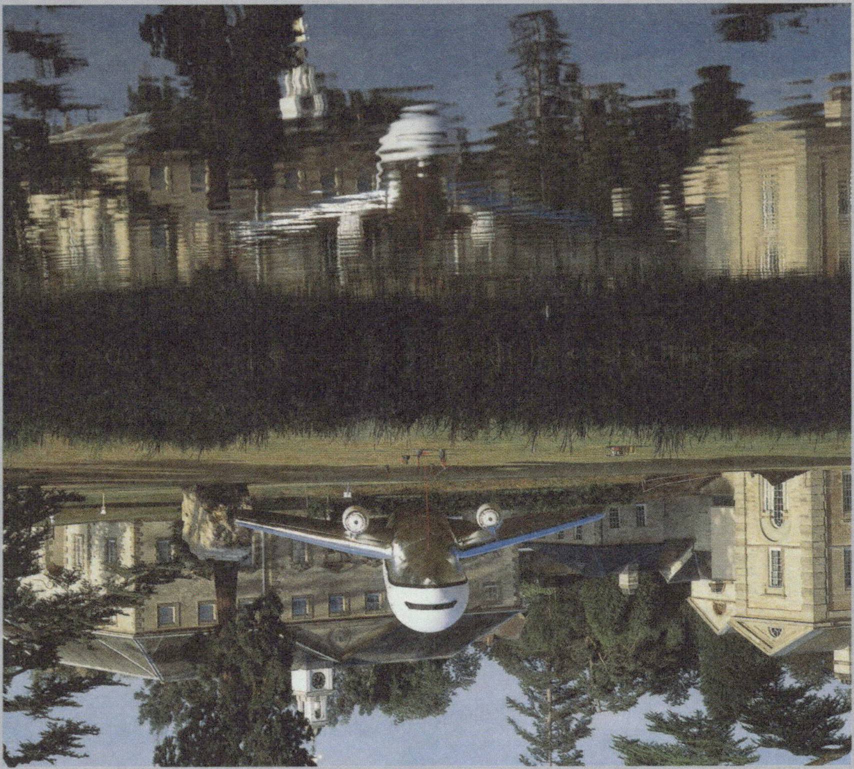

FB Okay now, you are the man in the know. So you will be able to tell me how big the plane actually is.

GH It's about approximately 60 feet long. And the whole thing weighs 91 kilos, and it's 106 cubic meters of helium. Well, it's a 737, and considering it is a fabric structure and it's helium filled, it looks very similar to the real thing. I think it's quite intricate but it's certainly quite challenging. And it's certainly the first plane that I've ever made. In total, with the design, the manufacturing, there were about eight people that worked on the plane at different stages. It's been very much a team effort.

RB A little bit earlier I spoke to Aleksandra Mir from her home in Manhattan, in New York. She's the artist behind the project. And I asked her where the idea for the balloon had come from.

Aleksandra Mir I was actually in England on a train going on my way to Bristol when I saw in the sky a few planes in the process of landing. And they were back-lit and they looked like they were standing still. And I thought it was an amazing visual. And I was wondering if it would be possible to actually create that visual. From there it became a very pragmatic process of actually trying to find a balloon manufacturer who could take it on. And the idea of actually producing a helium-inflatable jet plane that would be tethered to the ground and would be a kind of inverted sculpture.

RB And how did you get in touch with Cameron Balloons then?

AM Well it's funny because obviously I don't come from ballooning and I don't come from aviation. I'm a visual artist and I work in a wide variety of mediums. But every time I take on a new challenge in a new field that I have no clue about... so I do a lot of research. And I started actually sourcing the world for balloon manufacturers, and ironically, or maybe obviously, I ended up back in Bristol where Cameron Balloons is situated. They're a world-leading balloon manufacturer. We've been talking for two years and going back and forth, back and forth trying to figure this out. And now this object does exist. You know, we're hoping that it will work, but it's a huge experiment. But at least we have it, and we've done it and I'm very anxious to see it work myself.

RB You came to the very best place of all, coming to Cameron Balloons.

AM Yes, it was the absolutely obvious solution. I didn't have that information. I wasn't aware of that even when I started thinking about this.

RB As we've just been hearing, the actual engineering involved in this is terribly complicated. How much of that have you been involved in?

AM Nothing. I don't know anything about engineering. I've just been this sort of silly artist with a dumb idea, and that sort of brought the vision. Don Cameron's first question to me was, "What is the vision?" So, I don't feel I've been infantilised in that process, but it's been, you know, my whims and my kind of aesthetic kind of idea... it's something that they've had to translate and it's absolutely their knowledge and their insight.

RB That's the American artist Aleksandra Mir. Now, she's responsible for the concept behind this helium-filled jet plane. It's kind of hard to explain Rob, but it's going to appear as a hovering jet in landing position. And it's first 'fake flight' if you like, will be in a couple weekends' time. It's an event in Warwickshire.

Rob Salvidge You paint such a wonderful, vivid picture.

RB [chuckling] Don't I just? I spent a long time on the phone to her and I still couldn't get quite around it.

RS We look forward to seeing pictures of it. [laughter] It's 24 minutes past seven. Sport along very shortly.

BBC Radio Bristol interview, 8 July 2003, transcribed by Jacqui Sutton, New York.

In conversation

Aleksandra Mir and Claire Doherty

Claire Doherty *Plane Landing* occurred at Compton Verney in July 2003, some two years after your initial idea and proposal. Could you describe the process through which this project was realised?

Aleksandra Mir I had the idea and started doing research into ballooning and aviation whilst on a Delfina residency in London in 2001. It was then realised through a commission from the Compton Verney House Trust, on the initial invitation of curator Michael Stanley, who also raised a supporting grant from the Art Council of England that effectively paid for the bulk of the production of the project. The present curator John Leslie brought it to realisation in the grounds of Compton Verney in the summer of 2003.[1] I had by then written around 3000 emails and made about 15 trips to Bristol for meetings with the factory, Cameron Balloons, who built it. I am now continuing the active negotiation with hosts around the world who are interested in bringing the plane to new locations and add to its journey that way.

CD With a project such as this, are you able to articulate where for you the work resides? Are there aspects of the project that are purely production or is every aspect of the process another facet of the work?

AM I get this question more and more often which may be indicative of how all aspects of my practice are naturally blending into one seamless flow. *Plane Landing* is an object, which functions both as a sculpture and as a prop for a performance, situated in a ready-made landscape. I allow the audience as much insight into the process of preparations, the inflation and deflation as is practical and safe. I photograph all stages of the production and this material is made public, both as documentation and promotion of the event. Recently, documentary material of my past ephemeral works have also started to enter museum collections, as art history.

So in effect, there is really no distinction for myself between doing the research, drafting proposals, attending meetings, negotiating aesthetics, physics or money, travelling, being available for press, capturing the process as it happens or staging shoots to show it off from a particular angle that is of interest to me, following up in educational or gallery contexts, or doing interviews like this one. It all requires the same effort. So if I focus the question back on my self, my activity and engagement, I would say that as long as I am needed on the scene, as long as there is a resonance between me and the world and I am actively involved in the work, I create work.

CD If the plane in this project was to act (as you have said elsewhere) as a "catalyst to talk about landscape", could you give an indication of how and whether you think that occurred or is still occurring?

AM It occurred live and it is apparent in the photography. The plane is situated outdoors in an open-air situation. It is surrounded by a landscape; in this case, the Capability Brown designed parkland of the Compton Verney House. My further intentions are to take the plane to a variety of different surroundings; California desert, Manhattan skyline, Swiss Alps, Dutch flower fields, to offset these environments and make them apparent. As small human bodies we often take our surroundings for granted as natural entities, their size and permanence in relation to ours more or less demand that we adapt to them and not vice versa. But every landscape is also the result of previous human intervention and I am interested in making this resonant.

CD Your practice is often focused around an idea that must capture the imagination of a diversity of publics, media, producers and partners. Have there been moments during the development of a project when the idea has not been strong enough to carry that through–do you have a sense of the direction of a project and how to control the process or when to let go?

AM My ideas are constructed as paradoxes that will always evolve around themselves, so as far as my philosophy goes, it can't really be corrupted or fail. I can easily let other people project their desires, engage their opinions, use their economies and form their own meaning through individual or local relationships to the work without ruining my intentions. In fact, I completely rely on all these relations to be able to pull anything this complex off at all.

But of course communication also breaks down for many different reasons: human factors, money, and politics, often prompting the premature cancellation of a work. I'd say my success ratio is around 50%. If the process is already far-gone and I have lived with it for a long time, an aborted project can be very painful, but it's also fair enough. The successful realisation of a work is also the demonstration of a whole set of circumstances and relations that have been strong enough to sustain it. It is real that way. And if things don't work out, I may have a cancelled proposal in my hand that reflects on its own impossibility and hopefully makes it clear why. But then again, there is always the possibility to revisit cancelled ideas under a different set of new circumstances. I never really stop trying.

CD You mentioned (in your lecture in Bristol) the unexpected resonances of a piece like *First Woman on the Moon*, could you indicate what some of those have been and whether you seek those out?[2]

AM *First Woman on the Moon* was conceived as a direct commentary on the thirtieth anniversary of the original moon landing.[3] It was in essence a joke on the lack of the advancement of gender equality in our society, as reflected in my demonstration of a simulated moon landing. JFK turned his nation on to the space race by saying he wanted a man on the moon before the end of the decade (the 60s). I said I wanted a woman on the moon before the end of the millennium, knowing very well this wasn't going to happen. The documentary of the work has now been touring art institutions for five years. In the beginning it was used to comment on anything from gender and land art to conspiracy theory, but in quite an academic, and I would say, detached way from its populist origins. It had been very quiet around space exploration since the anniversary in 1999, but now suddenly, there is feverish interest again. The Mars landings and Bush's pronouncement of revisiting the moon, have all suddenly resonated with my work in new, unexpected ways. And this spring the tape of the work was shown at the launch of a new report on the future of the British Space Industry, as an example of how space can be democratised.

CD What has been your experience of working within group exhibitions; would you rather confine your participation in such projects to the documentation of projects such as *First Woman on the Moon* and *Plane Landing*, or do you think it's possible to produce a new work within the complex dynamic of a group project such as a biennale?

AM I participate in all sorts of exhibitions, high and low, central, peripheral, solo, collective, 'prestigious' or not. They all offer me very different things and very different work comes out of them. But those two works you mention could not have happened in a biennale context. In both cases the production structure was built up around the works themselves and not vice versa. *First Woman on the Moon* was in effect a zero-budget punk production orchestrated from the tiny, non-profit office of Casco Projects in Utrecht. I worked according to a real world context–the thirtieth anniversary of the original moon landing–so I was able to define the time in which my work happened, using that as a context and making reference to world history in that way. I could take weeks site scouting the Dutch beaches before settling on my location. I got to know people in the villages personally who were then instrumental in clearing an enormous amount of red tape that no bureaucratic art institution or 'big deal' show in the world would have had the capacity to do for me. I spent five months raising the goodwill needed and in the end we had a zoo of volunteer collaborators, ranging from a steel factory to street musicians, all indispensable.

On the back of this experience, I was able to realise *Plane Landing*, which is a serious commission from Compton Verney and the Arts Council of England, on a budget totalling around £60,000. But again, the idea was defined before there were any budgets–people got turned on and we had to go out and find the money to meet the project's requirements. The timing here was also left completely open due to the extremely experimental process that was going on at the factory. If they needed four months to order silver fabric, well that meant we had to postpone the intended launch date another six months and that was not a problem. So you can riff endlessly in a commission like this where the work itself is allowed maximum integrity.

My experience with biennale culture is quite different, not better or worse, but just a very different way of working. In a biennial, you are part of a huge preconceived scenario where you are asked to fill a slot, a pre-fixed economy and a bundle of rhetoric you may or may not necessarily agree with. There is rarely room for spontaneous effects as everything pretty much needs to be clear up front. But even this seemingly constricted scenario can be useful for particular works. I just made a piece for the *Whitney Biennial*, 2004, it cost $30. I'm very happy with this work, it works![4]

Aleksandra Mir, *First Woman on the Moon*, 1999
performance, land art, media spectacle, produced by Casco Projects on location in Wijk aan Zee, NL

[1] See www.planelanding.info.

[2] This lecture took place on 15 October 2003 in Bristol as part of the *Situations* lecture series.

[3] See www.aleksandramir.info/projects/moon/moon.html.

[4] See www.aleksandramir.info/projects/nosmoking/nosmoking.html.

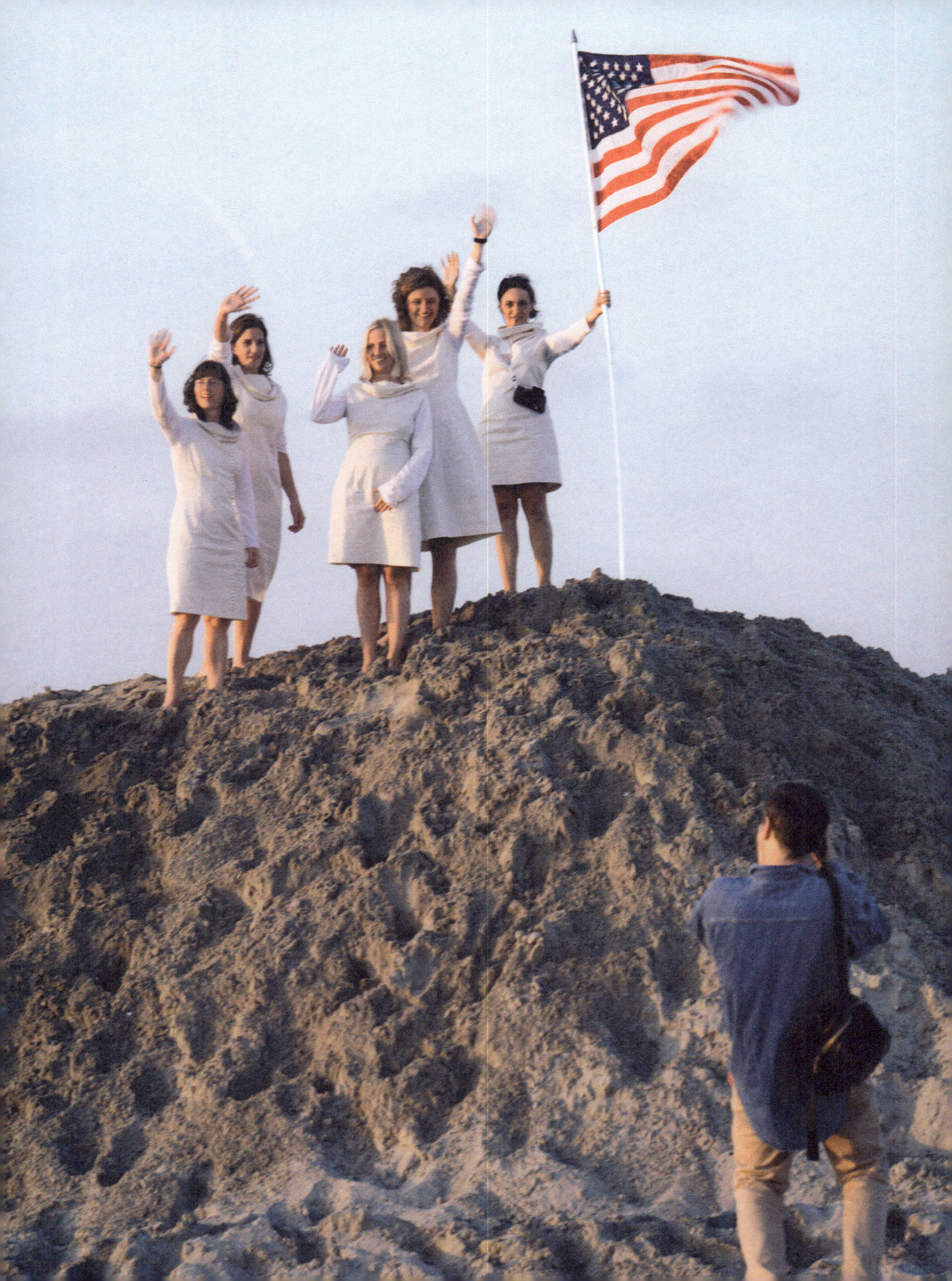

In conversation
Nathan Coley

Lockerbie is the result of Nathan Coley's project to be unofficial artist-in-residence at Kamp van Zeist in the Netherlands, the Scottish Court established in 2000 to try the two Libyan former intelligence agents charged with the bombing of flight PAN AM 103 over Lockerbie in 1988. The work includes a replica of the witness box used during the trial, displayed together with drawings of evidence presented to the court and a video. The original witness box is now, thanks to the artist's intervention, part of the Weapons and Firearms Collection of the Imperial War Museum in London.

In conversation

Nathan Coley and Claire Doherty

Claire Doherty I'm looking here at two images–one is a photograph of the witness box at the Lockerbie trial on 'Scottish land' in the Netherlands, the other is a photograph of the replica of the witness box in the galleries of Tate Britain some three years later. It seems to me that it is in the gap between these two places and these two objects, that your work *Lockerbie* comes into being, but where does the work itself reside? Do you think there's a difference between the research process that took you to Kamp van Zeist and the process of making the object?

Nathan Coley I like that we are starting with the question of place and ideas of meaning within that. For me, the two images (although similar visually) illustrate different intents. The witness box in Kamp van Zeist and the sculpture in Tate Britain have both been fabricated for very specific functions, in very specific places. The courtroom object could be seen as a space, we as a community have created, to enable us to find truth–an area outwith normal life from which to give evidence (in one sense, not unlike the museum). My thoughts on the work *Lockerbie Witness Box (Exhibition Version)*, 2003, are very clear. This is a sculpture that is the exact replica of the original piece of furniture from the courtroom. It has been made to exist as an object within the contemporary art space. Its function is to be an artwork: in this case on display in Tate Britain. We of course 'read' both objects differently due to context, both of which are extremely loaded. It gets interesting for me when we think about my sculpture being a 'fake' of an object which has been originally made (by ourselves) to enable us to find truth.

CD You didn't know what the outcome would be when you first left for Kamp van Zeist. You knew to some extent that you would be (as Alain de Botton has suggested) travelling with 'yourself', so do you think you arrived at that strange 'Scotland without Scotland' looking for the ready-made? Is there a process of investigation when faced with a place, or context, that you are aware of employing?

Nathan Coley *Lockerbie Witness Box (Exhibition Version)*, installation at Tate Britain, 2003

Research image of The Lockerbie Trial Court, Kamp Van Zeist, Holland, 2001. Courtesy Nathan Coley

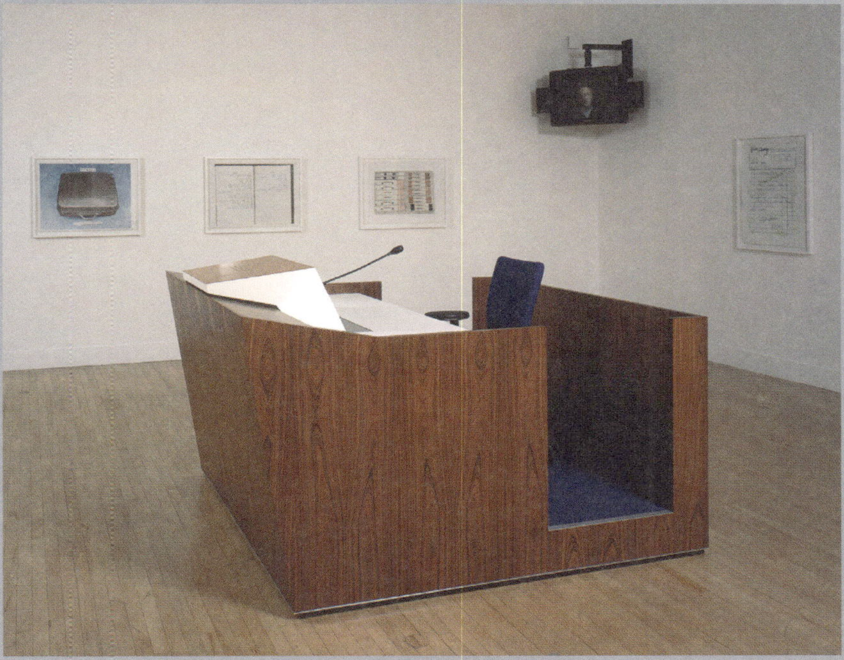

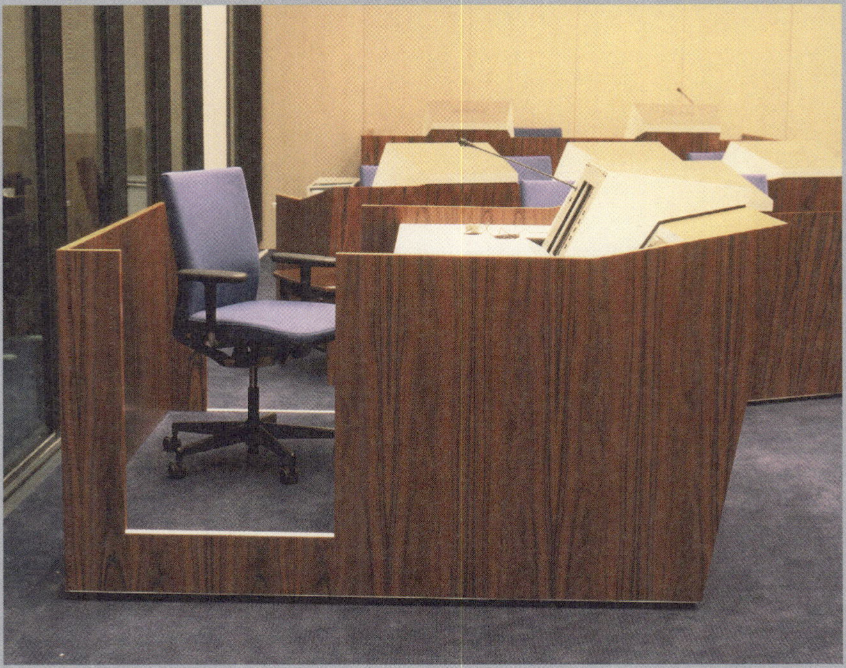

NC Initially I was just interested in going to the event of the trial–this place in the middle of Holland that was technically and legally 'Scottish'. I then thought it was important to set myself some rules. As no-one had asked me to be there, I had no brief or job to do, other than what I could make for myself. The first thing I said to myself was "try to forget that you are an artist", not to look directly at the situation as somewhere to make art from or in. This of course fell away towards the end, but for many months I was just there to witness this world event, in a strange constructed place in the middle of Europe. All that seemed to be interesting enough, without looking for cultural signals or ways to startwork. The second decision I made (which I feel now to have been a very important one) was not to make contact with any of the victims' families. On the busy days, the world press was there. From CNN to the BBC, many of them were looking for the 'human story', and I felt my position should be more removed than that.

CD So what did this distance allow you to do? What kinds of truths or untruths fascinated you?

NC Although I am sensitive to the horrors of the bombing, I hold no interest in who did or did not plant the bomb. In that sense (unlike a lot of the other people in the court) I had no interest in seeking or finding 'the truth' to what happened that day in 1988. However, I was and am interested in how we created a 'legal fiction' to look at the subject. It was the place in Holland that first interested me. I have never been to Lockerbie, and feel no need to visit. All of that said the starting point or ready-made that I was looking for (the witness box) was constructed under very specific conditions. The first step with the work was firstly to ask what would happen if this loaded historical object was repositioned in the art gallery and then subsequently, how would we deal with it if we were presented with a copy of the original–a fake?

CD I remember when you first spoke to me about the idea and at that point, you were in the midst of negotiations about how to acquire the original witness box. At that point, the potential work seemed to me to be closely related to Susan Stewart's notion of the souvenir. She says, "The souvenir distinguishes experiences... and speaks to a context of origin through a language of longing... we need and desire souvenirs of events that are reportable, events whose materiality has escaped us, events that thereby exist only through the invention of narrative."[1] I think I'd be right in saying that the initial proposal for the work to include the original witness box captured the imagination of colleagues and friends–because it involved this 'invention of narrative' around a relic, the dislocation of a piece of history from one non-place to another. But then, when one aspect of the outcome of your research process became the fabrication of a replica of the box, I think the work became something else. As you say, it became much more loaded, perhaps more complex. The replica is still a kind of souvenir, but also references the impossibility of translating your experience as witness to the trial. It short-circuits that process of memory, so that we don't know if to trust you as witness. I think this is what I find so intriguing about your responses to invitations to make new works in particular places or situations, that resistance to nostalgia that is certainly evident in *Showhome*.[2]

NC I agree. I think the work fundamentally changed of course, when I decided to make my own witness box rather than just re-contextualise the original. In truth I think of the whole project as being both invented (the original) and then remade (the exhibition version). The original (due to my endeavour) is now in the Imperial War Museum in London (interestingly in the Weapons and Firearms Department!) and the 'sister work' vibrates in the context of the contemporary art arena. What would happen if we exhibited both? Would they just cancel each other out, or become more than the sum of their parts? With that other point: can we ever (in Britain) really even get away from nostalgia?

Research image taken just outside Zeist, Holland, 2001. Courtesy Nathan Coley

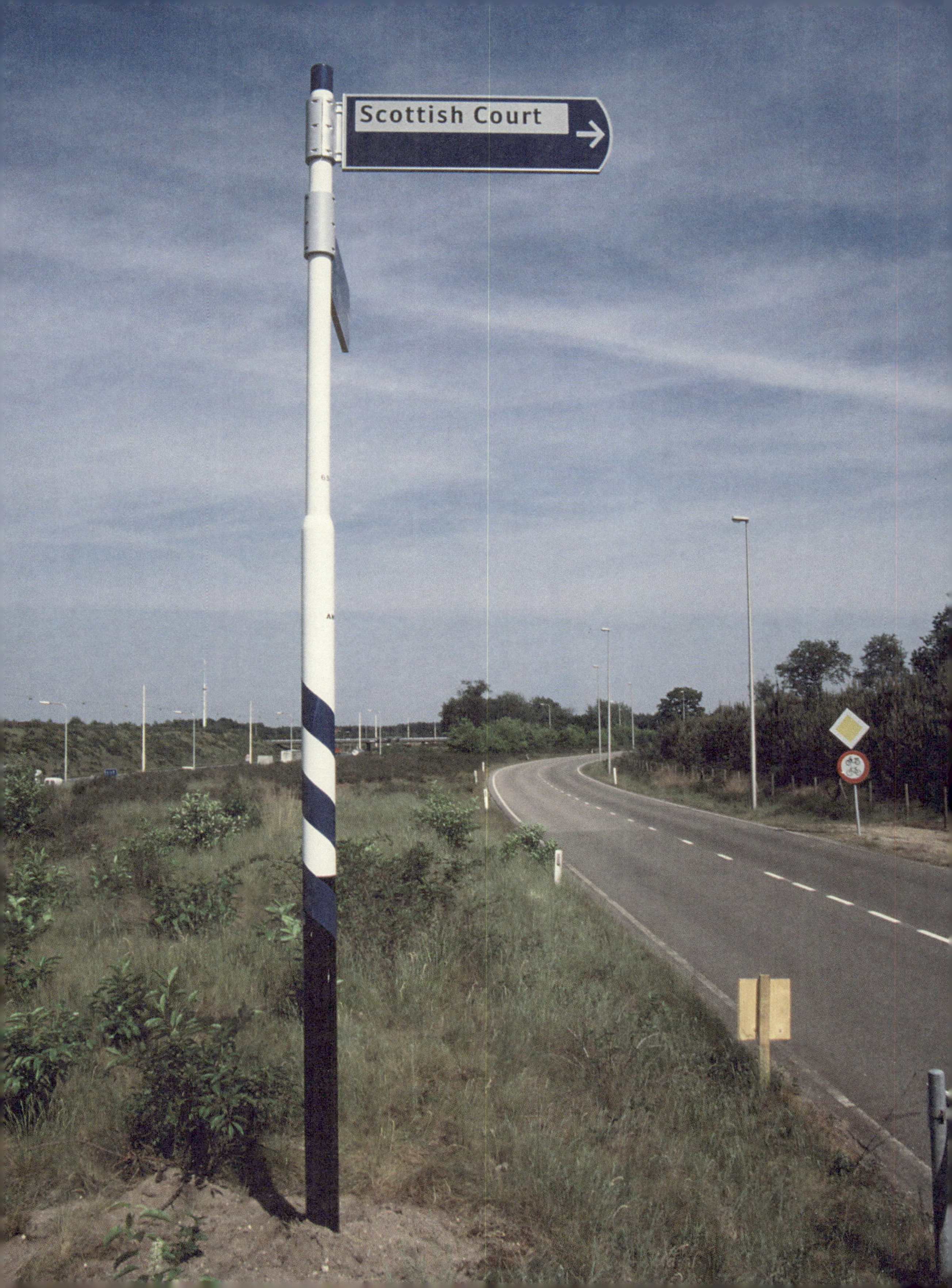
Scottish Court

CD I guess nostalgia is perhaps the wrong word in relation to your response to the Lockerbie trial–perhaps 'indulgence in the story' might be more appropriate to the ways in which such an event has been reported, consumed and digested. What I find particularly interesting about 'your' witness box is that, if you consider it outside the specifics of the drawings, it begins to operate outside the specifics of Lockerbie. It functions as a sign of the physical mechanics of truth or as Maria Lind suggests elsewhere in this publication–"the actualisation of space". I think this is particularly interesting if you consider this project as a way of responding to a very specific geographical and political situation without confining your response to the particulars of that place. For me, this is the problem with much commissioned art practice, particularly within a biennale culture, where the work is rarely able (for reasons of time, budget and support) to signify beyond the most obvious characterisation of place. I wanted to ask you though, whether you feel the work is finished–or whether you might actually still be refining the 'ideal' presentation of that work?

NC I think this work in particular has more to learn. It still has the capacity to understand itself better. I just recently included the sculpture and the drawings in my solo exhibition at Fruitmarket Gallery in Edinburgh. For me it was interesting seeing it alongside a number of other works that I have been making, and I think in some respects it was tough trying to make sense of it as something resolved. It was the first time it had been seen in Scotland. It was in Edinburgh, the political and legal centre of Scotland. I don't see that as a problem. The idea that artworks exist out of time is clearly absurd. Maybe its moment is yet to come. Perhaps we are too close to the events of the bombing for the ideas to transcend history.

As for this idea of making work for specific places. I have never been a fan of that way of thinking or looking. I guess I want the moment of looking to place you in the centre of the world, but that the ideas or discussion can be seen both here and everywhere at the same time. In any case, local history is generally exactly that.

CD I'm not sure about the here and everywhere though–I think it might be more that your work subverts the preconceptions of place, so that it reveals the systems–both personal and political–that begin to make a sense of place. In which case, it's an interrogation of the specifics of place–rather than an indulgence in them. I think this is different than saying that a work can have universal meaning.

I want to take you back a bit though–to what you were saying about forgetting that you were an artist, as a rule of engagement with that particular time and place. What does that mean–forgetting that you are an artist? Do you bring to bear other kinds of approaches, or use other kinds of tools–anthropological, architectural, and economic?

NC What is here? Who are these people? What's that horrible building over there? God, I'd love a drink! These are initial reactions and feelings that we all go through in relation to places that we're new to. We try to make sense of them physically, visually, personally, and of course (in the case of needing water) in terms of just getting through the day. I feel (and this happens without really thinking) that when I'm invited to start thinking about making art from or in a particular place, that it's best, at first, to stay as long as possible in this mode. Not to think about the sculpture or film or 'the work' too much. In my experience that gets in the way of the idea. What I mean is that for me, the start of the work is there to be found. There is a conversation over dinner, a street sign, a taxi ride or a 'Wimpy' show flat which might be the trigger for an idea. If I am too busy thinking about art, I feel I'll miss the reality of the situation. The whole thing about being an artist doesn't really come into it. It is hopefully about the idea which then manifests itself in the world somehow: the other way round seems too difficult to me. In any case

I get my best ideas driving home tired from the supermarket, not with all the site visit photographs in front of me.

CD And when the idea for the replica witness box emerged–from left of centre, maybe when your mind was 'off-duty', back home from witnessing the trial–what kinds of concerns did you have about remaking the ready-made? For instance, were you concerned about what might happen when it became displaced and recontextualised?

NC Not concerns really, more an excitement about what would happen. The witness box seemed to be a micro version of all that was happening at the trial in Holland. Ideas of ownership of space (both legal and personal), jurisdiction, sovereignty and its transference as well as the whole issue of the fetishisation of the object seemed to be contained within the box. It's important to say that had the original looked different, I imagine I would have felt less excited about it. Although designed by Dutch architects in 1999 for a very specific official task (the witness box for the most expensive trial in British legal history), it has a certain style to it. Some people imagine it to be an actual box when hearing about my project. When confronted by a 1970s-looking, spaceship-like piece of furniture, it works differently I think. One commentator said it looked as if was a collaboration between Duchamp and Richard Artschwager, which of course I enjoyed.

CD And now, as you've noted, it has been shown within the context of your other work–models and propositions of projects which deal with the nature of belief, of authority and memory in very different ways.[3] How do you think this replica operated in relation to the remaking of all the places of worship in Edinburgh in cardboard, for example?

NC I think in exactly that way. Both projects deal with how ideas of belief manifest themselves. They both set up a very deliberate relationship between you, the audience and the object: something which still excites me, and keep me wanting to make sculpture. In addition, seeing all the work together, I think something was being presented which if nothing else you could deal with in terms of 'skill'. A very dirty word in contemporary art!

CD What do you mean by skill? Whose skill?

NC Skill in terms of understanding what it can mean to present objects in public, and being able to make manifest ideas and thoughts able to withstand that. Also, in particular, the remaking of every place of worship in Edinburgh, presents a level of hand skill which was important to the actual idea of the sculpture. That piece in particular, for someone in my position, is a really radical work. To be an artist working in the UK in 2004, presenting a work with such an articulation of hand skill is, I think, quite a provocative, risky proposition.

CD And does this sense of testing out a proposition through a 'crafted' technique have an impact of how you work within a studio? What do you think the studio allows you to do? Is it simply a site of production and the ideas flow more readily 'driving home tired from the supermarket'?

NC For me the ideas are tried out in the studio, but never or rarely are they found there. I guess it's about finding the right balance. I don't think I would find it easy to make art without a working space, but being in the studio can be a bit restrictive for the development of ideas.
I'm interested in how the built environment is a reflection of our values, beliefs and social politics. When I get captured by the studio and the world of making art, I sometimes forget that.

[1] Susan Stewart, *On Longing: Narratives of the Miniature, the Gigantic, the Souvenir, the Collection*, Durham, North Carolina: Duke University Press, 1993, p. 63.

[2] *Showhome* is a temporary public art project by Nathan Coley, curated by Locus+. See www.showhome.org.uk.

[3] *Nathan Coley*, Fruitmarket Gallery, Edinburgh, 2004.

In conversation
Catherine David
and Irit Rogoff

Contemporary Arab Representations is a long-term project curated by Catherine David which includes meetings, publications, productions, and representations of visuals, texts, and discourses by various authors in many different cultural venues. The aim of the project is to stimulate locally-based critical platforms and exchanges in the Middle East, as well as between the different centres of the Arab world and the rest of the world. Irit Rogoff's recent book *Terra Infirma–Geography's Visual Culture* took up similar issues of location with regard to identity and attempted to undo the naturalised relations between subjects and places that traditional geography has established. Here Catherine David and Irit Rogoff discuss the implications of representation, of cross-cultural curatorial and artistic activity.

In conversation
Catherine David and Irit Rogoff

Since the 1990s, Catherine David's exhibitions and curatorial projects have in the most part examined art practice in relation to contemporary socio-political issues. This approach was made highly visible by her direction of Documenta *X, in Kassel in 1997, and more recently in her exhibition programme at the Witte de With, Rotterdam, of which the cumulative project* Contemporary Arab Representations *is one. David was one of 11 curators invited by Artistic Director, Francesco Bonami, to curate a component of the* fiftieth Venice Biennale. *The temporary presentation of* Contemporary Arab Representations *at Venice was conceived as an information platform and possible meeting place from 15 June-2 November 2003 and included contributions from the following 'authors': The Atlas Group / Walid Raad; Taysir Batniji; Tony Chakar; Bilal Khbeiz; Randa Shaath and Paola Yacoub / Michel Lasserre. As David has noted in the press material on this manifestation of the project, not all the authors contributing to* Contemporary Arab Representations *were able or willing to be present in the context of the* Venice Biennale.

Catherine David I think that for those who went to the *Venice Biennale* in 2003, it makes sense to state from the beginning that what we showed there was not an exhibition, but rather, a presentation of the project *Contemporary Arab Representations*. We took the *Venice Biennale* for what it is at best, a cultural fair. I had a long series of discussions with most of the participants of the project, mostly people living and working in Beirut, Lebanon and Cairo and some said, "we can't deal with the situation, because we would like to show works. We would like to enter in many different layers of our work and it's not a convenient place or situation to do so". They did agree, however, that we should make a simple booth, which provided one way of showing everybody in a series of projected images, rather than including specific works. *Contemporary Arab Representations* was developed after *Documenta X*. In the making of *Documenta X*, it became clear to me that exhaustive representation was out of the question, and that maybe it would be better to articulate a number of positions which were not all coming from the same geo-cultural perspective. Secondly, the *Documenta* production process didn't allow for travelling back and forth, spending time with people, reading a lot, to accede to very different sectors of cultural activity and so on and so forth. And finally (and this is more from the audience's perspective), though *Documenta* is a much quieter and more closely focused situation than the *Venice Biennale*, there are still not adequate conditions in this kind of exhibition for the audience to accede to a certain level of complexity, so this is why we came up with the idea of a cumulative series of projects and exhibitions, which became *Contemporary Arab Representations*. There were many questions about why we titled this project *Contemporary Arab Representations*, rather than *Contemporary Arab Art*. I think the notion of contemporary art is too precise and too predictive, if you really want to confront the contemporaneity of aesthetic practices, so I thought it would be more honest to look at our understanding of representation: of course this includes visual representations, but also ideological and political representations, especially at a time when there are so many misunderstandings and so much disinformation. I thought it was important to give access to a certain number of social/political discourses which have nothing to do with what is labelled daily as fundamentalist politics.

The articulation of the project occurs in many ways, so you can have seminars, exhibitions and 'travelling meetings'–there are many possible manifestations which do not fit the conventional idea of an exhibition. Sometimes we have included people who are not able or not allowed to travel, through recordings or documentation. This is vital to the project. You have to integrate the possibility that they might not be able to get a visa, into the cultural process. I have a French passport and so have access.

One of the explicit intentions of the project is to facilitate circulation in two directions–to and from the Arab world. This is a world that is very heterogeneous with many dissenters, with many conflicting situations. It is less about censorship than it is about a precarious economic situation, with poor levels of education, non-existent public space or spaces for debate. There are certainly a number of critical platforms which have been developed in the Arab world for a long time. These platforms have, however, been systematically censored both by regional countries, and by the West, but saying that is not saying that critical ideas and articulations don't exist. So again, part of the implicit intention of the *Contemporary Arab Representations* is to do everything possible to consolidate these critical platforms, wherever they exist, respecting the way these platforms have been articulated. So I'd say that our method is far more along the lines of co-producing and co-organising events whether seminars, travels or publications.

Irit Rogoff What I find most interesting about this discussion is that it seems that we can put forward different bodies of work that are agitating around the notion of how you get 'at a place'. I'm familiar with some of the work of *Contemporary Arab Representations* and it's very obviously not corrective work, so it doesn't start from a perspective that says, there is this set of circulating representations and now we will correct it through exhaustive local knowledge. It starts–not from the kind of import/export dynamic where I might go some place, find vast amounts of stuff, bring it over here and inform 'over here' about 'over there'–but rather puts forward a notion of research. It's not about encountering finished bodies of culture produced somewhere and looking at it passively, but rather almost any interesting artistic practice and curatorial practice should now force you to enter a research project, through it and with it, so that what gets fore-grounded are not artistic products from elsewhere, but rather, it puts forward a series of research questions, a series of research methodologies and asks you to track those with you.

I think that's one important way of thinking 'place' whereas I have a very different way of thinking 'place'. What interested me about the potential of this conversation was that we come from fairly similar kinds of geo-political concerns but follow extremely different methodologies. Maybe I should talk about two things.

My entry point into all of this is a very long research project on the relation between geographies and contemporary visual practices, which culminated in a book *Terra Infirma*, that in part has moved onto a current research project (*Translating the Image–Cross Cultural Contemporary Arts*) which is on the 'terroristic' (not terrorism), a project that wants to understand how we could possibly think about relations between subjects and places in a post-colonial, post-migratory, post-communist world in which the forces of globalisation seem to deny the possibility of a fixed locale.

The whole project started a long time ago, actually in the middle of the first Gulf War… I was having a discussion with a German friend. We were in California and there was no hard news of any kind beyond celebratory bragging about 'smart' bombs. Each one of us was deeply worried for very different reasons. We had a discussion which quickly turned into an argument which quickly turned into a shouting match and, at a certain point, he said to me, "well of course you would think that. You come from the Middle East". I suddenly thought, "the middle of whose bloody East do I come from?" Who determined the proximity and the distance that placed me in something called 'the Middle East'? At a distance from what and in relation to whose fantasies about proximity and distance? So that was at the beginning, a project on how we could rethink the relations between subject and places away from something called geography, that organises us around nation states, that organises us in the heritages of empires, that organises us regionally and linguistically, and which in the process of all that determines the privileges, the rights, the exclusions, the mobilities and lack of mobilities that are afforded to us. All of this seemed to organise itself around a question of geography and what really interested me was how do we get out of a geographical relation that is determined by the nation state? It seemed an almost impossible conundrum and I think that *Contemporary Arab Representations* put forward one model, which is one of a kind of inter-relationality.

My project was very focused on what I call 'un-belonging'. How can we make un-belonging a kind of active realm by which to somehow relate to place and not through the identifications demanded by the nation state? How can we find a whole set of strategies by which we relate to a particular place by actively 'un-belonging' ourselves from it? For me, it's a very active, almost daily process by which you are constantly trying to think of positionality–one's constantly contingent, constantly shifting positionality towards place.

The last time we had a conversation about *Contemporary Arab Representations* was at a discussion that we ran in London that was part of the research project *A European Conversation on Cultural Difference*. It's a small, closed forum comprising a group of 20 people from across Europe–expanded Europe, not just old Western industrialised Europe–talking about local, shared and different conflicts and issues around cultural difference through cultural politics. Catherine introduced the Beirut component of the *Contemporary Arab Representations* and I asked, "how do you approach a project that is under such demonisation? How do you even begin to think the world of *Contemporary Arab Representations* when it's under a daily assault of the 'War on Terror'?" You, Catherine, said that you bypassed that assault; you enter it at a different register. I think that is significant. I would probably spend

 Tamáss 1. Courtesy Witte de With

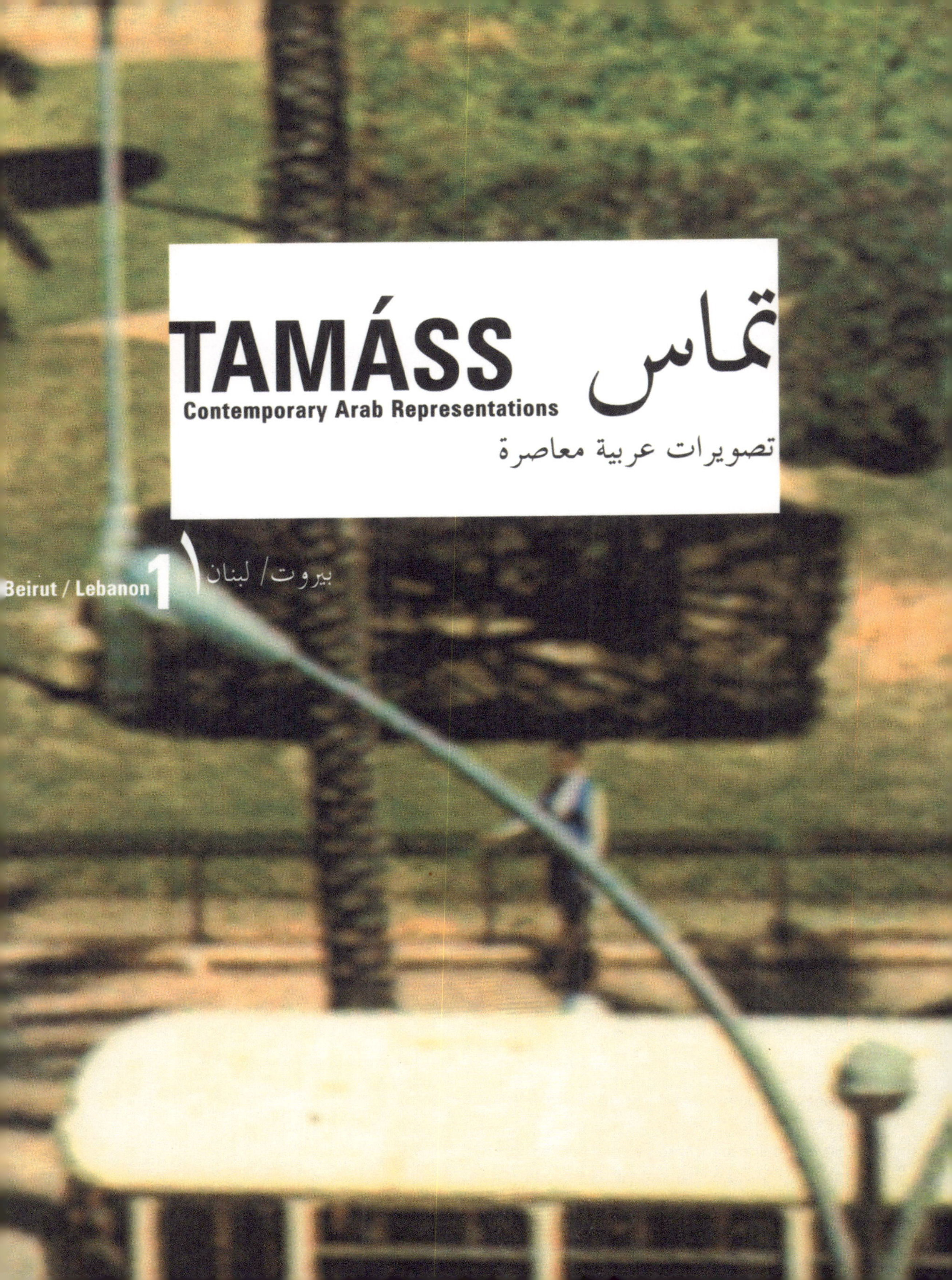
TAMÁSS
تماس
Contemporary Arab Representations
تصويرات عربية معاصرة
Beirut / Lebanon 1
١ بيروت/ لبنان

two years thinking about one's positionality in relation to *Contemporary Arab Representations* and worrying about it so that would actually hamper the ability to get in there and delve into that world. This I guess is part of the difference between doing and reading, which are different practices, even as they circulate around the same problems. That's one way in which I think about the politics of place and the location of art.

The other is more current and it has to do with developing a notion that we have of fieldwork and fieldwork is something that my colleagues, in our research group at Goldsmiths, have been preoccupied with. It's a term borrowed from anthropology but it doesn't mean what anthropology wants it to mean. This is not a practice of going out in the field, finding facts and then using them as the material base for an argument. For us, it's the work of fields, and those fields have a kind of relationality between artistic practices, modes of research and modes of knowing (this is one of the things that I've taken from contemporary critical cultural anthropology, primarily the work of George Marcus, particularly his book *Fieldwork Through Thick and Thin*).[1] In it, he says that the real crisis in fieldwork was the distinction between fieldwork that is done through a mode of rapport, of proximity and a sense of having rapport with the place, and fieldwork that is done through an understanding of one's complicity with the work. So in rapport we have all kinds of conceits, we have all kinds of illusions. We have a notion of understanding. We have a notion of insight. There is a kind of empathy that is foregrounded, there's a notion of investigation.

Our conference, *Field Work*, last year investigated this shift in fieldwork between rapport and complicity.[2] So in this model of rapport I found a great proximity to what is called 'site-specific art'.

Site-specific art seemed to me to function in the model of rapport. It goes into something that is apparently located and specific and it works at uncovering and unveiling and revealing hidden mechanisms and assumptions. The actual artwork that gets produced through that model has a whole set of assumptions about having an empathy with the locale, and coming in and being able to expose and reveal and uncover and make explicit things that might have lain uncovered. I'm thinking of a huge range of work from, let's say, Martha Rosler's work in The Bowery in New York and Hans Haacke's work on MOMA NY Real Estate interests, work that uncovered and linked a whole set of social and cultural relations. The breakdown of that work in anthropology which is based in rapport, and I think the breakdown of that parallel work in contemporary art practices, comes with this emergent notion of complicity.

Complicity is an understanding that all work is undertaken in the form of a collusion and that it's a collusion that is operating at several levels. There's the collusion that you just talked about, Catherine, which is between artists and institutions, between enabling contexts or enabling situations. Then, there's a collusion with tropes and narrative structures and modes of actual representation, with language. You could simply say that's it's a collusion with language. There's a notion of collusions with sites and locations.

There is an Israeli artist, Avital Geva, I've been thinking about. He created a huge closed ecosystem in which water was circulated and things grew for the *Venice Biennale* of 1997. He's not an artist, he's actually an agronomist. He studied agriculture and makes his living as a teacher of agriculture on a kibbutz. Together with his class of students, about 14 or 15 year olds from the kibbutz where he teaches, he would go to the major cities in Israel and they would carry rucksacks with a little bit of earth and some string and a few plants and little bit of fertiliser and then, between parked cars in the city, they would erect instant little agricultural settlements. They would pull a piece of string between two cars, put down some earth and plant a few seedlings and water them. They were always vegetables, they weren't ornamental. They were meant to be of use.

This was in a culture where the national rhetoric was about reclaiming the land and making it productive and bringing modern agriculture to the region. He was playing with it wonderfully because of course five minutes after they completed their little performance of claiming the land, some car would back over this little garden, or two cars would pull the string. (I think the strings were always attached to the bumpers.)

Thinking about the collusion between sites and locations, we might think about the way in which the rhetoric of the site can be taken up and made to work against itself rather than the analytical work of exposing it. I think between us, Catherine, what we have is a series of ways of addressing location that has to do with trying to understand it in a whole set of different ways, none of them determined by a national rhetoric. I think where there's a common ground is the fact that national rhetoric is never the point of departure.

Catherine David At the beginning of your statement, you mention the demonisation of the Arab World. I should say that I began to work on the project much before September 11th. In fact I was in Beirut on that date and, perversely, I can say that it was really a privilege because it was really a completely different situation than the one seen on western TV screens. It was very important for me to live it from another perspective, with people with other references, with other tools for estimating what was happening. I never saw anybody dancing in the street, but I saw people shocked by the world's sympathy for people dying in New York, when they were left without any assistance during the Lebanese wars and Israeli invasion and killings of the 1980s. No pathos, no hysteria but strong political analysis and thinking at a very early stage of the drama. I also have to mention that I am working with people who have to confront the systematic disinformation produced by the majority of the media on a daily basis. Some respond with distance, others more with anger. But what I understand is that I can't take this demonisation of the Arab world seriously. The simple fact of 'being there' with people is a devastating answer to all this. I feel sorry for those who are accepting being brainwashed but I have no fear. And I am really tired seeing any Arab activist and/or radical Arab discourse stamped as 'terrorist'. I believe, on the contrary, that it is time to circulate radical discourses when people are put in impossible circumstances. Of course I am working with people who are more knowledgeable in terms of translating and circulating a certain number of discourses.
A famous Spanish islamologist was telling me the other day, with a lot of humour, "[T]his one, you'd better not invite him now; it would be like giving him a ticket to Guantanamo".

So this said, I move now to the question of locality. First of all, I think there are many ways of dealing with locality. As a 'fast' visitor or tourist or as a more concerned and empathic partner (and here I would like to quote Asef Bayat, an Iranian sociologist who lived for many years in Cairo, who mentioned this simple and crucial part of the experience "being there with people"), there is no problem as long as people are able to understand and admit that the local/global is not reserved to the non-European and non-Western situations.
But what is probably the most interesting and (apparently) paradoxical aspect of dealing with locality is that most of these processes have to do with idiosyncrasy, to do with phenomena, with elements of reality, with references which are very precisely, very directly attached to a place or to a situation, or to a memory or to a history common to a group of people. For example, it was amazing to see in the Lebanese and Beirut situation, how many decodings you need in a day, how people are experts in micro phenomenology and analysis, how 'palimpsestic' the entire city is.

It was totally different in Cairo where the entire political, social and cultural situation and the relationship between time and space are very different. Egypt is a very old country, with a strong pre-Islamic, pharonic culture. They have no problems in terms of identity, frontiers and sovereignty, unless you admit that the country is *de facto* under American control. The major problem in Egypt at the moment is political, an authoritarian regime backed by the West, a complete freezing of debate and public space, a very degraded economical and social situation, a near final erasure of the middle class, all this is of course is causing major damage to culture and cultural production.

This is probably most striking when you look carefully at the large series of portraits made by the artist, Randa Shaath, over the past 20 years. There you can see something like time not passing, a culture frozen, energies constrained, and a lot of sadness too. All this you can read in Shaath's portraits of people involved in Cairo's cultural and artistic scene in the last 20 years. When you go back to Beirut, you can see these idiosyncratic references and articulations in Elias Khoury's novels as well as in Mohammed Soueid's movies. I don't want to enter here into a discussion about the whether literature and writing have a more 'universalist' status over other mediums, but rather, I'd like to make clear that the power of Mohammed Soueid's films and stories is closely related to the idiosyncrasy of his references. *Nightfall*, for instance, is entirely built on the living memory of a group of people and friends who participated in the war in the same militias. Most of the names, places and events which people are referring to are unknown to anyone who didn't experience the civil war in Beirut, but the strong poetic impact of the movie goes beyond these facts.

It seems to me that both Elias Khoury and Mohammed Soueid have are dealing with an idea of *communauté* [a term meaning community used by Maurice Blanchot, Jean-Luc Nancy and Giorgio Agamben] as opposed to any *communautarism.* And this should take us to more concrete, but also deeply political, questions. Idiosyncrasy has to do with time, priorities, resistance to a dominant system of representations and values. And the point then is how you present these works so that people are ready for the necessary translation?

Irit Rogoff You mean using images of local horror and....

Catherine David I think that things are more complex. In the Beirut situation, for instance, it is amazing to see the complexities of narratives developed by people like Elias Khoury and Mohammed Soueid, but also by younger artists like Walid Sadek or Rabih Mroué. I would like to quote Walid Sadek here:

> For to remain in Beirut today requires a marked resilience in travelling the circuitous complexity of a city where the roaming of artistic intent is preceded and overlapped by the murderous roaming of political speech.

My point is more about what is the aesthetical act? What is the ethics of it? When I'm working with some of my Lebanese partners, I really feel that I'm not doing the same work as many of my colleagues. I don't feel I am a 'curator' and I think that on this level, the question is not really the question of place, but more about aesthetical experience and practice today, in very different geo-political circumstances. In Portuguese, I would say it has to do with the radical specificity of *vivencias*.

Irit Rogoff 'Experiential'?

Catherine David 'Experimental', you can put it like that. Meaning that you are deeply involved with certain elements of cultural life in a place, because preceding cultural production there is something like cultural life and experience. It seems to me that part of the project *Contemporary Arab Representations* is also dealing with this more ambiguous, maybe obscure–level of experience.

Irit Rogoff We're talking about two work processes and in the background there is the archive or the cumulus of *Documentas* over the last seven years. The very explicit and precisely located work processes that we're trying to talk about here may get their permission from two very large exhibitions. So I think what's important in relation to a lot of the specifically located projects that we're involved in is that they get permission, they get animated through these exhibitions that refuse to locate artistic practices on a purely aesthetic realm. Visual culture is as issue-driven as anything else in the world, but it doesn't necessarily reflect it. It isn't an illustration of the issues that it's driven by, so let's try and work out another relation between issues and aesthetic practices. We've had seven or eight years of that because each one of these *Documentas* is not just an exhibition, it is the events, in the case of Catherine's *Documenta,* the 100 days and, in the case of Enwezor's *Documenta,* the platforms that took place around the world and the publications that came out of them. The problem is the prevalent attitude that the international exhibition, rather than the smaller, cumulative research projects or events, can deal with issue-driven practices.

Catherine David I think that the long term effect(s) of *Documenta* is positive. I also think that we should be aware that *Documenta* is indeed one, if not the only, platform of this size where you can still work seriously. But the point Irit is raising here, is a different thing. And she is completely right underlining the possible limitations of showing local projects in the frame of big exhibitions when part of it has to do with processes, cumulative experience, slow learning of differences, etc.. She is also right to point out the paradox that big international exhibitions are attracting more attention to local situations. We have to deal with this, but it is also clear that a smaller scale is more appropriate to long term projects, which can articulate temporarily within bigger contexts. I don't see this as black and white, even if I am more and more convinced that more heterogeneity in the scale and form of such events, as well as in the ways of addressing different audiences, is an urgent matter. For the rest, I think that wherever the works are coming from, there is a major distinction between a critical attitude and the illustration or 'aesthetisation' of the problems. It may also take time to identify different critical paradigms and agendas and to make it understandable and profitable to those who may take the time to pay attention.

1 George Marcus, *Fieldwork Through Thick and Thin,* Princeton: Princeton University Press, 1998.

2 *Field Work: Reports from the Fields of Visual Culture* was held from 16-17 May 2003 at Victoria Miro Gallery and was organised by the AHRB Research Project: *Translating the Image–Cross Cultural Contemporary Arts,* Goldsmiths College, London.

In conversation
Jeremy Deller

Jeremy Deller occupies various roles as an artist: curator, social entrepreneur, actor, and producer. His work almost always involves collaborative elements and takes on various forms. He produces books, video, performances, recordings and photography. Perhaps most famous for *The Battle of Orgreave*, a public re-enactment of the notorious clash between pickets and police during the 1984 UK miners' strike, Deller's works continually ask witty but telling questions about cultural identity and social groupings; they intrigue and provoke their viewers.

In conversation

Jeremy Deller and Claire Doherty

In 1984 the National Union of Mineworkers went on strike. The dispute lasted for over a year and was the most bitterly fought since the general strike of 1926, marking a turning point in the struggle between the government and the trade union movement. On the 18 June 1984, there occurred at the Orgreave coking plant one of the strike's most violent confrontations, begun in a field near to the plant and culminating in a cavalry charge through the village of Orgreave. Jeremy Deller's The Battle of Orgreave *was a spectacular re-enactment of what happened on that day, orchestrated by Howard Giles, historical re-enactment expert and former director of English Heritage's event programme, on 17 June 2001.* The Battle of Orgreave *was filmed under the direction of Mike Figgis for Artangel Media and Channel 4, and was aired on Sunday 20 October 2002 and has subsequently been screened world-wide.*

Deller also published The English Civil War Part II: Personal accounts of the 1984-1985 miners' strike, *an anthology of new texts, interviews, original documents, pamphlets, news clippings, anecdotes and photographs. Though the re-enactment is documented, the main body of the book is a work of historical research. Almost all contributions are written in first person, documenting the impact of the strike on people's lives. This approach is representative of Deller's interest in the essence of a place or a particular event (as revealed in the newsletter, the hand-made banner, the lyrics of a chant, the fanzine) and his privileging of personal history over the institutional or mediated reality.* After the Gold Rush, *a guidebook, was Deller's response to a residency at Capp Street in San Francisco and like* The English Civil War Part II *incorporates a diversity of voices, responses and memories, as guides to the state of California.*

Claire Doherty I'd like to start by asking how you position yourself, going into situations such as Orgreave? What processes do you use and are you aware of particular strategies?

Jeremy Deller, *The Battle of Orgreave,* produced and commissioned by Artangel, 2001
Photos: Martin Jenkinson

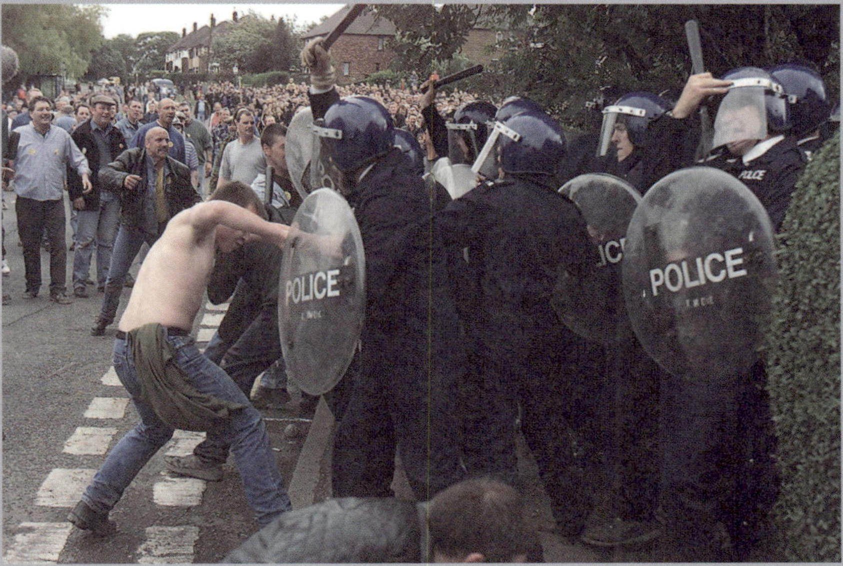

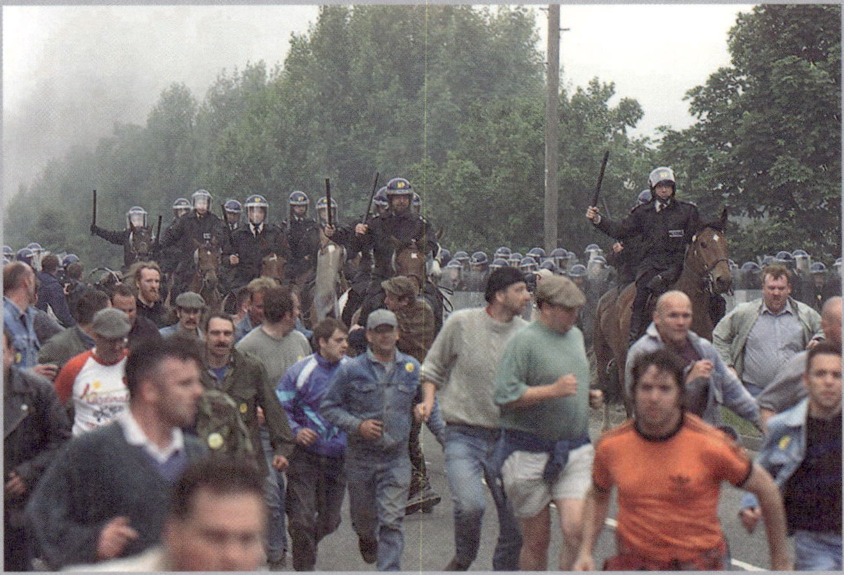

Jeremy Deller Orgeave involved a year and a half's research prior to the project, involving discussions with people in Sheffield and the area of South Yorkshire. I'd chat with people informally, one to one, getting information from them. It involved a range of other people, such as the production company subsequently, but initially it was just me.

CD And when you were talking to people, explaining that you wanted to stage a re-enactment, did you mention that you were an artist?

JD Yes. I always said that I was an artist, though no-one was ever interested in the work that I made and I was never challenged about the project being art–which was good. I think it was probably because the idea was so striking that it didn't really matter to anyone that I was an artist. People were interested in how the idea could be made to happen. It caught people's imaginations.

CD Do you think that was because this was a situation where certain participants had not had a voice previously?

JD I think that is certainly an element, but also people understood instinctively why it would be a good thing to happen, far more than people in London I should say. Some of my friends in the art world were horrified.

CD Why because they were concerned about exploitation?

JD Yes, but also because of the subject matter in general. They didn't seem able to get their heads round it initially, though people locally understood it instinctively. They were more in tune with me than people in my world, as it were.

CD After that long period of research, as you were coming closer to the days of the re-enactment, did you begin to let go?

JD Yes, you have to. I know what my limitations are and there were other people there who were far better experienced in making the thing happen than me. I had already done the work and set the situation up and so it was up to the experts to get on with it. Also, I was interested in how other people would interpret the idea, where it would go to. I knew it had its own life. I had no ownership over it.

CD Do you think that's a common trait in your work?

JD Yes, I think it is. I'm always interested in seeing what other people can bring to the work, how they can improve on or improvise with an idea. It's partly laziness on my part and partly that I'm interested in what other people will do. The best moment is when you are surprised by what someone can do to your idea, though I'm sure many artists would be offended if someone deviated from what they expected.

CD So there is a clear distinction between those practices that require participants to deliver something the artist has in mind, rather than your approach which means that the work can reside in many different outcomes.

JD There's no set outcome. It existed in the public domain before it existed in the art world, and it doesn't need [the art world's] approval. There is no art product for sale, which is characteristic of what I do. With the *Folk Archive*, even though it is an evolving exhibition, it is not something that can be bought *en masse*.[1] So there is rarely just one outcome.

At Orgreave, it could have been a disaster. A lot of members of historical re-enactment societies were terrified of the miners. During the 80s, they had obviously believed what they read in the press and had the idea that the men that they would be working with on the re-enactment were going to be outright hooligans or revolutionaries. They thought it would turn into one huge real battle. It wouldn't have been that difficult for it to go wrong, but it didn't. It was an experiment and I think a lot of what I do are experiments rather than artworks; social situations which are set up.

CD You mention, in your introduction to the book

The English Civil War Part II, "I was interested in how far an idea could be taken, especially one that is on the face of it a contradiction in terms, a recreation of something that was essentially chaos", that tension in finding a form where there can't be one.[2] I wondered in that regard, how you felt about the film, which of course is edited to tell a particular story?

JD There are elements I'd change about the film, but really not that many. I had a lot to do with the editing and I did all the interviews as well, so I knew what I wanted from it and the film pretty much delivered it.

CD Which was?

JD I wanted to make a political film about the miners' strike on the back of an artwork. I didn't want to be in the film initially. (I was put in later.) I'm usually really bad at documentation, but this is such a good piece of evidence of the event. It has its own life–it's now being shown world-wide from New York to Tel Aviv and Bordeaux.

CD Do you have a sense of how it's received in those locations?

JD Well I don't often go to screenings abroad, but I think it's a universal story of the state versus the people. So it will have echoes with the historical or social context in those places.

CD Having completed *The Battle of Orgreave*, and given its iconic status since, would you say that the success of this project allows you to do other things?

JD The year after we did it, I didn't have any projects. But now it's gaining a wider profile and that's having an effect on the invitations I'm getting to do certain things. It's achieved a high profile this year, because of the twentieth anniversary, though I never wanted to stage it as an anniversary event or screening.

CD Why not?

JD I didn't want to peg it in that way. It's the way media deals with events such as this, but it becomes nostalgic.

CD In the book, you speak about 'living history' and the way in which you wanted to collapse that gap between the historical event (be it Roman or Cromwellian) and its re-enactment. But there were still 17 years between the miners' strike and your re-enactment.

JD I don't think you could have done the project five years after the strike. It was before its time if anything. I think that's why artists are around–to push things–to do things before a TV company would commission something. It was so unfashionable at the time (this was prior to the twentieth anniversary of course).

CD So is the sense of freedom you experience, one of the reasons why you choose to be an artist. Why not be a documentary filmmaker, for example?

JD Being an artist gives you space. You can move across different disciplines. Your role is far more fluid.

CD Do you think your art history training influences your working process? I've always thought about your work as investigative and analytical.

JD It's certainly there in projects such as *After the Gold Rush*. You can see it in the combination between history and contemporary life. But the history is not obvious, but rather revealed through the contributors' lives in California.

CD In the introduction to that book, you mention that you'd "had enough of Britain" when you took up the residency in San Francisco.[3] Was that because of Orgreave?

JD I felt that I'd 'done' Britain at that time. I wanted to go somewhere where it wouldn't necessarily be about my own history. I guess it was a way in which to challenge my own limits. Initially the residency was for three months but I ended up staying a year. I wanted to do something that was really about 'place' and so it involved a far deeper process of research. This meant that I had to self-fund the project (in fact I lost money on it), as I only had money for the three-month residency, but this resulted in a more complex project–the book–than an exhibition could ever have been.

CD In such a project as this, you are exploring and representing a place as an outsider. How does your work relate to investigative journalism or TV documentaries, such as the sub-cultural investigations of Louis Theroux?

JD I think Theroux does it with a very specific agenda and a wry smile. He looks for very particular people to illustrate a particular narrative. I was drawn to California as it is on 'the edge' in all senses: a meeting of all these different people, migrants and cultures. The history of the US is intricately tied up with travel and exile. Historical examples are plenty beginning with the arrival of the Pilgrims, the enforced displacement of Native Americans, and the victims of the slave trade. They continue with the Mormons and the Gold Rush, as well as the more recent phenomena of the Dust Bowl, Route 66, Hells Angels, Jack Kerouac and the seasonal migrations of retired 'snowbirds' right up to the present day, where every time a road trip is taken, it becomes part of the tradition. But I didn't set out to find particular people, I just came across them. It was a road trip of sorts and the encounters that I experienced were genuine and thus are a genuine reflection of that place and that time. I never force anyone to be involved in the projects I do.

CD In many of your projects, particularly *Folk Archive* and your new work for *Manifesta 5* in San Sebastian, you open up the project to a range of different people, and I understand have experienced problems where the authorship of the project may be brought into question by the art institution once the project is presented in a more formal, exhibition setting.[4] Can you tell me a bit about how you address that?

JD It comes down to whether or not it is the genuine article. For example, the documentation of the parade by local interest groups in San Sebastian was made by a video group and so that is also the work, but it is made by this group of young people. It also means that the work doesn't become the product of a particular celebrity.

CD So what is the impact then of being nominated for the Turner Prize 2004?

JD Well, I think people look at me differently! But specifically, the work I'm planning moves beyond the gallery and I'm trying to break up the presentation space and make it feel more comfortable. Overall, it gives me the opportunity to make new work. It took me seven years to make *The Battle of Orgreave* happen, so the success of that project gives me the opportunity to take certain projects forward now that have been germinating for some time.

[1] See www.folkarchive.co.uk.

[2] Jeremy Deller, "Foreword", *The English Civil War Part II, Personal accounts of the 1984-85 miners' strike*, London: Artangel, 2004

[3] Jeremy Deller, "Happiness is a 4x4", *After the Gold Rush*, San Francisco: CCAC Wattis Institute for Contemporary Arts, 2002, p. 6.

[4] For *Manifesta 5*, Deller organised a parade in San Sebastian. See www.manifesta.es.

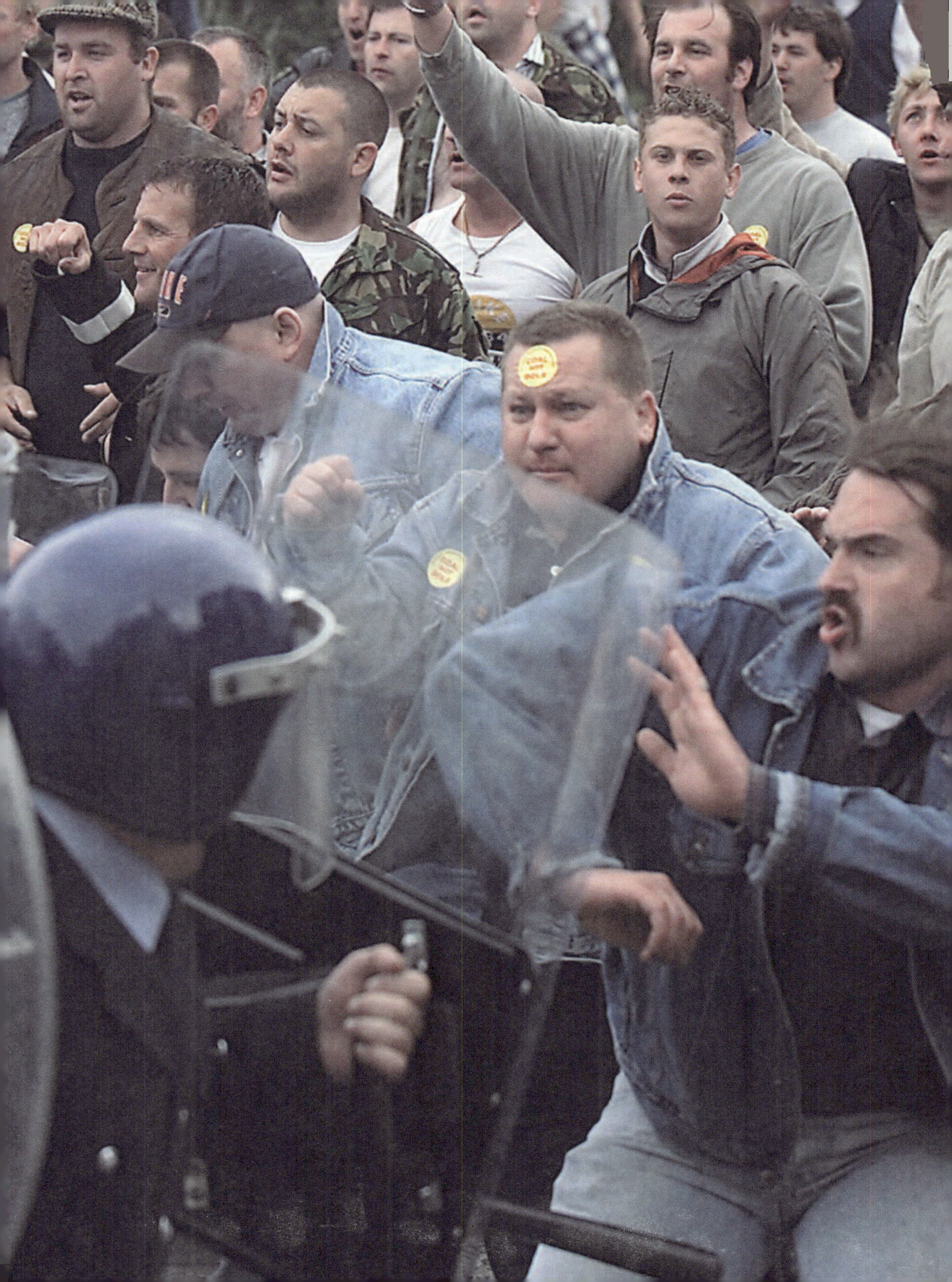

In conversation

James Lingwood and Richard Wentworth

Sculptor, photographer and 'urban explorer', Richard Wentworth has lived in King's Cross for some 25 years. Wentworth's work is an ongoing conversation with his native habitat. At a moment of huge upheaval in this particular transient part of London, Wentworth temporarily inhabited a vacated General Plumbing Supplies store overlooking the railway tracks and the building sites of King's Cross station in autumn 2002. Inside he installed maps and plans and films, ping-pong tables and a periscope in an evolving excavation of the fugitive nature of the inner city. A wide-ranging interaction programme, fed into and out of Wentworth's King's Cross HQ. *An Area of Outstanding Unnatural Beauty* was commissioned by Artangel and here the artist looks back on the genesis of the project with Co-Director of Artangel, James Lingwood.

In conversation

James Lingwood and Richard Wentworth with Claire Doherty

Richard Wentworth I know a good place to start, which is to ask you James at what point did it occur to you that there might be a project in me?

James Lingwood I guess our conversation was quite meandering to start with, and then it gradually became more directed. In my mind, it was probably implicit from our first meetings that we wanted you to work with us and at a certain point it must have become explicit–but I can't remember exactly when!

RW It felt like an incredibly long incubation. It was certainly more than two years, perhaps as much as four!

JL Well for us that would not seem like an overlong incubation for a project. Each one takes the time it needs.

RW Ah well, that's interesting; because I've always felt guilty about the length of time my project took to come to fruition. I've always felt that I have something wrong with me, or maybe right with me, when somebody asks me to do something. How artists edit is really intriguing: when to say yes, when to say no, and how to develop the necessary reciprocity. Did I say yes too quickly? Did I then create a sort of resistance?
I don't know how other artists do it–maybe it's something to do with the necessary tension, like lovers! I remember recognising that we probably could work together quite well, but then there's a sort of shy thing–perhaps born of mutual recognition.

Claire Doherty Is there also a problem in finding a starting point? To a degree, an exhibition gives you a framework and a public commission–a brief, but it seems to me Artangel's starting points might be very different? What's the trigger?

JL I think that's one of the reasons why the incubation period can be so long. We don't base these projects on a kind of 'pointing' relationship: we rarely point the artist towards a certain site or even a certain situation. There is no specific time-frame, no demarcated slot in an exhibition

Richard Wentworth, *An Area of Outstanding Unnatural Beauty*, 2002 (detail). Courtesy Artangel

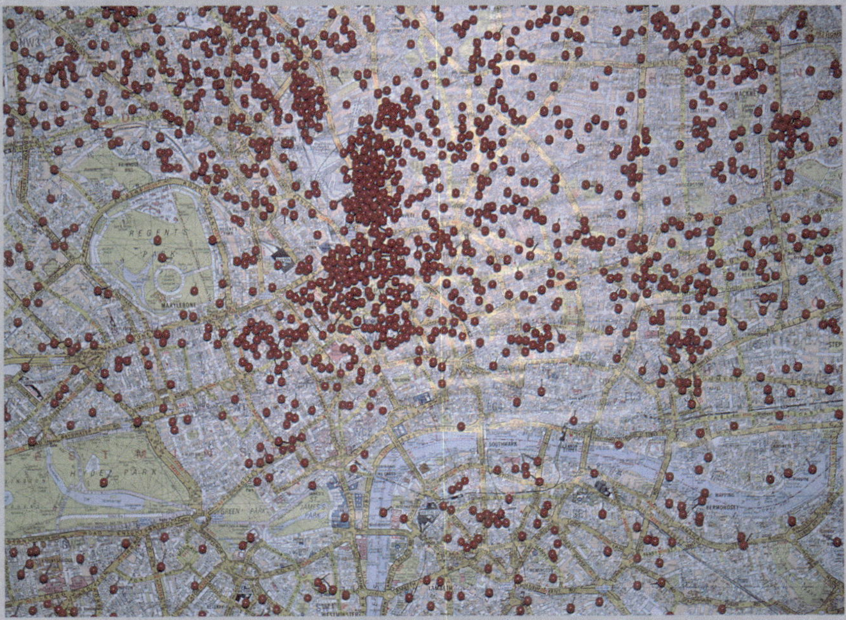

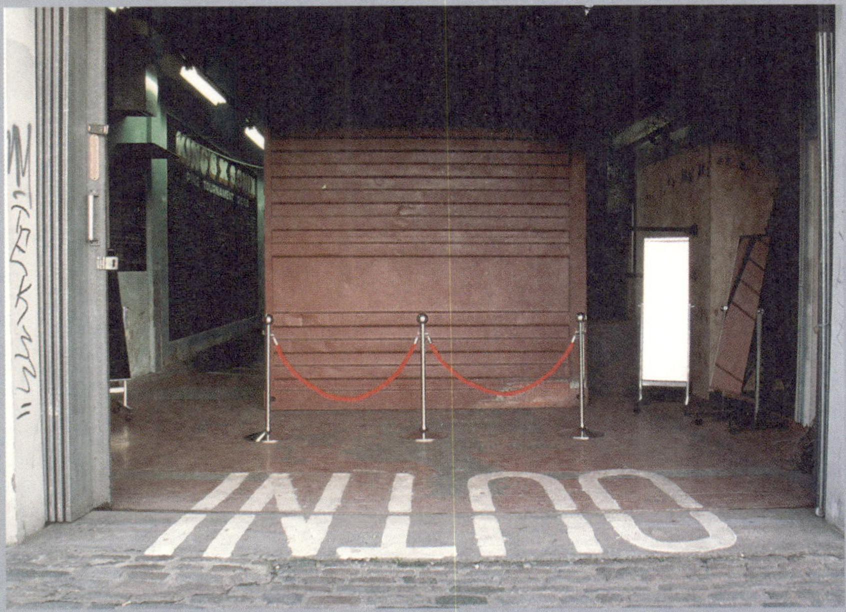

programme. We don't give them a brief as such. That means there can be a bewildering range of possibilities, but we hope that through a number of conversations that the profile of a possible project slowly comes into view. I had been to Richard's talks with slides on a number of occasions. They represent a very distinctive way of seeing and reading the world–the accumulation of images and insights and asides can be quite exhilarating. I think I was interested in seeing whether this kind of feeling could be transposed to a particular situation, and somehow stretched in time and space. I didn't know how or even where, but a great many of Richard's photos have been made in his 'native habitat'–King's Cross and we fairly naturally gravitated towards this part of the world.

RW It's intriguing to know somewhere like King's Cross for more than 30 years. I used to buy steel from where the British Library is now. My earliest knowledge of King's Cross was as a 'doing' place and a supplying place and if you look at the map (well you don't even have to look at the map, you just experience it), it really is the proper Hyde Park Corner of London. It's where all the mercantile forces meet and only five minutes from the mercantile City. I had always known it in decline. Knowing this piece of the city–I see that it was always 'falling'. When we were first talking about it, neither of us was much aware of urban planning initiatives or anything like that, we just saw this thing as a constantly 'falling' thing and some of the images that came up in conversations were 'outside-the-city-wall' images, things like the mini-cab office. It has a strange atmosphere–sort of scummy, and run-down but immensely wired, almost literally because so much infrastructure meets there. It's really a grubby nineteenth century 'airport', with the scale of topographic disturbance to match. The River Fleet flows north to south, underground from King's Cross to Blackfriars Bridge. To me this is where London folds, 'east' from 'west'.

What James did was to release a bigger response from me. Somebody said to me the other day that I take photographs of details and I was mortified. I don't see the table, I see the crack, but there can be no table without the crack and if I ever make a picture of the crack, I'd always want to imply the whole table by photographing the cracks. I think James was re-wiring me a little bit to look at King's Cross as a totality.

CD I've heard you speak in the past about your DAAD year in Berlin, where you were clearly off your home turf, invited to make work and respond as a visitor rather than as a resident. How did that instance differ from this project?

RW Well actually that's funny because I think of my time in Berlin as a major 'hinge' in my life. That was 1993 to 1994. It was incredibly stressful and exhilarating. I'm not a studio artist and yet there I was on a studio residency. I know how to work very well in a studio and I've got lots of conventional studio skills but it doesn't really engage me week in week out. When I came back, I was lost. I wasn't sure how to begin again. I would say that was the first time that I realised that what I am really interested in is the tourism outside my front door. It's quite banal that you have to go away to understand such a thing. But I realised this is what I've always done. I think those anxieties were rekindled a little bit by the Artangel invitation. Perhaps, you recognised that, James?

JL I think one of the things that Richard does in his work is engage with completely different senses of time. The French historian Fernand Braudel talks about three different aspects of time: *La Longue Durée*, the very slow glacial speed of geological time: historical time, the speed of the industrial revolution, and human time, which is the time that it takes you to walk down the street. Richard's way of looking at King's Cross engages us with all of these different time scales–most notably of course the time of history and its interface with individual lives. At a certain moment the project needed a situation or site for it to develop a shape or a form. That was very difficult to achieve. I had naively thought that in King's Cross–a part of London which was undergoing huge change with vast building projects occurring all over the place–that it would be relatively easy to find somewhere appropriate, particularly because we were not looking for an extraordinary place. But we found it difficult to find the right place. Although I said I try to avoid a 'pointing' relationship with an artist, at a certain stage in the discussion you do need to offer suggestions–as a kind of prompt if nothing else. One of the suggestions that I made to Richard was to visit a place called Container City down on the River Thames near the Lea Estuary, because we thought that we could perhaps create our own provisional structure somewhere within King's Cross, where there are already huge numbers of indigenous porta-cabins and containers, to temporarily house the project, and add to it as it grew.

RW That was completely born of the fact that we were not wanted in any of the existing buildings wasn't it? What was great about Container City is that it's actually very late Archigram. There were two things that came out of the visit. One is that there was a rising sense of ambition five months before the project actually happened and secondly it gave me a chance to be somewhere totally unexpected. Artangel are incredibly good at breaking that permissions barrier. A particular instance I remember was walking around on the roof of the Scala (an Edwardian cinema, which is built on stilts over the railway lines at King's Cross). We were up there on top of the world. We felt like kings. You're very good, James, at what I'd call boyhood moments like that.

But going back to Container City–it was very important physically and metaphorically. I think it had implications of mobility. I am not at all drawn to containers as objects, but being amongst all of this stuff you realised how pliant it was and consequently how pliant King's Cross could be. Perhaps there are now more containers in the world than cars, all in less than 40 years. Treating them as ready-mades, Container City are very imaginative with them spatially. I fell in love with a prototype staircase in an upended container: a magnificent piece of 'thinking on its feet'. So during this time Artangel really acted as my cultural estate agents.

CD When you were looking at various sites, what kinds of criteria did you have in mind?

JL I think by then, through talking to Richard quite a bit, I realised the project should not, could not be one thing. It needed to be a situation in which different kinds of material could work off against each other. His photography and slide talks are all about building up the layers of experience and observation. I was also interested in enabling a situation which would be sufficiently open for Richard to be able to continue to improvise.

RW And by that time, through a process of poring over *A-Z* books etc., we had some quite in-depth discussions about maps and map rooms, which of course I'd used quite a lot in the exhibition *Thinking Aloud*. I was interested in what happens in your head when you look at a plan or map or diagram.

JL We began to see that if we were going to be showing maps, it would have to have a direct relationship to the outside.

CD I want to just stay on process for a minute because I'm interested to what extent you were seeking out ideas Richard and then coming back to James and to what extent the project developed in dialogue through your joint visits?

RW I think it was both. I would say that there was a sense of mounting responsibility between us. You've gone through the goodwill moment and you've moved through a certain kind of elementary trust onto something which is actually ambitious but is not necessarily being articulated. Of course what actually came from all those site visits and trawling through maps and archives wasn't any one thing in particular, but rather the picturisation of space, of King's Cross. It began to form the character of the place where I live. You can see the traffic going in and out of the airport and you can see the aeroplanes lined up and to me it's just like the map of the economy of the city and the pool of London distributed in the sky.

CD Were there any questions in your mind about whether or not it should be made public and for how long?

JL Well I think there was a sense that this would be a project that would accumulate and develop over time. That it would not necessarily open in a finished form. I was really attracted to that and we kept the project open for about 12 weeks but I think if we existed within a different cultural economy, it could have been a project which could have had a longer time-span. In retrospect, its life was prematurely cut short. It was still growing.

Maybe it's just worth saying how it came about that we identified that particular location on York Way. Richard had begun to think that the upended container he so much admired could be a fantastic viewing platform to look out over King's Cross, so I wanted to find somewhere in King's Cross where we could site this upended container vertically. We wanted it to look out over the working wasteland. So I went to see these guys who owned a car park to see if we could negotiate the use of a corner to install the container. And one of them said it could be problematic in the car park but did I want to look at the warehouse next door. When we went inside, I recognised quite quickly that this could work. It was unusually high, in fact it had a very odd shape, which I thought Richard might like and it was right on the edge of the King's Cross development, next to the railways. Then Richard had the brilliant idea of installing the container inside the building and puncturing its roof with a periscope.

RW I remember it being much more about the idea of stacking up the containers and then the staircase would deliver you to the different stacks. I was caught by that image–the horizontal staircase. Then a call from James saying I don't know about the car park but there is this one empty building, and then going to look at it and realising that I knew it really well. I had stood in there for countless hours to buy plumbing parts, or solder for sculpture etc.. It was a plumbers' merchants in an abandoned Bentley and Rolls Royce service garage. Its sign, *General Plumbing Supplies*, was displayed in wonderful neon which was broken for years. When you sat in the train at King's Cross all you could see against the sky were the words "Plumbers… lies" because that was the only bit that worked. All the marks on the floor were all still there. And of course plumbing is just infrastructure as well. Plumbing is just buckets turned into tubes and people don't have to carry water anymore. An image which joins everything together, just like the canals before the railways took over. Standing there I realised, the roof is so high, so that's why it was always so cold in there. I thought immediately about bringing in the much desired stairwell.

I also remember being slightly shy about the money. "God I bet it'll cost a lot to get a container up here and look… the door isn't big enough and how would you get it through the roof?" But then I realised that this is what Artangel does, it just loves to solve a problem, especially if the problem is culturally sexy. I remember thinking; imagine getting up to the top of the building. An architect friend of mine came to the space and counted the bricks and sent me a drawing which showed you can have this much of your staircase and you will come out right by those dusty purlins and you will be in the roof space. It was then, and only then, in zeal and imagined space, that I knew this was our project…. What I didn't know (and I think this is very typical of all sorts of incubated imaginative moments) was that you wouldn't just be up there–but you'd also be looking down and therefore you would have that same sense as walking on the Scala roof, but you'd also be a witness to what was going on down below. And it was then that I realised that I had to make something happen downstairs. The sea of ping-pong tables and the tournament were all generated by this moment.

 Richard Wentworth, *An Area of Outstanding Unnatural Beauty*, 2002 (detail). Courtesy Artangel

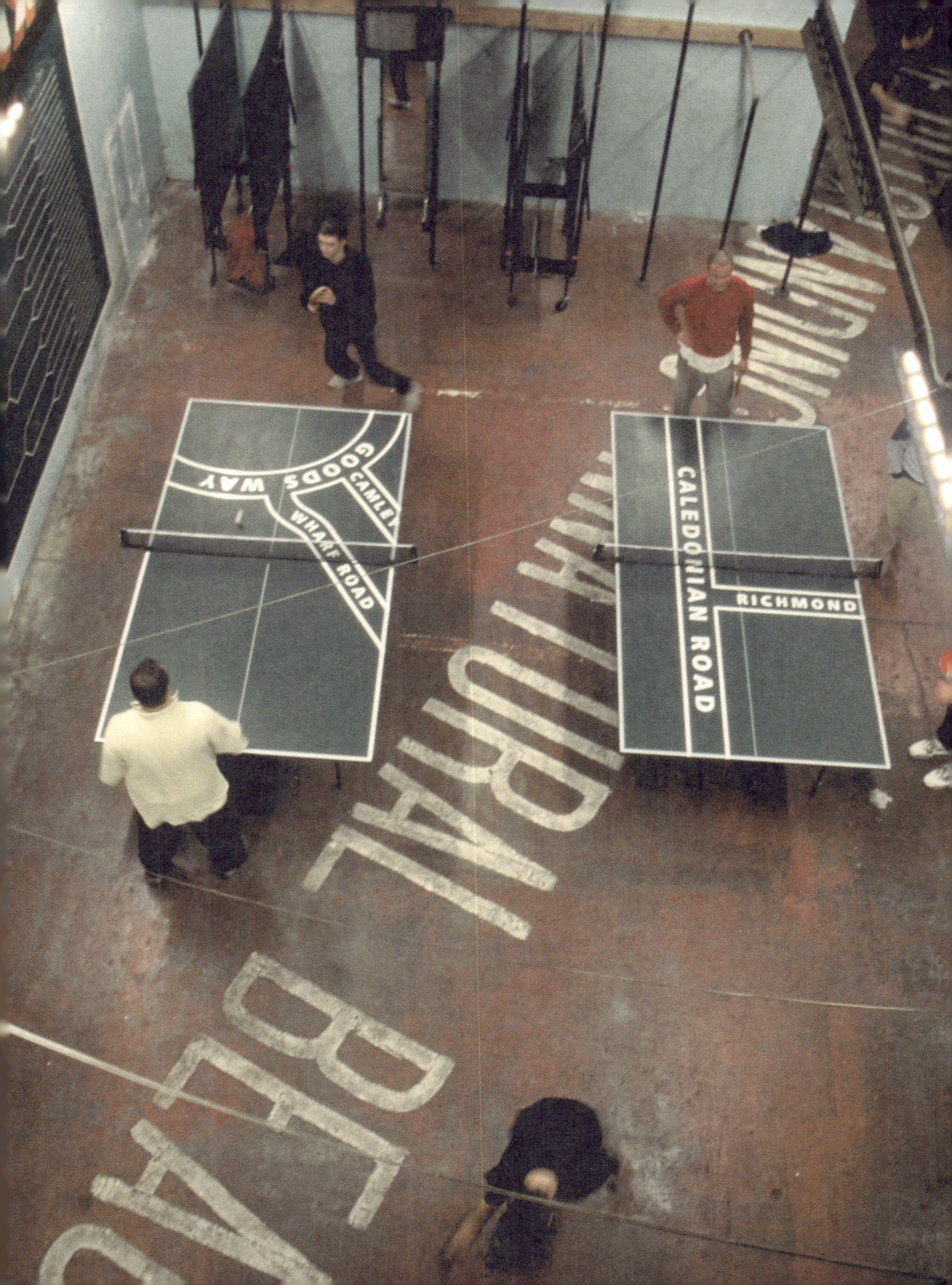
GOODS WAY
CAMLEY
WHARF ROAD
CALEDONIAN ROAD
RICHMOND

JL It was something to do with the angles of looking that led to the idea of the periscope, that sense of all-in-the-round surveillance. There was the constructivist view from above which was something I related to things like [Alexander] Rodchenko or [Lazlo] Moholy-Nagy photos and their dynamic picturing of space. The fact that you were looking down on people playing ping-pong on tables painted with fragments of the *A-Z* reinforced this idea. Then there was an intimate looking, just poring over the details of different kinds of maps. Then there was the looking involved in playing. Richard came up with quite a few ideas distinct from his previous projects, for example, to film the *A-Z* being made.

RW James didn't know how much I admire the Moholy-Nagy pictures or early aerial photography. It was important that Artangel gave me the freedom to explore certain avenues. The day we went to see the *A-Z* being printed was one of the best days ever, though I have one huge regret. We went with a film crew and noticed that the printers clean the plates or drums with the same paper, so there were palimpsest piles of excerpts of the *A-Z*. There were motorways crossing Hyde Park. There were rivers through Knightsbridge. Dead centre in a huge pile of them was King's Cross. And there we were salivating at the incredible find. They even had the pile 'ready' on the day of our visit.

JL There was a degree of suspicion amongst the *A-Z* people about what we might want to do with their material and it was quite difficult to secure permission to go there with a film crew. We were really chaperoned around.

RW And time was running out....

JL But we failed to come away with these overlaid, discarded maps–or at least not the one with King's Cross in it.

RW They were gorgeous. How close does desire come to pain? Perhaps desire as possession is a kind of failure?

JL I suppose if we'd continued to push it we might have arrived at some agreement. They didn't seem too keen for Richard to show anything that was unfinished, that looked like a mistake. The film that came out of the cutting of the *A-Z* maps prior to printing was very good though.

CD Do you think that perfectionism something that's reflected in what you do as director of Artangel and also as curator–you want to show the finished product and not any of those difficult decisions or those cul-de-sacs, the throw-aways of a project?

JL What you show depends on the artist. The cul-de-sacs may be interesting to us, but whether they are integral to the finished work is open to question. You need to make decisions as to what aspects of that process could and should be made public. I would always respect an artist's take on that process. I'm not really interested in privileging process for the sake of it. I do believe that the projects we're involved in need to find a form. In the case of this project it was a particularly open-ended form, but nonetheless it was still a form. I think there is too much emphasis given to process as an end in itself. Michael Landy's project *Break Down* for example, was based on a huge amount of research but was not illustrative of the research process.

RW It's great to hear somebody speak so well about process in relation to form, in relation to imagery and narrative. What was so funny about alighting on this desirable object of the stack of throw-away maps was that I wasn't sure, even if we had got hold of the pile, whether it would ever really have approached anything like the moment of discovery. Maybe that's the loss–the loss of the moment of discovery. I was hurt for about ten days afterwards, saying to James, "What do you mean we're not going to get them?" But of course the subject matter of the project wasn't lost. Yearning is part of the process.

CD And maybe what your relationship with Artangel did was to allow for those moments of discovery to be revealed in that final form so that in turn there were a series of moments of discovery in the final project for visitors to the York Way premises.

RW Oh yes. It was all about loss. There was this peripatetic crowd of visitors. You could hear the railway outside, you could hear the announcements, and see the aeroplanes in the sky. The chief invigilator, Tracey Ferguson, became very important as a kind of navigator in the space, who so well understood what she had to do; or rather maybe she didn't understand what she had to do. She invented what she did and it was impeccable. People would say "Where is the work?" and she would answer, "You're standing in it" and those people would always stay an hour. They would say, "Oh, it's like being in a library, or being allowed to walk around a shop and knowing that you can just look as much as you like, no one expects you to buy anything." People would climb the staircase unaware that you could look down. So gradually there would be people looking up and down and down and up, and then, of course, there were always people who didn't know why they were there. All this to the sounds of mass ping-pong.

CD So it was important that you might not know that this was a destination of sorts.

RW Definitely. I am still terribly disappointed in many ways that we closed it when we did because it had hit a stride. I loved the way people would happen upon the place as much as those who sought it out.

CD Do you feel that that through the process of the project and its final form, the relationship with James and Artangel, that it shifted your approach to other projects? Are you aware yet of how this project effected your work as a whole?

RW Well the usual rules continue to apply–work with the best people at all levels, and edit thoughtfully. I think *An Area of Outstanding Unnatural Beauty* set all sorts of new standards. It set new standards for me. Artists live with a hybrid of overconfidence and the terror of doubt. That's their choice, and their distinction.

JL One of the issues for Richard is that he performs so brilliantly that he's always going to be asked to do another gig but without necessarily being given the time and the space to really move the ideas forward. I hope that's one of the things that we were able to do with this project, to show the complexity and the richness of his work, integrating his performative skills with his practice as a sculptor.

CD So perhaps contrary to other projects in which the artist is remote, this was a project in which you or all of your capacities of an artist were revealed.

RW I hadn't even thought of it like that. I feel rather shy in the face of something like that. But I see it's true. People were generous with me, of course.

CD Perhaps you were not only the instigator of this project, but that your presence was required as an instigator of discussion.

RW It's an interesting question because I was never quite comfortable there. I have always thought that conventional public art is an attempt to possess the street, what artists of that sort are really doing is emptying a private patio culture out into the public realm (and ruining it). I like to feel that I'm just another person on the street and I always felt the project was just that–an occurrence in some part of London. It wasn't as if it was very physically substantial. It felt modest and underplayed I hope, but it gathered an extraordinary set of people, objects, moments, seasons and different times of the day together into one place. Perhaps that's what cities are, but you don't get many chances to see it.

An Area of Outstanding Unnatural Beauty
4 September-17 November 2002, General Plumbing Supplies, 66 York Way, London N1

Maria Lind

Actualisation of Space: The Case of Oda Projesi

The Oda Projesi team of artists is composed of Özge Acikkol, Gunes Savas and Secil Yersel. They began working together in 1997 and in 2000 set up a project in an apartment in Galata, Istanbul. The main aim of their work is to draw on aspects of everyday life–social gatherings, meal-times, discussions–to expand the possibilities for a social sculpture in process, shaped by the relationships between people and spaces.

Oda Projesi have extended their practice by initiating process-based and participatory projects worldwide and in 2003 were invited by Kunstverein München and Kunstprojekte_Riem to initiate a project in Munich as the first part in the series *Dispositiv Workshop*. Maria Lind, former Director of Kunstverein München, here discusses the case of Oda Projesi. The images and captions included here are written by the artists and adapted from material available as part of *The Room Revisted* at Kunstverein München.

A long, high-ceilinged room with small trees in boxes in the middle. The walls are punctuated by doors and windows, on all three storeys of the building. Here and there are shoes outside the doors and you glimpse curtains through the windows. One or two pushchairs are parked beside the shoes. Daylight floods the space through a glass ceiling and also filters it through the glass on the narrow sides of the room. If it weren't for the shoes and the pushchairs you might think of a hospital, or even an American-style prison. In the middle of the room a group of men play Turkish music on instruments, others dance. A little girl, dressed in yellow, attracts attention to herself as she dances an elegant solo. Tinkles of laughter. Suddenly a roll of paper is dropped from a balcony, winding down like a great snake, and some children begin to draw on it.

The location is a passage and a gathering place in Galeriahaus, a block of flats in Messestadt Riem in the outskirts of Munich. The occasion is one of many modest events that Oda Projesi organised during their visit there in spring 2003. Just as the name indicates ('oda' means room/space and 'projesi' project in Turkish), the point of departure of Oda Projesi's work is space; how one can create and recreate different places and spatial situations through using them in a number of different ways. For example, how, together with various groups of people, can you find new functions for a public space such as a square? Or an empty space in a flat? Or an architect-designed passage, like the atrium in Galeriahaus, which was closed by the authorities to non-residents and forbidden as a play area?

The three artists, Özge Acikkol, Gunes Savas and Secil Yersel, have been working together since 1997. They began by taking advantage of the possibilities offered by the public spaces in their hometown, Istanbul, by doing workshops together with groups of children, where they drew, painted and then exhibited their works on site.[1] In 2000 they adopted the name Oda Projesi and rented a three-room flat in Galata, the same district where they started their workshops. Galata lies near the famous pedestrian street, *Istiklal*, and an entertainment district where many immigrants from Turkey's eastern regions arrive when they first come to the city and was at that time still an 'ungentrified' quarter of Istanbul. The streets are narrow, courtyards small and street life lively and crowded.[2] However, none of the artists live in the flat, which functions as a meeting place for neighbours and simultaneously as a platform for the projects, inside and outside its walls, which are generated in cooperation with the people of the district and others.

The artists have become familiar with the surroundings in Galata and built up relationships with neighbours, especially with the children who, during my visits there in October 2001 and September 2003, obviously felt at home and at peace in the flat. Activities vary, but a common denominator is that they are not about showing or exhibiting a work of art but about using art as a means for creating and recreating new relations between people through diverse investigations and the shaping of both private and public space. Oda Projesi have been inspired by the ways in which Istanbul residents use their city, getting around rules and regulations: for example, how shopkeepers find clever solutions for showing their wares outside the shop without extra cost, or how additions are made to residential buildings.

One of the rooms in the Galata flat is used as a meeting place and contains drawing materials, art books and children's books. Another room is sometimes used for art projects and a third room functions as an archive, but the invited artists can also avail themselves of the rest of the flat and change the usages. The surroundings may also be utilised–for instance, when the artist Erik Göngrich, as part of his study of Istanbul as a 'picnic city', invited all the neighbours for a picnic in the little courtyard. The Istanbul-based architect group, Heterotopya, recently held discussions with children about how the enclosed, stone-covered courtyard could be rebuilt. Proposals for a swimming pool have been developing, as have ideas for a garden with swings.

The Room We used a flat near the Bewohnertreff (citizens' meeting point) organised by Kunstprojekte_Riem as the project space. The flat consists of one room and a kitchen. Before the start of the project all the inhabitants of Messestadt Riem received information about us and this space–such things as, they could meet us there every day from 9am to 12pm from 20 March to 20 April 2003. The Room was empty at first. During the project a group of people shaped it in various ways by painting it, giving a Tupperware party, filling a wall with photographs that had been taken by them and us; by working on a 40 metre long roll of paper, organising dinners, participating in a talk–all various ways of dealing with a space when you do not have 'responsibility' for it, but are trying to make it your own, to make it comfortable to be in. Throughout the project we all tried to find out what and how The Room should be, constantly searching for its use.

The Galeriahaus Galeriahaus is a residential building with fairly small flats for nearly 600 residents with a large public space in the middle. The public area was originally meant to function as a passageway open to more people than the residents. But over time (and for different reasons) the main doors to the building became locked so that only the residents can enter. From time to time, the public area of Galeriahaus is used for art exhibitions, organised by the caretaker of the building. We wanted to create and add other uses together with the residents by, for instance, utilising the public area for a big tea party, trying to reshape the space with some children and families using the 40 metre long roll of paper that people have written or drawn on. Thereby, for some time, the Galeriahaus functioned as another kind of social space. We shared residents' comments about the building with the architect, Karl-Heinz Ropke, and discussed how he might design the building in comparison with how it is today.

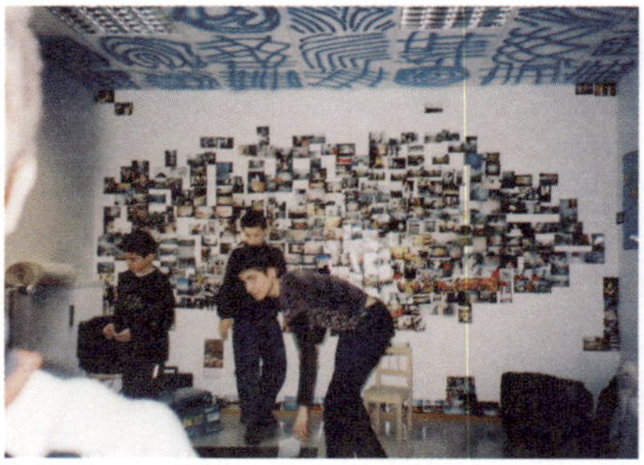

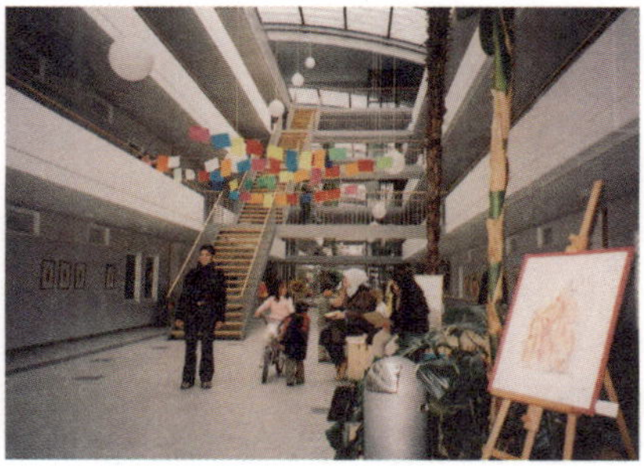

Oda Projesi is an ongoing project, initiated and financed by the artists themselves. It is not part of a programme or campaign; it has neither opening hours nor is advertised. When artists are invited to participate, there are openings to which the local art crowd come, but otherwise it is possible to make arrangements to drop in by word-of-mouth. When the members of Oda Projesi are away, the key is kept by a neighbour who looks after the flat and lets in children and others who want to use it. In this way, the flat becomes a place with both private and public features. Oda Projesi's understanding and use of space lies close to Michel de Certeau's use-oriented, pragmatic approach: space is an effect of the activities that influence–and even determine it–that place it in a time frame. Thus space is about actualisation, about active utilisation, and about the ambivalences and internal dependencies that arise in the very use of it, just as when a word is articulated it acquires layers of meaning through its specific context.[3]

Oda Projesi's work is part of the varied contemporary art that operates interactively and utilises public (or 'semi-public') space. They set up situations for various types of exchange in which intimacy and personal contact are stressed. Their work has even been described as a reflection of what public art is–and what it can be–and how it functions within contemporary art.[4] As the field is so varied it seems even more important to try and pin down some specifics in relation to each practice. At first glance, Suzanne Lacy's definition of the 'new genre public art' might be applied to Oda Projesi: "New genre public art calls for an integrative critical language through which values, ethics and social responsibility can be discussed in terms of art".[5]

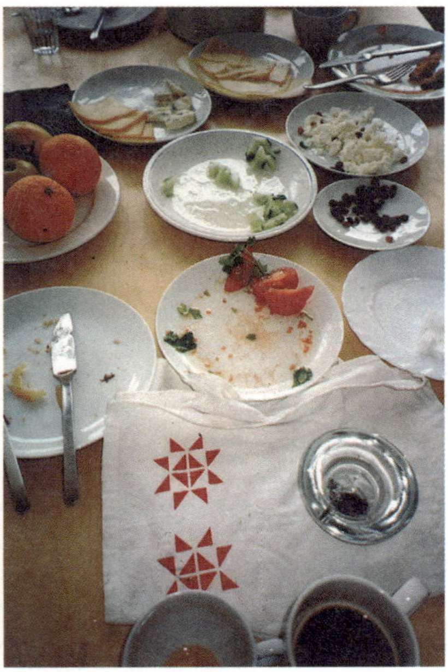

The Kitchen There is a kitchen next to The Room. Like The Room, The Kitchen was also experienced in different ways. Events such as hair cutting and make-up sessions, playing with the colour of the walls, cooking and small tea parties took place there, without curtains so that all the activity could be seen from outside. The Kitchen faces a construction area which will be the heart of Messestadt Riem with a shopping mall, cinemas and other facilities. Thus, The Kitchen could be seen from the outside, from the road, from other buildings and houses. This meant the space became active at different times whenever there was light inside.

It is a working model based on relations between people and on social creativity rather than on self-expression, and it is characterised by cooperation. It is community-based, often relating to marginalised groups; it is socially-engaged, interactive and aimed at another, less anonymous public than that of art institutions. 'New genre public art' is about creative participation in a process. Activities are primarily pursued far from established art institutions, in other social contexts such as housing areas or schools. In this way, a kind of reverse exclusiveness arises: those who are attracted to and captured by the project have more access to this art than the usual art public.

An important difference in relation to most 'new genre public art' is, however, that Oda Projesi is not reactive; that is, they do not respond to a social or cultural problem. Neither are those they work with (the target group) treated or described as 'the other'; it is rather the traditional art public that is placed in the position of 'the other'. Oda Projesi are not out to campaign to improve the world–therefore, activism in the same vein as a group such as *Park Fiktion* is also lacking.[6] Neither do they have any connection to the spiritual and 'healing' traditions in art, which Suzanne Lacy discerns in the 'new genre public art'. Even if Oda Projesi often allow their projects to take place in public or semi-public space, it is not 'public art' in any real sense since they lack public commissioners and do not distinctly thematise public space. Despite their occasionally friendly image, their work is not didactic (for example, it is not aimed direclty at target groups of underprivileged citizens). Nevertheless, like the 'grand old man' of social and somewhat behaviourist neighbourhood projects, Stephen Willats, Oda Projesi want to contribute to social change,

The Kindergarten Sadiye, a resident of Messestadt Riem, works in a kindergarten. We spent one day in the kindergarten to meet with the people employed there and work with them and with the children on a 40 metre long roll of paper.

The Classroom One of the residents of Messestadt Riem, Sadiye, made a presentation entitled *Türkische Lebensart* (the Turkish way of life) in a school for kindergarten teachers in the city centre of Munich. She brought different kinds of objects to explain several Turkish traditions. She invited us to her presentation.

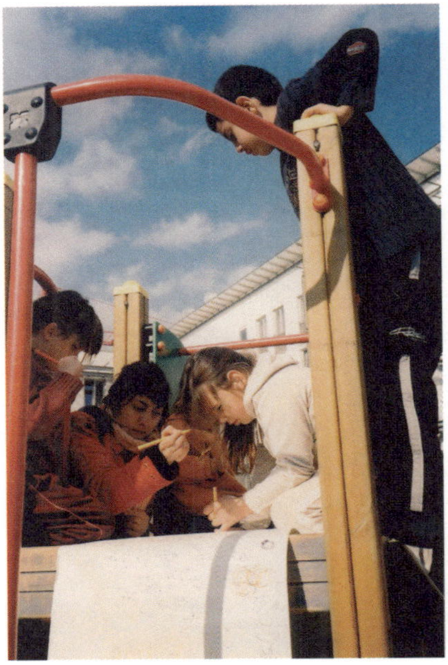

albeit from a micro perspective. For Willats, the relationship between the work and the public is the work itself, but this is difficult to apply to Oda Projesi since their understanding of what constitutes the public is more differentiated and their concept of the artwork more open and less object-based.[7]

Except for their documentation, Oda Projesi take great care not to leave behind objects that might be interpreted as art to be exhibited. Documentation becomes, instead, a diary of sorts, where activities are registered and evaluated in person. Even so, paradoxically enough, Oda Projesi have discussed their work in terms of "building a monument". They say they want to create "a monument composed of gestures from everyday life and layers of memories of the community", and they point out that this always occurs together with, and not for, the participants.[8] What they have in mind is an abstract monument, fluid in form but concrete in memory, dedicated to the participants' efforts to investigate space and formulate suggestions for alternative uses, which in turn, can contribute to recoding and restructuring human relations.

Here Oda Projesi's understanding departs radically from one of the recently most debated (and therefore 'iconic') monument-related works, which took place in a residential neighbourhood and involved the residents, namely Thomas Hirschhorn's *Bataille Monument* in Friedrich-Wöhler-Siedlung, a part of *Documenta 11* in Kassel, summer 2002 (see Hirschhorn in this publication). Both Oda Projesi and Hirschhorn refer to and question ideas about classic monuments. Thomas Hirschhorn's strategy includes using 'low' and perishable materials to build his monuments in out-of-the-way places, which are dedicated to 'great' men like Spinoza and Deleuze. His aim is to create art. For the *Bataille Monument,* he had already prepared, and in part also executed, a plan on which he needed help to implement. His participants were paid for their work and their role was that of the 'executor' and not 'co-creator'.

In my opinion, the residents in the working class neighbourhood appeared as a different and colourful element in a project that was primarily a criticism of an art genre and not of social structures. Hirschhorn's work has therefore understandably been criticised for 'exhibiting' and making exotic marginalised groups and thereby contributing to a form of a social pornography. Thomas

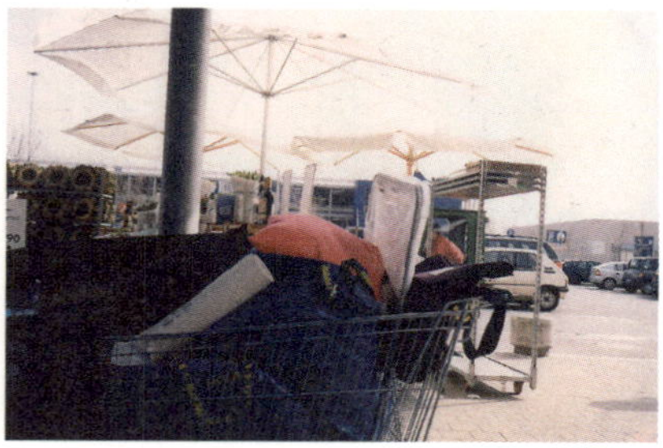

IKEA One of the first places in Munich that we went to was IKEA to buy material for the project space. We had a little tour with a group of Turkish women from Riem as well as with Rudi, whom we had agreed to help redecorate his flat.

Hirschhorn himself wanted to test what is possible within the framework of the world's most prestigious contemporary art exhibition.[9] Where Thomas Hirschhorn makes a distinction between social projects and art projects–his own work clearly belonging to the second category–such a distinction is more difficult to make for Oda Projesi. They have loose connections with the art world and are less occupied with discussing what is and what is not art; it seems to suffice that art offers a method and a zone for certain types of activities. At the same time, they work with groups of people in their immediate environments and allow them to wield great influence on the project. Therefore, Oda Projesi's work is both social and artistic, but often without an official commissioner–for instance, a local authority–that expects social reform or measurable improvements.

This double-sided nature of their work was expressed and thematised in their project in Messestadt Riem, following an invitation from Kunstprojekte_Riem and made in collaboration with Kunstverein München.[10] Although the flat in Galata is the hub of Oda Projesi's activities, it is not its entirety. During recent years, at the invitation of art institutions and organisations, the artists have carried out projects briefer than the Galata project, often taking place in other cultural and socio-political contexts.[11] The inhabitants of Messestadt Riem were notified that Oda Projesi would be available for three hours a day for one month in the project room that Kunstprojekte_Riem had at its disposal–a space, which lies next to the official and often deserted *Bewohnertreff* (citizens' meeting point) and the adjacent kitchen.[12] Together with the participants, the artists tried to find a use for the space: arranging hairdressing, Tupperware parties and making food. The Turkish women showed were expecially appreciative of the kitchen as a meeting place. The furnishings of the space were altered, partly in conjunction with each individual event, and consequently the place had a different appearance at the end than in the beginning.

Most of the social contacts were made thanks to a Turkish couple who run a little grocery across the street from Bewohnertreff. As none of the members of Oda Projesi speak German, most of the participants were Turkish-speaking. Over and above the activities in the project space and kitchen, videos were made of the quarter which were shown in the grocery. There were guided tours led by the residents and a tea party with music and dance in Galeriahaus. A long roll of paper functioned as a social instrument on several of these occasions: people were encouraged to use the paper to write and draw on, and this stimulated more conversations. As is so often the case with Oda Projesi, the 'audience' on these occasions was basically the participants, all of whom had met the artists. This minimises the degree of theatricality–there is seldom an outside, purely observing, audience. Those present participate and the artists' own presence is also central, creating an unusually intimate relationship that is sometimes difficult to grasp by 'outsiders'.

Oda Projesi shares the emphasis on human relations with a very diverse group of artists covered by what Nicolas Bourriaud has termed 'relational aesthetics'. According to him the basic material of these artists is human relations. They, stress social exchange, thematise communication processes and interact with the spectator.[13] As with Oda Projesi's activities, Dan Peterman and his project, *The Shop*, in Chicago, is oriented towards a specific community and is based on shared activities that are not 'exhibited'–in Peterman's case, a bicycle workshop in a run-down area of the city, though I would rather link Oda Projesi to another artist connected to relational aesthetics: Rirkrit Tiravanija. Like Oda Projesi, Tiravanija's work involves a great amount of openness in the sense that a social situation is created, shaped very much by the participants, and focused on new uses of space and restructuring of everyday actions.

Both Oda Projesi and Rirkrit Tiravanija deliberately mix the private and the public, with all that means in terms of informality and intimacy. The initiative lies with the public, quite often children or young people, a group that more easily avoid anticipated behaviour and predetermined ways of using things.[14] Collaboration and participation are at the core of their activities. Although both Oda Projesi and Rirkrit Tiravanija lack grand political pretensions, they do not lose sight of the idea of change. As always where human relations are pivotal, it is difficult, if not impossible, to describe exactly what happens and to judge whether it is successful or not. It is nevertheless clear that this method is decisive: with Oda Projesi, the method of social interaction in combination with a focus on concrete space is itself the essence of their work.

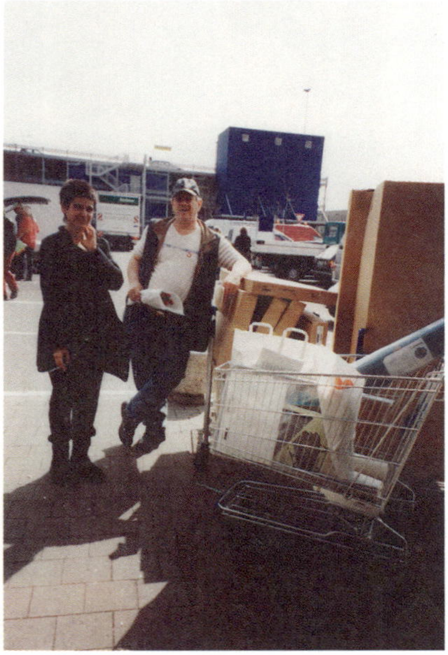

Rudi's Room We met Rudi through Turhan, the owner of the local supermarket, *Galeria Früchtehaus*, who had told Rudi about us, about us being artists. This prompted Rudi to ask us to help him redecorate his flat. In return he made and designed a website for us which mostly includes photographs he took during our stay in Messestadt Riem (www.odaprojesi.com).

In this context, the Vienna-based critic Christian Kravagna's distinction between four different working methods in contemporary art concerned with human interaction may be useful: working with others, interactive activities, collective action, and participatory practice. Written in 1998, his text, "Modelle partizipatorischer Praxis" (Models of participatory practice), sketches a picture of a society where a feeling of political powerlessness reigns, and where real or imagined unemployment lurks around the corner.[15] Kravagna considers sociologist Ulrich Beck's notion of "Bürgerarbeit" (citizen's work), which implies activating unused potential for political engagement in order to create an engaged civil society. "Bürgerarbeit" would involve people on state subsidies engaging in community work, everything from helping the dying to working with the homeless and becoming involved in art and culture. For Christian Kravagna this is nothing less than a trick: where the reduced possibilities for political participation is compensated for by 'social activity', work which citizens do for free. In effect under Ulrich Beck's model people have something meaningful to do, they are rewarded, and therefore they keep quiet. And the state saves money.

Although Christian Kravagna's view might be both too black and white, too infused with conspiracy theory, it could help us clarify the position of Oda Projesi among the different participatory art approaches. As he rightly remarks, participation as a method takes on a significance within twentieth century art whenever art is engaged in self-critique, with the position of the author being questioned or when the relationship between art and life is being disputed. His first category–'working together'–is exemplified with artists like Rirkrit Tiravanija, Irene and Christine Hohenbüchler and Jens Haaning. In his opinion this practice is merely fashionably 'socio-chic' and should be excluded from the discussion altogether. He quotes the artists Alice Creischer and Andreas Siekkmann who write that this practice has a "pronounced exploitation character" as these artists outsource the production of the work but still get the surplus value themselves.

The second category–interactive art–permits one or more reactions that can influence the appearance of the work without deeply affecting its structure. Christian Kravagna does not give any examples here but we can imagine that he has 'push the button' works in so-called 'new media' in mind, as well as works where you accept an offer to consume something. The idea behind the third category–collective action–is that a group of people formulate an idea and then carry it out together. Again he skips examples but *Park Fiktion* could be one. His fourth category–participatory practice–presumes that there is a difference between the producer and receiver but the focus is on the latter, to which a significant part of the development of the work is transferred. This fourth category provides the focus for his discussion, including works such as Adrian Piper's *Funk Lessons* 1982-1984, Clegg & Guttman's *Offene Bibliothek* (Open library) 1991 and 1993, Stephen Willat's *Vertical Living,* 1978 as well as the so-called 'new genre public art'.[16] Whereas the first three works are considered successful, 'new genre public art' is dismissed as traditional, essentialist, moralising, mystifying and pastoral.

Both in terms of art production and curating, Christian Kravagna's very first category–'working together'–can function as an umbrella for the other three categories. Yet it retains some specificities lacking in the others, among which 'openness' seems to be the most disputed but also the most relevant in relation to Oda Projesi's activities. The issue of exploitation is complicated but if Rirkrit Tiravanija, Irene and Christine Hohenbüchler and Jens Haaning can be said to keep the surplus value then the same should undoubtedly go for the quoted works of Adrian Piper, Clegg & Guttman and Stephen Willats. Oda Projesi's work may be said to represent a hybrid form: it encompasses all four categories, but with a more open concept of a work of art, sometimes in separate projects, sometimes in one and the same project. And perhaps it is here that the strength and weakness of their work lies: from their everyday–often spatial–points of departure, working in different ways with people in their immediate environs creating not so small shifts in how we think about and relate to each other. However, the nature of the political discourse around this activity requires further development.

Oda Projesi's approach throws up more than one obstacle. For institution-based curating it raises the dilemma of how to work with contemporary art such as this which originates in and functions outside institutions, as part of public, or semi-public space, in direct relation to everyday life. Since Oda Projesi's involvement with the art system is distant, and since they don't produce objects or images aimed at being exhibited in institutions, they have a vague relationship to the exhibition as medium and partly also to the institution as coded place. This came to the fore when as, a continuation and discussion of the project in Messestadt Riem, the documentation of the project was shown under the title *The Room Revisited* at Kunstverein München.[17] The situation was thereby radically altered and Oda Projesi were, for instance, confronted with outside spectators who had no direct contact with the project. The presentation was adjusted to this situation; beside various forms of documentation they designed the space to resemble the project space in Messestadt Riem–a usage of space which does not correspond to the 'white cube'.

The 14-minute long video *Riem Rooms* was shown in the 'cabinet', an intimate room in the otherwise purpose-built grand gallery space from the late eighteenth century, which was furnished with a carpet, cloth and pillows on the floor. There were also small snapshots on the floor which the visitors were encouraged to take with them, well produced official information material from the district and a *Notebook of Space*, photocopied documentation and notebook, designed by the artists, which visitors could take away with them. Large colour photographs of some of the rooms that Oda Projesi have used in their work over the past few years were mounted on a wall outside the 'cabinet'. *The Room Revisited* was neither an exhibition, nor strictly documentation of Oda Projesi's experience in Messestadt Riem. In a way it was a bit 'out of place', to which a number of reactions from both the general audience and some critics testified. There have been various attempts to transform art exhibition spaces (particularly since the 1990s), to challenge the white cube, into something other than rigid, sometimes authoritarian show places, something beyond a 'showroom'. Inspired by club culture and bar atmospheres, these spaces have been turned into, among other things, places for 'hanging out'–undramatic, relaxing areas–but also they have become sewing workshops, tattooing studios, dating agencies, etc.. Exhibition spaces have also been used as offices and meeting places for activists, thereby taking on some responsibilities normally assigned to community centres or Kulturläden (cultural shops)–thanks to the work of artists. Mostly neglected but equally important for altering the notion of institutions for contemporary art are their own intitiatives to fund and produce projects which have very little or nothing to do with the physical institutional space. In an indirect but palpable way, they contribute to the erosion of the conventional understanding of the institution as a place for the display of art objects by underlining the institution as a structure for support, for production and distribution through alternative channels. In short, they help 'de-Duchampify' the institution.

One year after working with Oda Projesi and doing *The Room Revisited* at Kunstverein München, I am still busy wondering how we can involve the type of–very important–work which Oda Projesi do, in institutional programming. It is the kind of work which is carried out within the field of art but which resembles (or is it even the same) as activities happening within other areas of society. Typically Oda Projesi would not spend a lot of time discussing what is and isn't art. Instead they take advantage of being able to operate within its specific field of action. Their work is based on regular, long-term, personal engagement and presence. In light of all these dilemmas should we leave this kind of work to itself, and to the few organisations supporting it? Or should we (the art institution and curators of contemporary art) insist on engaging with it and

The Market Galeria Früchtehaus, owned by a Turkish family, is the first place we started to spend time and through which we got to know Messestadt Riem and some of its residents. We used this local supermarket as the starting point for our research about daily structures in Messestadt Riem. A video recorded in the supermarket and Galeriahaus next door, was shown in the supermarket during the last week of the project.

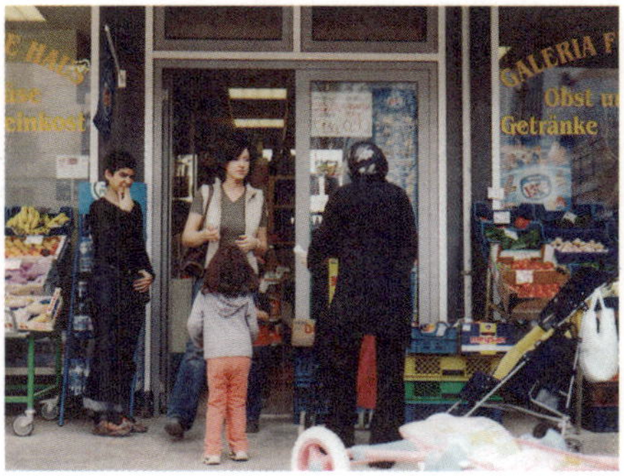

thereby run the risk of compromising the work, as well as annoying both the general audience and colleagues?

Institutional politics should not be overlooked in a situation like this. Oda Projesi's project began with Kunstprojekte_Riem contacting us at Kunstverein München and asking if we could collaborate on one of their many projects. At the time they were under political pressure to be more visible within the city centre. We mentioned Oda Projesi as an interesting possibility, particularly as we had not succeeded in raising enough funds for them to do something in Munich in conjunction with their participation in the group exhibition *Exchange & Transform (Arbeitstitel)* in 2002.[18] Eventually Kunstprojekte_Riem did invite Oda Projesi and we offered them the spaces of Kunstverein München. This process raised questions about to what extent inviting artists like this fulfils the institution's desire to justify its support of community-related work. My initial reply would be to support it in its 'natural' habitat, i.e. the places from where it springs. This is not usually popular with trustees and funders, who expect things to appear in the exhibition spaces rather than in distant suburbs. However, at the end of the day I'd like to see *The Room Revisited* as yet another example of how Oda Projesi continuously question the conventional uses of space in a 'de Certeauan' way: how they even actualise space by staging activities which engage with the ambiguous, often incompatible uses and understandings of the institution.

The Room Revisited, 2003 Exhibition space at the Kunstverein München with video documentation and pictures about Oda Projesi's stay in Messestadt Riem.

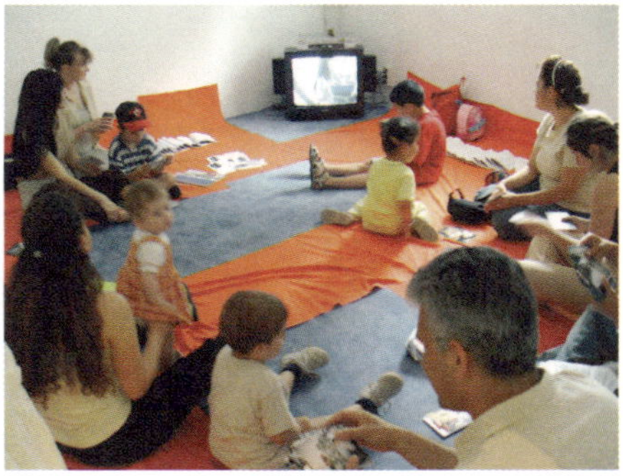

[1] At that time in Turkey, no museums, art or otherwise, had educational workshops for children or adults.

[2] Galata has been documented in the film *Windows* by the film maker Belmin Soylemez. Oda Projesi have used the film in exhibitions as part of the presentation of their activities, for instance in the exhibition, *Exchange & Transform (Arbeitstitel)* at Kunstverein München in the summer of 2002.

[3] See Michel de Certeau, *The Practice of Everyday Life*, Berkeley, Los Angeles: University of California Press, 1988.

[4] Ana Paula Cohen, "Dispositiv Workshop–Part 1: Oda Projesi", *Drucksache Spring 03*, Munich: Kunstverein München, 2003.

[5] Suzanne Lacy, *Mapping the Terrain: New Genre Public Art*, Seattle, Washington: Bay Press, 1995, p. 43. Lacy uses the term to discuss a number of very different projects in the US from the 1970s to the 1990s.

[6] See, for example, Christoph Schäfer and Cathy Skene, "Aufruhr auf Ebene p: St. Pauli Elbpark O-100%" in Marius Babias, and Achim Könneke, *Die Kunst des Öffentlichen*, Amsterdam and Dresden: Verlag der Kunst, 1998. *Park Fiktion* is an activist initiative, started by a group of artists and other local residents, to stop gentrification in Hamburg's St. Pauli district and specifically to preserve a park.

[7] See, for example, Stephen Willats, *Living Together*, exh. cat., Glasgow: Tramway, 1995. Despite focusing on co-operation and process, Willats produced object-based art, which is regularly exhibited in 'white cube' spaces.

[8] Ana Paula Cohen, "Dispositiv Workshop–Part 1: Oda Projesi", *Drucksache Spring 03*, Munich: Kunstverein München, 2003.

[9] See Michaela Pöschl, *Hirschhorn's Wurst* at www.igkultur.at, 2002.

[10] Oda Projesi's project was the first part in the series *Dispositiv Workshop*, initiated by Kunstverein München in 2003. The subsequent parts were: *Dispositiv Workshop Part 2* with Annika Eriksson, Autumn 2003; *Dispositiv Workshop Part 3* with Katya Sander, Summer 2004; *Dispositiv Workshop Part* 4, a colloquium on collaborative practice with artistic and curatorial initiatives from all over Europe, Summer 2004; *Dispositiv Workshop Part 5* with Ruth Kaasserer, Summer 2004 and finally *Dispositiv Workshop Part 6* with Rirkrit Tiravanija, a retrospective project, Autumn 2004. *Dispositiv Workshop* is a project series, where artists are invited to realise projects in collaboration with a group of people from Munich. See Katharina Schlieben, "Dispositiv Workshop", *Drucksache Fall 03*, Munich: Künstverein München, 2003.

[11] Two of these invitations came from an institution in Istanbul: the new contemporary art museum Proje4L, located in Gültepe in between a financial district and a so-called '24-hour house district', where one can build additions to residential housing without building permits as long as it only takes 24 hours. The first invitation resulted in Oda Projesi renting a flat for six months in one of these '24-hour' buildings neighbouring the museum, where they had similar activities to those going on in Galata. The second led to co-operating with an adjacent school for two years. A little later, in spring 2002, Oda Projesi participated in the *Gwangju Biennale* in South Korea, where they reconstructed the Galata flat in its actual size in the exhibition space.

[12] Kunstprojekte_Riem was an ambitious project, which ran from 2002-2003, where the city of Munich, through the curator Claudia Büttner, commissioned artworks in and for a newly developed housing area on the old airport ground. See www.kunstprojekte-riem.de

[13] Nicolas Bourriaud, "An Introduction to Relational Aesthetics", in *Traffic*, exh. cat., Bordeaux: CAPC Musée d'Art Contemporain, 1995.

[14] See Nina Möntman, *Kunst als sozialer Raum*, Cologne: Verlag der Buchhandlung Walther König, 2002. Whereas Tiravanija stages a majority of his works, which often contain rooms or spaces, in art institutions that are used in ways unusual for them, Oda Projesi has worked less often in such contexts.

[15] See Christian Kravagna, "Modelle partizipatorischer Praxis"in Marius Babias and Achim Könneke, eds., *Die Kunst des Öffentlichen*, Amsterdam and Dresden: Verlag der Kunst, 1998.

[16] The question of context has come to the fore, also beyond the institution. To the extent that there is a German term *Kontextkunst* (context art), coined by Peter Weibel for an exhibition in Graz in 1993, and highly contested by particularly the Cologne-based leftist art scene. *Kontextkunst* is, if you wish a German parallel to the so-called 'relational aesthetics' but more programmatically political and academic. Both imply a more dynamic notion of art, which actively takes the context into consideration and which often goes beyond the exhibition space. Some of the artists used as 'good' examples by Christian Kravagna have been associated with Kontextkunst. See Peter Weibel: *Kontextkunst–Kunst der 90er Jahre*, Cologne: DuMont Verlag, 1994.

[17] *The Room Revisited* at Kunstverein München, 5 June-31 August 2003.

[18] See note 2.

Paul Domela

FURTHER Up in the Air

FURTHER is a long-term project, spanning half a decade, developed and run by artist/curators Leo Fitzmaurice and Neville Gabie in Liverpool. Evolving from an earlier project *Up in the Air*, *FURTHER* expanded the vision of the project with nationally and internationally recognised artists and writers responding to the same Sheil Park housing estate in North Liverpool. The last tower block of flats on this site, Linosa Close, was home to 18 artists and writers from a broad spectrum of disciplines working in three phases of residencies in 2002-2003, including Catherine Bertola, Leo Fitzmaurice, Stephen Gec, Neville Gabie, Gary Perkins, Will Self, Tom Woolford, Elizabeth Wright, Lothar Gotz, David Mabb, Greg Streak, Paul Rooney and Bill Drummond. Their studios were open to visitors on 27 and 28 September 2002. Here Paul Domela, Deputy Chief Executive of the *Liverpool Biennial*, places the project within its wider social and cultural context.

A lack of stated political ambition for *FURTHER Up in the Air* can be misconstrued as problematic, in terms of the engagement of the project with the socio-economic and urbanistic changes affecting the residential community of Sheil Park. Perhaps this is a residue of dialectical belligerence that obscures an appreciation for the extensive relations between artists and residents that brings forth the project. It also points to a set of expectations that has become associated with 'situated practices'–fixing the discursive production of the subject into a new orthodoxy, and thereby adding to the menu of categories which 'situatedness' sought to overcome. Over five years the artists Neville Gabie and Leo Fitzmaurice (and the artist Kelly Large initially) have built up confidence with a community of high rise tenants to engage with contemporary art, artists and writers in an unstable transitionary context. The proposal was simple, to give 18 artists the opportunity to spend one month living and working in Linosa Close, a 22-storey flat destined for demolition, with an open invitation to comment and reflect on this experience.

This can (and in some ways should) be understood as a fairly conventional invitation until one brings into focus the extraordinary setting of the city of Liverpool, which since the 1930s has lost half its population, almost 500,000 people. Linosa Close is the last of three tower blocks in Sheil Park. In the late 1960s, 67 tower blocks had been built as part of a large programme to redress overcrowding and poor living conditions in Liverpool's city centre. The *tabula rasa* demolition of back-to-back Victorian terraces and tenement buildings dispersed close-knit communities to the new high rises and further out to new towns such as Skelmersdale, Netherton or Speke. Over time a new vertical community grew up behind a single front door, around stairs, elevators and on balconies with views stretching for miles: Mount Snowdon to the West, the Irish Sea to the North, the Pennines to the East and to the South the Mersey Estuary. But 20 years later modernist progress had left Liverpool well behind. A catastrophic conflation of de-industrialisation, suburbanisation, and containerisation of shipping and the dissolution of the British Empire washed out the riches, leaving the city disorientated and decentred, eroding its economic base and draining its financial power to London. The city barely escaped bankruptcy and in the 1980s it was close to destitution. Like much council housing, many of the blocks suffered from poor maintenance and falling occupancy. At the time of *FURTHER Up in the Air* Linosa Close only housed 90 residents in 172 flats, most of them elderly, most of them women. But we have to tread carefully to understand the micropolitics of this situation.

FURTHER Up in the Air is marked by the absence of any interventionist strategy of empowerment, capacity building or attempts to thematise the potential for communicative action often associated with community-based projects. I am reminded of *Dead House Walking*, a recent project by Social Impact that accompanied the move of 1500 residents out of two high rise blocks in Linz, Austria, which were set for demolition.[1] *Dead House Walking* tried to set up communication between residents to better represent their interests to the owners in the determination of their new homes. On the surface, two comparable conditions in which 1960s tower blocks are destroyed to be replaced by low rise housing, with all the contingent social and psychological problems for the residents involved. However, the circumstances are very different. Whereas the project in Linz supported the residents in setting up communication, *FURTHER Up in the Air* cannot be considered without the work the Liverpool High Rise Tenants Group (LHRTG), the association of tenants which was instrumental in establishing the government-funded Housing Action Trust (HAT) that now manages Liverpool's high rise tower blocks. Established in 1993, HAT was originally charged with refurbishment, but forecasts for a continuing decline in population forced it to reformulate its policy and demolish 49 of the 67 tower blocks, with the remainder being handed over to housing corporations. The occupancy of the flats had fallen so dramatically that in most cases the residents could be rehoused in semi-detached one and two-storey bungalows on the footprint of the existing flats. The more serpentine meanderings of this contemporary housing corporation estate has the houses facing inward onto a community centre, erasing any aspiration to the clear lines of vision afforded by modernity. Alongside this process, HAT set up a Community Development Programme that saw the involvement of artists as an integral part of its policy. Apart from more finite projects such as *Outhouse* by artist Vong Phaophanit, HAT together with the LHRTG also started the Superchannel project *tenantspin* (www.tenantspin.org.uk) producing a weekly webcast with and by the tenants. It is this articulate and politically aware setting that allowed *FURTHER Up in the Air* an unusual degree of freedom both in process and in terms of its outcomes–unusual, for in Britain increasingly art production, distribution and reception are validated by politicised briefs or quantifiable objectives, be it inclusivity, diversity, participation or visitor numbers.

FURTHER Up in the Air was never conceived with *a priori* outputs in mind but emerged out of a sustained conversation between the three artists/curators, the residents and the housing association. Though seen by HAT within a regeneration context, the project successfully avoids the trappings of a participatory rhetoric that can obfuscate the real power relations between commissioners, artists and the conditionally-invited participants. Not a singular vision then but a coincidental meeting of linking minds.

How does one translate the local? Let there be no mistake, the local has no objective existence. The local as place emerges as a dynamic pattern of relations with a palpable density of affect, which is produced and continuously regenerated. As a concept it exists only within the domain of the observer in order to distinguish and describe within a discursive field and not as a property of the observed domain. *FURTHER Up in the Air* is inextricably bound up with the local conditions that have co-determined its emergence. In an important

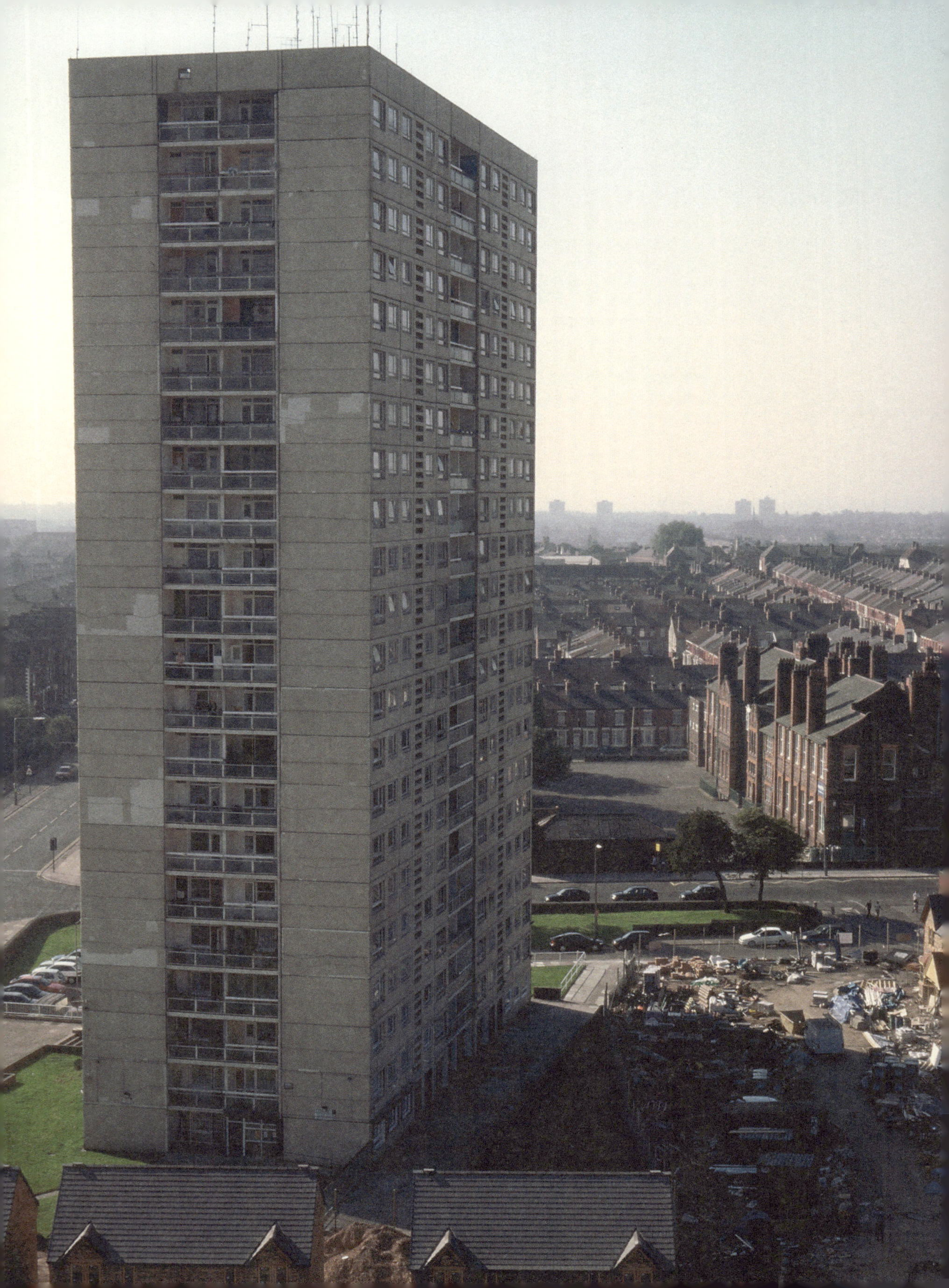

sense the project is self-referential for it was not conceived in relation to other models. This is important because the critical attention the project has received has put great pressure on the organisers to replicate or represent the project in places as diverse as Berlin, Johannesburg or Gaungzhou. It seems self-evident that initial conditions in these three places are entirely different and that the reception of any translation or modelisation of the project would need to be open to the emergence of very different relational patterns and organisational processes which would engender new possibilities for artistic production.

As the relational dynamics of the project appear to be its determining characteristic, it is tempting to understand the project in terms of Nicolas Bourriaud's 'relational aesthetics', discussed in this publication, but this would require a significant reformulation. If *FURTHER Up in the Air* echoes certain relational refrains it does so on the level of the project as a whole, not on the level of the individual artists. Many artists in the project are interested in the notion of individual creation and do not explicitly invite participation from the audience, even though they may well subscribe to a Duchampian formulation of the role of the viewer in completing the work of art. In order to understand the role of interpersonal relations in this project we may require a different meaning of it, perhaps less ceremonial, less rarefied and exclusive to the celebration of the work in the moment of its becoming, but rather an understanding of interpersonal relations, of meeting the 'other', that is more tangential, grounded in the everyday of eating, drinking and sleeping, thus resisting the immanence of mediation. As Neville Gabie notes, "[c]asual as much of it was, in the lift, returning from the pub, walking the dog on the patch of grass in front of the building, or just changing a light bulb, this gave us a uniquely different insight in to the life and community of the block...."[2] How can we translate the insights of relationality outside the scripted enclave of the art institutional framework?

FURTHER Up in the Air does not offer itself 'at a glance' as totality. It presents a choreography of spaces and processes that need to be traversed to glean a partial and contingent view. Its significance lies not only in the possibility it afforded the artists to experience the life in the block but also the chance for the community to exercise its hospitality. The project temporarily broke open the stasis of the residential community that had arisen as a consequence of the city's recent history. To a community brought inadvertently to a position of closure, the 18 artists' residencies point to the heterogeneity, dissociation and separation that are the necessary conditions for the possibility of any community. In a text written for Carnegie International Jean Fisher writes: "If artistic practices have a role here, it is to unpick the languages of habitual discourse, to present us with new ways of seeing, other stories that offer different insights into the experiences of the world, so that we can begin again the task of remaking it."[3] To the residents of Sheil Park moving into their new homes, *FURTHER Up in the Air* affirmed the possibility of beginning anew.

[1] See http://www.social-impact.at/dhw/.

[2] Neville Gabie, "Introduction", *Up in the Air*, Liverpool: Further A Field, p. 6. *Up in the Air* took place in 2000 in Kenley Close after a nine-month dialogue with the residents. Its success led to *FURTHER Up in the Air*.

[3] Jean Fisher, "Conversation Pieces", *Vampire in the Text Narratives of Contemporary Art*, London: inIVA, 2003, p. 277.

Linosa Close: Liverpool. All images courtesy *FURTHER Up in the Air* Archive

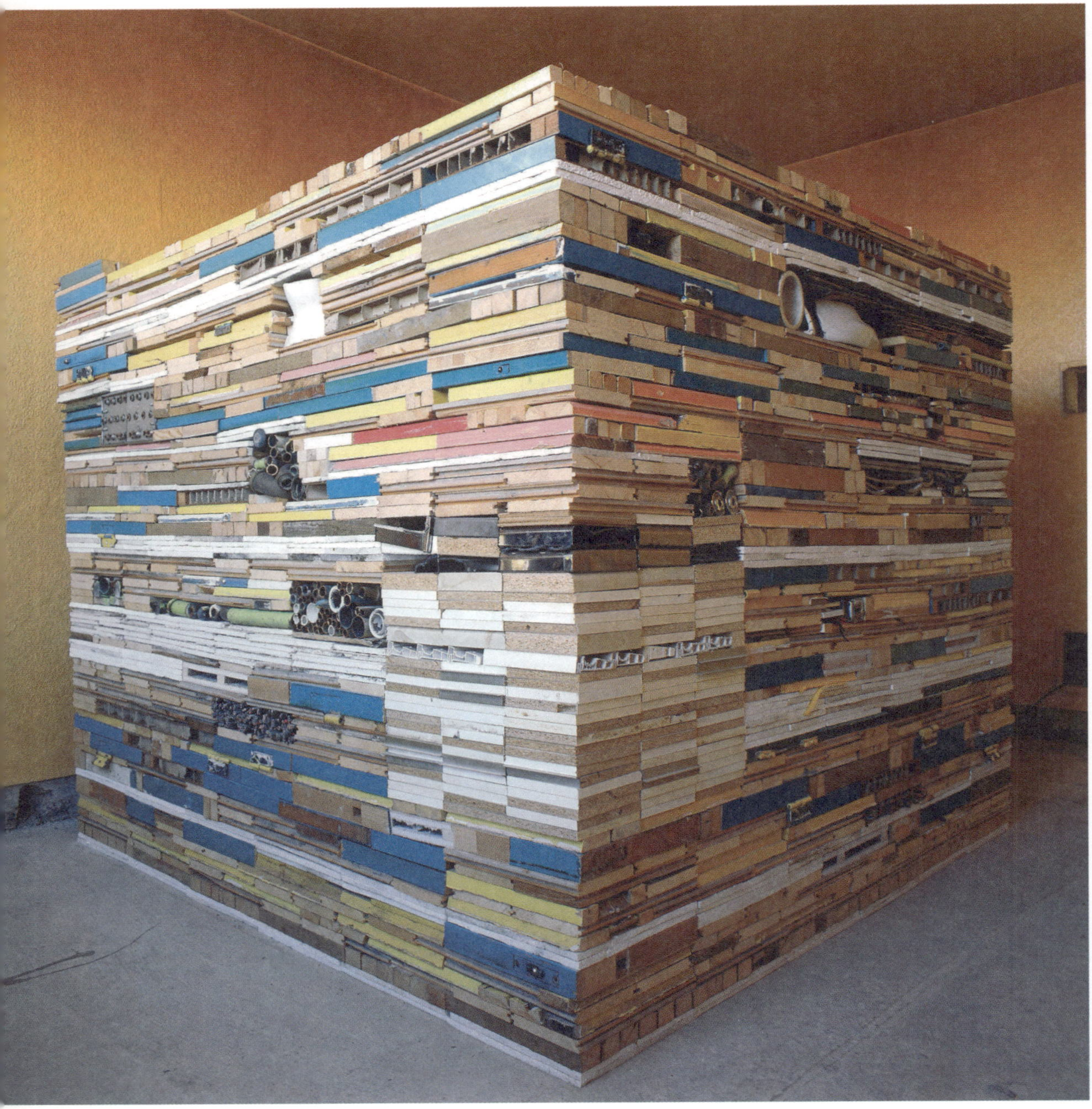

Marcus Coates. Photo: Nick David

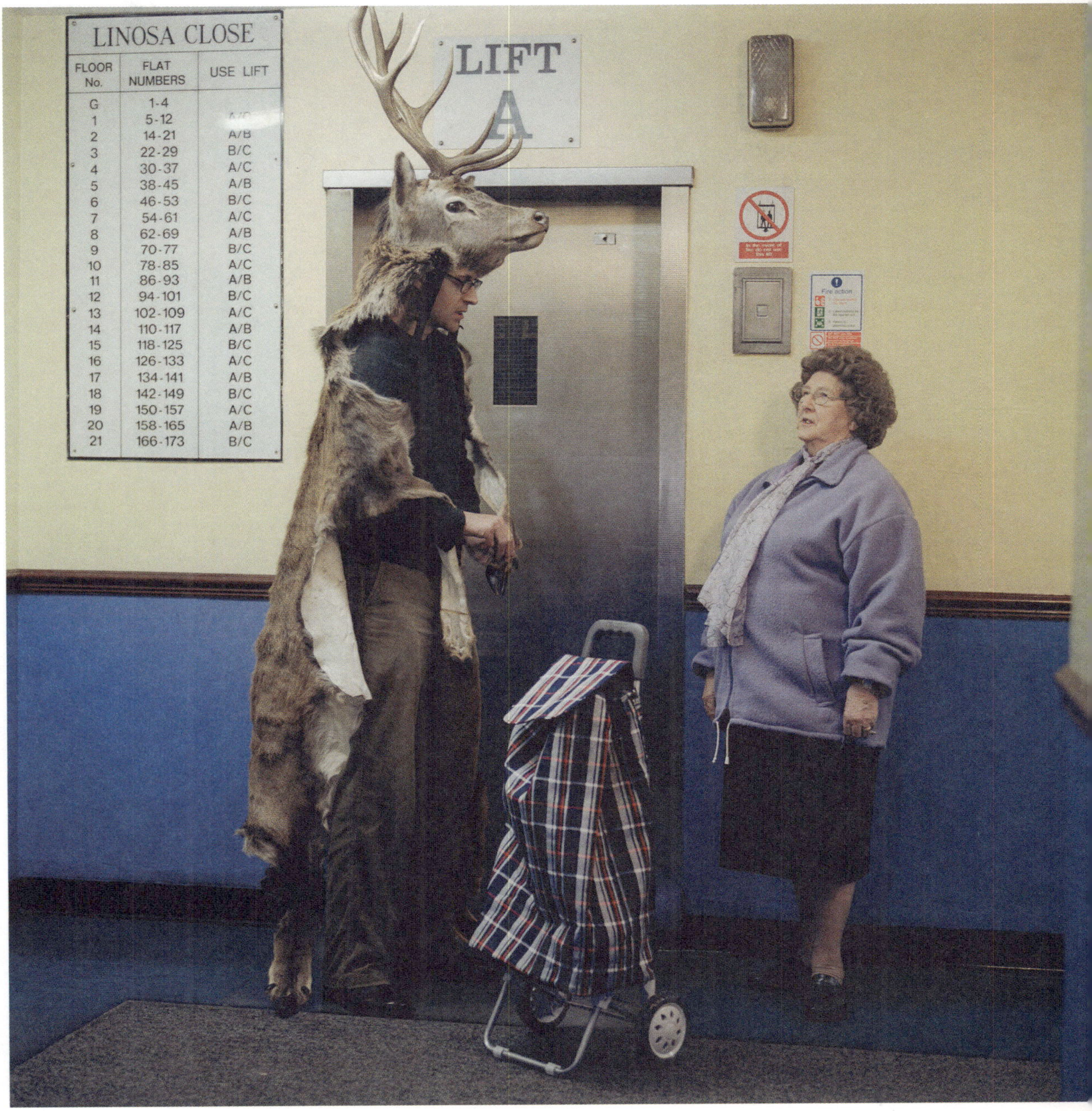

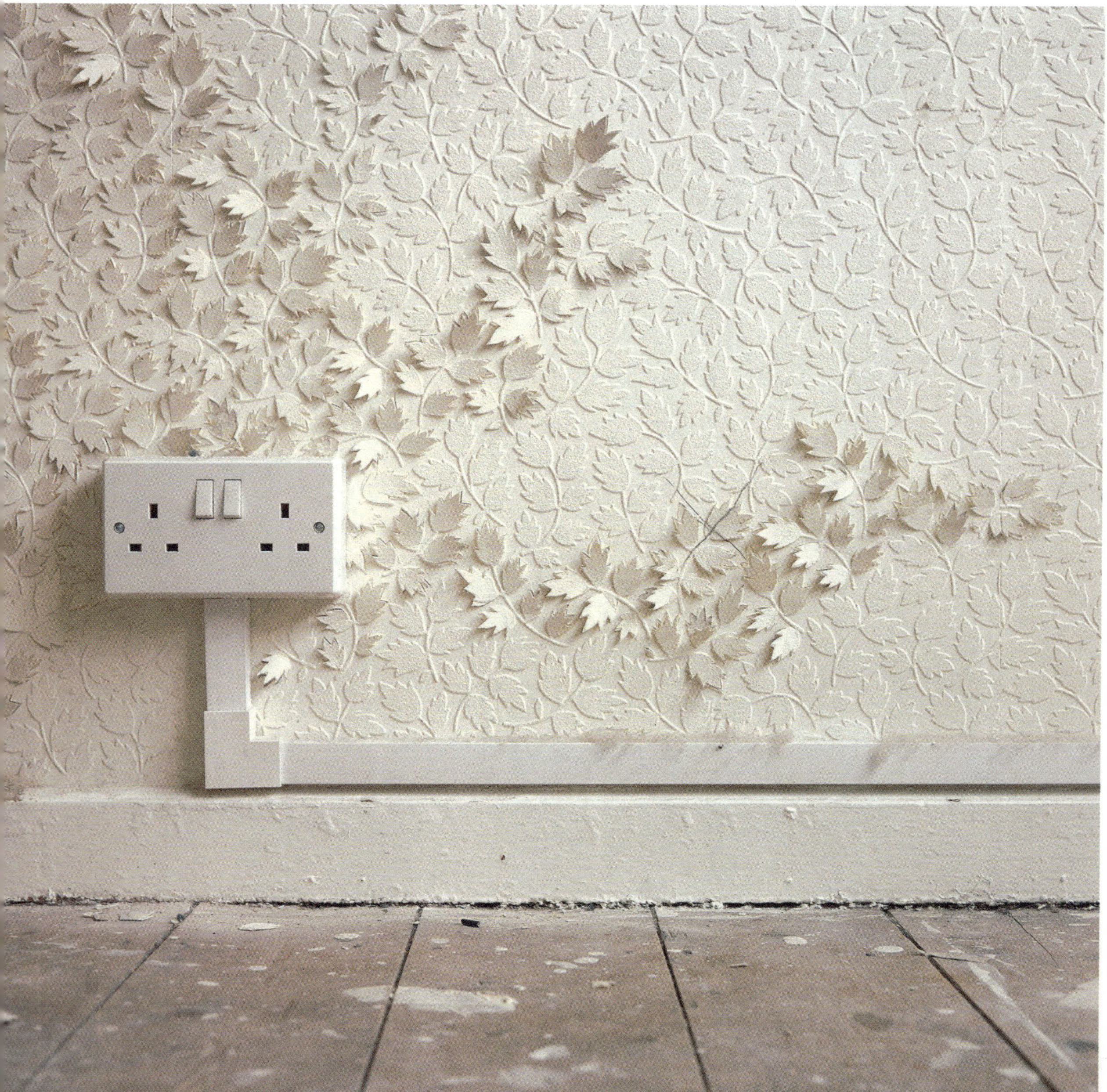

Will Self

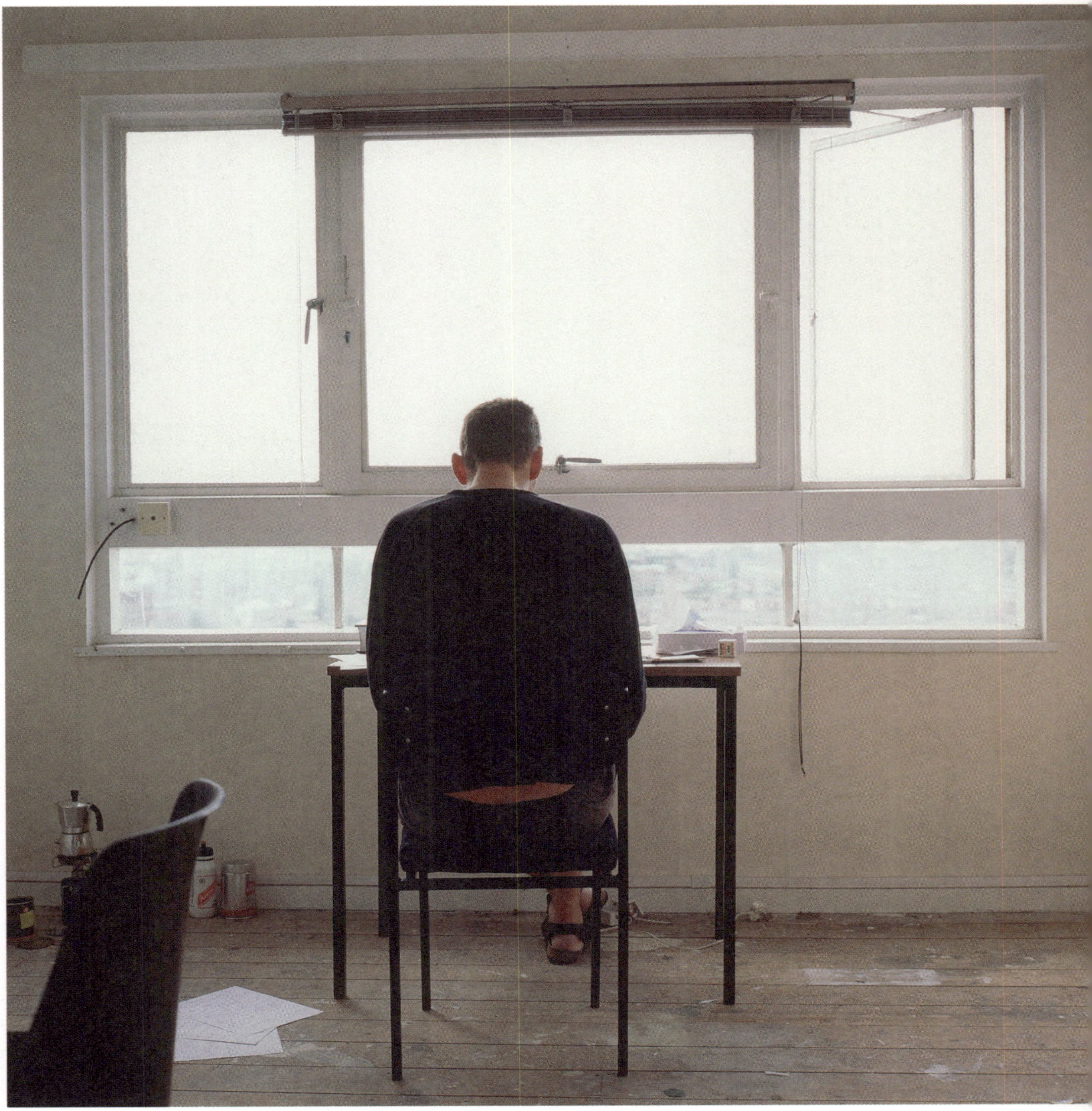

Thomas Hirschhorn
Bataille Monument

Thomas Hirschhorn is best known for constructions of foil, plastic, cardboard and packing tape that appear both in art institutions and in public places. They gather together references to philosophy and popular culture, economics and poetry, artists and fashion designers, in a bombardment of information and imagery. His *Bataille Monument,* 2002, was one of the most-discussed contributions to *Documenta 11* in Kassel. Here Hirschhorn offers a critical examination of the development and presentation of the project in the context of the exhibition event, the housing complex where it took place and his broader practice. This text is translated from German.

Preparation From my experience with projects in public spaces–so far I've worked on 44 projects–I know that the preparation phase is extremely important. For the *Bataille Monument* project, two aspects had to be prepared at the same time. On the one hand, there was the preparation on the ground in Kassel, which encompassed the selection of a site for the project, looking for potential partners, on-site organisation, and generally, getting to know the city of Kassel. On the other hand, there was the preparation in Paris, including substantive research on Georges Bataille.

Together with *Documenta 11* Artistic Director, Okwui Enwezor, I set the basic features of the project early on: it would be a project in a public space, a monument as part of the 'monuments' series. Before even visiting Kassel in November 2000, I had already decided that I wanted to make the *Bataille Monument*. I had realised the *Spinoza Monument* in Amsterdam in 1999 and the *Deleuze Monument* in Avignon in 2000. And in the future, I want to make the fourth and last monument in the series for Antonio Gramsci. The *Bataille Monument* was the third in the series and is dedicated to the French writer Georges Bataille (1897-1962).

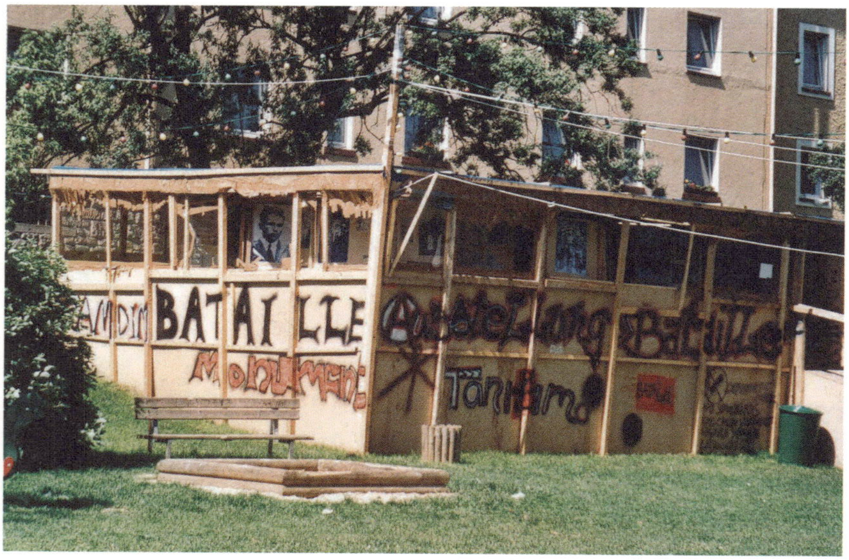

The most important aspect of selecting a location in Kassel was the potential helpers: the residents. Getting to know Lothar Kannenberg, the independent initiator of the Philippinenhof Boxing Camp, was of prime importance. After meeting and talking with him and the young people who box with him, I was certain that the boxing camp and the charismatic and exemplary position of Kannenberg had to be an important consideration in the choice of a site for the project. It was up to me to convince him and the youngsters of the seriousness of my project.

Thomas Hirschhorn
Bataille Monument (Exhibition)
Documenta 11, Kassel, 2002

The preparations in Paris, and in France included working with Christophe Fiat, a poet who explained the work of Georges Bataille to me. I encouraged him to map out Bataille's work visually. Together with Christophe I made four trips to 'stations' in Georges Bataille's life: St. Germain en Laye; Vezelay, Lacoste; the castle of the Marquis de Sade and the caves at Lascaux. I am a fan of Georges Bataille, especially his book *La part maudite* and his text "La notion de dépense": he is at once a role model and pretext for this project. Bataille explored and developed the principles of loss, of overexertion, of the gift, and of excess. Choosing Bataille meant opening up a broad and complex field between economy, politics, literature, art, erotica, and archaeology. Bataille had nothing to do with Kassel: the *Bataille Monument* is not a contextual work; rather, the monument could as easily be shown in another neighbourhood, in another city, in another country, or on another continent.

The *Bataille Monument* demanded friendship and sociability and was intended to impart knowledge and information, to make links and create connections. It was to be divided into eight elements: a shuttle service, a library, an exhibition, a snack bar, a TV studio, workshops, four web cams and a sculpture. I was looking for a site where construction and maintenance could be achieved, where friction and engagement might be possible. I was looking for a site that is itself a piece of reality. I wanted to make it where people were living, in a housing complex. I wanted to work with the residents; especially considering what I had learnt on the construction of the other two monuments. I wanted to supervise and follow the project myself for the duration of the exhibition and I also wanted to be there when it was dismantled.

All in all I made ten trips to Kassel in the period from November 2000 to April 2002. I knew I wanted to devote as much personal energy as possible to this project; travelling there without assistants from my studio. Although I spent all in all more than two months in Kassel, I didn't really know the city, so I needed every piece of information possible from residents, acquaintances, city authorities, and of course by visiting and discussing with people resident in the chosen location. Finally I decided to setup the monument in a mixed Turkish-German housing complex, the Friedrich-Wöhler-Siedlung.

Construction It took two months to set up the *Bataille Monument*. There were between 20 and 30 young people and other residents from the housing complex working on it. My project required no experts, no technicians, art students nor other art connoisseurs to help build it. Instead, I wanted to build it with residents of the Friedrich-Wöhler-Siedlung. There certainly wasn't a problem finding young people and other residents wanting to work on the project. One of the incentives was the eight euros that was paid as an hourly wage. For me, it was vital that everyone would be paid for their work on the project. I hate volunteerism for the sake of art. I refuse to appeal to volunteers, that is, unpaid workers, in order to implement my work of art.

Constructing the *Bataille Monument* was the hardest project I have ever created. I went beyond my limits; I was worn out. The construction was greatly taxing, in terms of technical efforts, organisation, group dynamics. The group that came together was very diverse, with respect to age, cultural and social background and attitude toward work. But I did not want to exclude anyone. I said, "If you live here, you can work on the project!"

When, despite all the hold-ups, we made it through the first week of construction, I went home (I had moved into an apartment in the housing-complex) to discover that my apartment had been broken into and my personal hi-fi, laptop, camera and video equipment had been stolen. I knew that it had to be one of the group and I knew that the continuation of the project was thus uncertain. I started to have serious doubts, and knew that I would have to find a solution since this was a test of my project's contact with reality. In other words, was my project too out of touch with reality? I also had to take responsibility for what happened. Either this was a test that my project would pass, or it would be the end of it. I could pass the test only if I got back all of the stolen property without having to look for the thief or thieves and without calling in the police. The project did pass this test–all stolen material was given back. From this point on I knew that whilst my project was perhaps difficult and complex, it was not out of touch with reality. I thought if art is not capable of resisting this normative pressure of exclusion, then nothing and no one will be able to!

But one thing that occurred during the project is what I call the 'satellite formation'. This is a negative experience which has happened to me more than once, where I isolate myself from the group exhibition project. On the one hand there were practical reasons for this satellite formation: the geographical distance between my project and the main venues of *Documenta 11*, the increasing stress as opening date approached, and the growing, clear-cut hierarchies that were forming, which had a negative effect on the technical help since our project was further way.

Opening The opening of the *Bataille Monument*, like the rest of the *Documenta 11*, took place over the course of three days. I decided that we would also celebrate it in the housing complex for those three days, with free drinks and food at the snack bar. I wanted to thank the residents of the Friedrich-Wöhler housing complex, who accepted the project in spite of the noise and encroachment on their space. Most importantly, the opening celebration in the complex served to create the project's first mixed audience. On these three days the invitation to the locals resulted in the mix of residents and *Documenta 11* opening visitors, as opposed to the regular visitors to *Documenta* during its ten-week duration.

Although it took a lot of time to visit the *Bataille Monument* and the programme schedule was very full, I noticed the seriousness and genuine curiosity of many visitors during this opening period. On the opening day, I realised that earlier–during planning, preparations, and set-up–I had never thought the *Bataille Monument* could be discussed and criticised as a social art project. However, I do think social issues can be raised through an art project. It is a question of the surroundings, the environment, the reality. That is a goal of my work. I am not afraid of false interpretations, misunderstandings, or over-interpretations. But one thing has always been clear for me: I am an artist and not a social worker. My project is an art project that aims to assert its autonomy as an art project. This was the starting point and cornerstone of all discussions I had with people working on the project as well as the visitors. Precisely because the *Bataille Monument* is an art project, it was not possible to exclude anyone from working on it. My guideline was: as the artist, I am not asking, can I help you? What can I do for you? Instead, as the artist, I am asking, can you and do you want to help me complete my project?

Shuttle Service I wanted the shuttle service to and from the main *Documenta* site to be an element of the *Bataille Monument*. The shuttle service was to create an actual link to go from the housing complex to the Binding Brewery and vice versa. I posted a quotation by artist David Hammons on the free standing panels set up at the two shuttle stops, one in the Friedrich-Wöhler housing complex and one in front of the entrance to the Binding Brewery. The quote was:

> The art audience is the worst audience in the world. It's overly educated, its conservative, it's out to criticise, not to understand and it never has any fun. Why should I spend my time playing to that audience? That's like going into a lion's den. So I refuse to deal with that audience, and I'll play with street audience. That audience is much more human and their

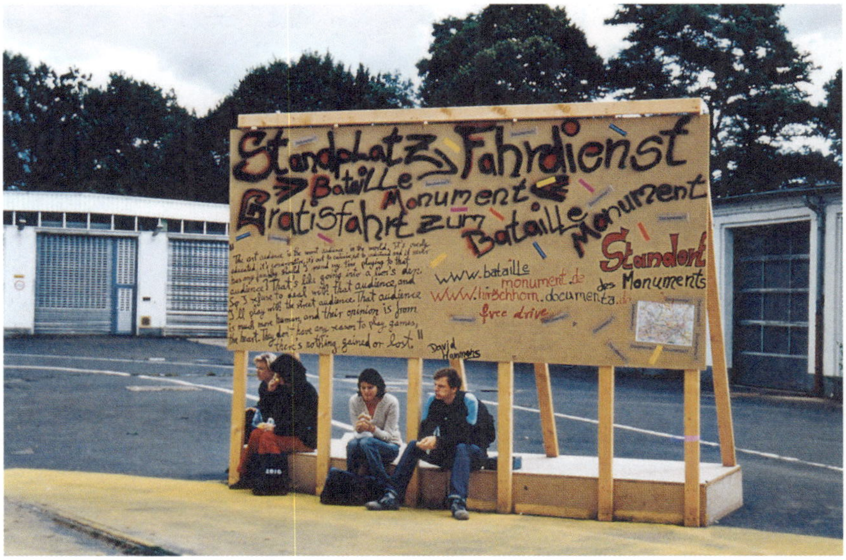

Thomas Hirschhorn
Bataille Monument (Shuttle Service), Documenta 11,
Kassel, 2002

> opinion is from the heart. They don't have any reason to play games; there's nothing gained or lost.

This quote is both problematic and contradictory, but it strikes at the core of the complexity of work in public space and the audience for publicly sited works. David Hammons is part of the art world and his work is part of the art market. Nonetheless, these sentences also assert defiantly the autonomy of a work of art. I wanted to propose it as an appeal for reflection and as a physical link between the two stops of the shuttle service. What I see in this quote in terms of the *Bataille Monument* project is that it also has nothing to win or lose. Work in public space is never a total success and never a total failure. Instead, it is about an experience, about exposing oneself, about enduring and creating an experience.

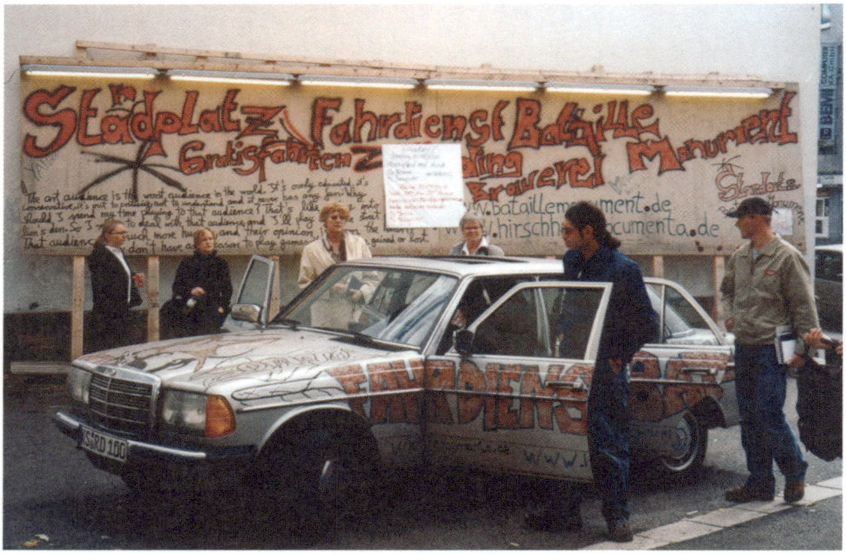

Thomas Hirschhorn
Bataille Monument (Shuttle Service), Documenta 11,
Kassel, 2002

The shuttle service was intended as a space of exchange and a means of regulating the flow of visitors. I did not want visitors to come to the *Bataille Monument* by buses or tourist vans. There were no *Documenta* guides at the *Bataille Monument.* I wanted the visitors to come by themselves. A maximum of four people fitted in our two Mercedes, which I thought would facilitate conversations and would protect the housing complex from large groups. Groups of art tourists could not of course be totally avoided, but at least it was left up to the initiative of the respective groups and nothing was done to encourage them. Five drivers (from the housing complex and the Philippinenhof Boxing Camp) were trained and the shuttle service became one element of the monument through the transportation of visitors and engaging with them during the drive. The drivers themselves contributed a great deal, making the journey to the *Bataille Monument* an event in itself!

Library The Georges Bataille Library was intended to facilitate connections with the work of Georges Bataille. For this reason there were no books in the library by or about Georges Bataille. Instead, there were books on five subjects: word, image, art, sports and sex. These thematics were supposed to expand and develop the work of Bataille. Uwe Fleckner, an art historian who proposed these categories and selected most of the books and cassettes, put together the list of books in an extremely precise but subjective manner. I am pleased that he insisted that no compromises were made on his selection. Photocopies of the list were available to visitors, so that the book list was not just a formality, but also a programme that could make sense even when separate from the library.

The 'library' space with chairs, sofas, and armchairs was a reading room and a meeting place for the young people from the housing complex. In some cases the library led to residents of the complex borrowing books. For instance, I recall Elfriede, who borrowed and read all the books by Marquis de Sade, not having previously known this author. The greatest demand was for the porno videos. What impressed me regarding the pornographic videos was that no one said anything moralising about them to me. Aside from the initial discussions about people under 18 watching them, the subject of 'sex' in the library seemed to regulate itself, insofar as within a few days all that was left in the library of the pornographic videos were the empty cases.

Exhibition The aim of the Bataille exhibition was to convey information about the life and work of Georges Bataille. Four parts of the exhibition were devoted to this goal. The centre of the room housed two superimposed maps: the diagram of Georges Bataille's work and the relief map of the city of Kassel. The books of Georges Bataille were placed on the map to represent the buildings; that is, the works were the structures. With four integrated videos and the videos on the 'Papuans', I wanted to depict the movement, the dynamic forces in the life of Georges Bataille, as well as what is considered his topical relevance. Ultimately these videos worked well throughout the exhibition. The third part of the exhibition was the freestanding panels. The materials on them were supposed to shed light on essential points in the work of Bataille. On reflection there was too much information here that was only in French. I paid too little attention during the planning phase in Paris to these written materials. Criticism expressed in this regard was totally justified.

The fourth and most important part of the exhibition space were the books by and about Georges Bataille. I tried to have all books in German, English, French, and Turkish available to look through. The exhibition room was too small, so the books were not easily accessible, with no real seating available which made it an uncomfortable environment in which to read. The books were there but their presentation was hardly more than symbolic. I also think the role played by the respective workers at the exhibition was not sufficiently active. They were the only ones involved in the *Bataille Monument* who had only a passive role. It was not possible for them to become actively involved; just like in a museum, they only paid attention to what was going on around them. One thing I liked about the exhibition as well as the other sections (library, TV studio and snack bar) was the writing, graffiti, and drawings that began to cover more and more of the empty spaces on the panels over the course of the exhibition. That form of appropriation is beautiful in the way it gets increasingly dense and takes over. This was not planned or intended. Some of these added statements could then be discussed, but they were also a formal enrichment. At the same time it brought greater complexity to the content of the work.

Snack bar I had gained considerable experience from my previous monument projects. For example, in discussion with residents in Avignon about the *Deleuze Monument*, the suggestion was made to have a beverage stand or a place to sit with refreshments outside the monument.

In planning the *Bataille Monument* I thought from the beginning of having a snack bar–not outside the monument, but as an element integrated into it. The idea of the snack bar was not primarily about offering food and drinks, but about offering visitors an opportunity to meet, converse and spend time together. At the same time the snack bar was a further anchor for the housing complex and the residents. The snack bar was a door, a way into the monument, as well as simultaneously being part of the monument.

I assumed that whoever only drank a beer or ate a kebab at the snack bar would also use the monument. For me it was clear that the snack bar would be run by residents of the housing complex. At first it was difficult to find someone to run it because those who expressed interest were afraid of the financial risk. There would be no rental fee for the stand and no water or electricity bills. The

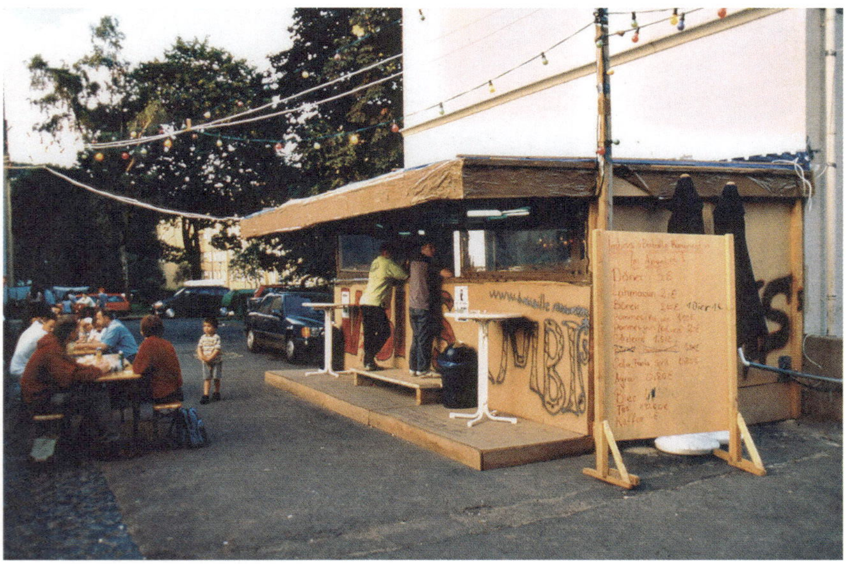

Thomas Hirschhorn
Bataille Monument (Snack Bar)
Documenta 11, Kassel, 2002

operators could keep all the money taken in by the snack bar. But they had to organise all the food and beverages and, most importantly, the snack bar had to be open twelve hours a day, every day of the week, just like the other elements of the monument. This scared potential operators. But in the end a solution was found, as was often the case in the complex, by having a discussion with the residents. The Kaban family decided to run the snack bar. The commitment and realism of this family played a major role in creating a snack bar as a meeting place and a place to converse. The friendliness and availability of the Kabans (mother, father, sons, grandmother, uncle, and aunt) often stood out. They operated the snack bar independently with Turkish and German refreshments. I was happy that they took this task so seriously. Every evening they cleaned up until 11pm and prepared for the next day, when they reopened at 10am. The last guests to leave were usually from the housing complex. I have to say that I had not considered any additional shared systems of distributing risk and profits. But through this experience it has to be seriously considered as a future option, as that would have increased participation by housing complex residents.

TV studio The aim of the TV studio was to create reports, approximately ten minutes in length, from the Friedrich-Wöhler housing complex and to broadcast them in the Open Channel–a public TV channel from the city of Kassel.

These TV reports would be produced and edited by the young people and other residents and workers on the ground, and then transmitted to the open channel. The programmes had to have something to do with Georges Bataille, and to report on the housing complex, its residents, a worker or a visitor to the *Bataille Monument*. We did not do any reports in the city centre. All programmes were to be local, from the housing complex and about the complex and events happening here directly. I was very happy to see the accumulation of video cassettes and we were able to broadcast a new cassette every production day over 72 days (excluding Saturdays and Sundays). There were some very dense reports, such as those in which the young people took advantage to talk about themselves, their problems, their critics, their views; and those of readings by Christophe Fiat, Jean-Charles Masséra, Manuel Joseph, the poets; Uwe Fleckner, the art historian; and Marcus Steinweg, the philosopher.

But not all of the reports had the same intensity, necessity, and urgency as too many were not discussed and assessed sufficiently in advance. Too often we chose the easiest and fastest solution in order to expend the least amount of effort. I often lacked sufficient energy to tackle the more difficult subjects. Sometimes I was content with the absolute minimum, that is, the daily production of a cassette.

Over time the TV studio became an active meeting place owing to its central geographic location in the housing complex, the proximity to the residents, and the *Bataille Monument* workers. I recall the evenings with Reinhold, Gudrum and friends sitting in front of the TV studio. These situations made the TV studio into a pillar of the *Bataille Monument*, open to both visitors and residents alike, though the *Documenta 11* visitors sat inside, in the TV studio, and the residents sat outside, in front of the studio.

The Workshops The motivation for the workshops was that I wanted the *Bataille Monument* to be lasting, that is, I wanted small events to be held during the exhibition in the Friedrich-Wöhler housing complex that would have a legacy. Something was created, produced–here and now–that had some relationship to Georges Bataille.

The two debates by Jean-Charles Massera, who worked with the young people to perform texts he had written, led to intense discussion. Jean-Charles' understanding, humour, and ambition created a basis for group work that was important for the continued cohesion and for the seriousness of our project. The ten forged letters "Sculpture as a Bullfight" by Manuel Joseph and his goal of bringing them to the citizens of Kassel by distributing them throughout the city was concrete. Thanks to the *HNA* daily newspaper, almost 100,000 copies of these letters were placed in mailboxes of Kassel households.

My opinion of the workshops was divided. The workshops I organised ahead of time–the workshops of Jean-Charles Massera, Manuel Joseph, and Marcus Steinweg–were truly enriching, evidence of the claim that the *Bataille Monument* could produce something significant. On the other hand, I imagined there would be many more workshops, run by the housing complex: a boxing event, small concerts with the residents, a capoeira-dance event, a conversation with the person working for the city of Kassel in charge of Joseph Beuys' *7000 Oaks* project. None of these workshops took place. I was too busy with all the daily tasks of supervising and maintaining the *Bataille Monument* that there was no energy left over to organise and carry out more workshops. I underestimated that without preparation or organisational assistance there were limits to my energy. The only workshop that took place that was not planned in advance was the *Alternative-Anarchist-Construction-Trailer* that docked onto the *Bataille Monument* for a week. I was surprised at the tolerance shown by the majority of residents with respect to this protest action.

The workshop by Marcus Steinweg, with his idea of text output, and his understanding of the *Bataille Monument* as a machine, as a 'Bataille Machine' was good. It was a pleasure to see the exhibition panel on *The Ontological Cinema* in the library continue to expand, and to realise that a lot of people took two copies of Marcus' texts away with them. This satisfied Marcus' goal. Philosophy confronts reality, immediately and directly. Philosophy acts. Philosophy is necessary. The numerous, multiple day visits that Marcus took to the housing complex and his confrontation with my work and with art, in its

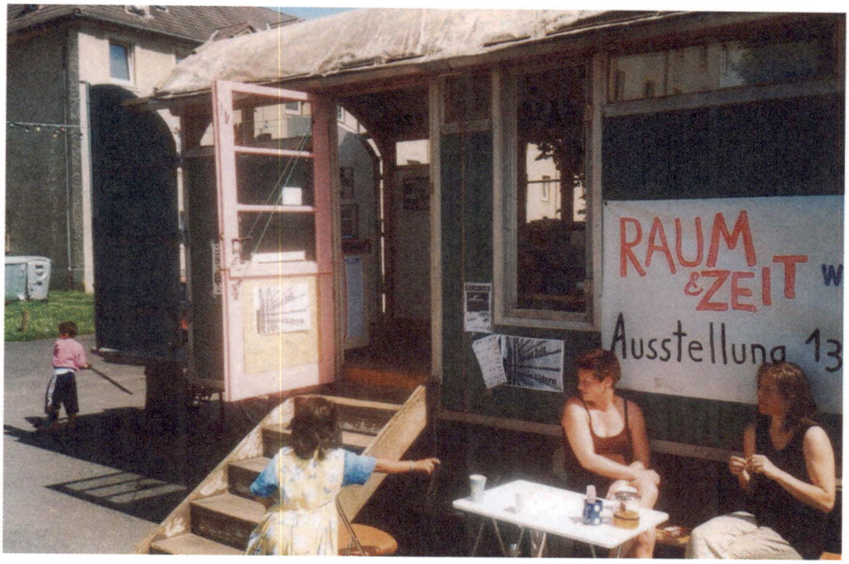

intensity, the severity of the questioning, and also in his life-affirming joy were stimulating moments.

Web cams I was not pleased with this element: the web cams were intended to create a link to the world, to non-visitors. Aside from any criticism as regards particular content or interest, what I really like about the internet in all its unspeakable poorness are the web cameras and the illusion of connectedness, of communication, of creating a feeling of simultaneity with another location. I like this idea, this unreflected and simplistic idea of letting someone participate. That is what I wanted to achieve with the web cameras and the website www.bataillemonument.de. It became impossible for me to work out this format. I wanted the absolute basics–just a web cam, pure simultaneous communication or non-communication. I wanted that to be possible without any text or framing so that people would be able to look quickly at *Bataille Monument* at the same time from Africa, Asia, or wherever. This was not possible because the websites were designed uniformly by graphic designers, including a biography, project description, a couple of photos, etc.. The website became an illustration. Even worse, it became 'information' instead of 'impossible communication' through a web camera.

I think this was also the reason why I received the least amount of feedback or critique regarding this element of the project. The web cams were supposed to be an element of the *Bataille Monument*, but they became information about it.

Thomas Hirschhorn
Bataille Monument (Workshop)
Documenta 11, Kassel, 2002

Sculpture The 'sculpture' element in the *Bataille Monument* was intended to isolate the object, the exterior, that which is generally referred to as 'a monument'. The sculpture was supposed to be only the sculpture of the monument and not the monument itself. This was often not properly

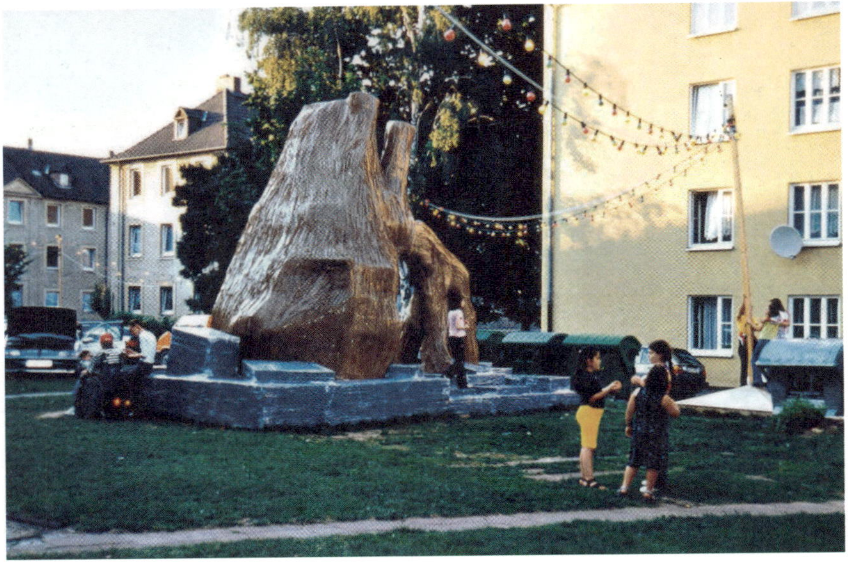

understood, or rather, it was understood in a very superficial and cursory manner. Yet it was precisely the questions that emerged from the misunderstanding that led to discussion about the sculpture.

Once it was isolated from the monument, the sculpture took on the function of a meeting place, a playground or rather a romping ground as well as a place to sit, used mostly during the evening hours. Many viewers raised questions as to what statement it was making, what it intended to represent. There was no way to avoid this, even though its form developed superficially. Once it was decided that the main goal was to create a sculpture that posed the question of the monument, it no longer mattered what the sculpture looked like. I did not want to copy the human figure or the head as was done for the Spinoza and Deluze monuments. The sculpture of wood, plastic and cardboard, covered with packing tape survived in good condition for the duration of the exhibition only thanks to the repair team that retaped and retouched the places where it was torn or scraped each and every day. This repair service was necessary, because without the daily repairs, replacing and reinforcing parts of the sculpture including other elements of the monument, this project would not have lasted through the entire exhibition period.

Confrontation There was a considerable degree of discussion about the *Bataille Monument*. I was surprised since we calculated that only about 5% of the *Documenta 11* visitors came to the Friedrich-Wöhler housing complex. I think there was so much discussion since this project was complex, problematic and beautiful. This carried over to the temporary visitors, and questions evolved in a way I had never experienced before. I think the fact that the *Bataille Monument* was set up as an experience in public space throughout the duration of *Documenta 11*, led to this situation. Also, I do think it was very

Thomas Hirschhorn
Bataille Monument (Sculpture)
Documenta 11, Kassel, 2002

important to be on the ground in the housing complex for the whole time. I wanted to offer a sign that I care about my work and I wouldn't leave the complex alone with my work. On the other hand it was necessary to solve the everyday problems that arose–technical, organisational, and personal. I appreciated this confrontation with the everyday reality of such a project. I was virtually ever-present because I wanted everything to work all the time. An important confrontation through and with my work was what I call the 'zoo' discussion. The 'zoo' criticism is something that has arisen in relation to other projects that I have made in public spaces. The criticism assumes that either the visitors to the housing complex find themselves in a zoo or feel like visitors to a zoo. Obviously the question of who feels as if they are in the zoo was not clearly and definitively answered. Who is on display? Who is the tourist? I reject this 'zoo' criticism, because it is only a question of over-sensitivity and bad conscience. It is a matter for the individual, and the over-sensitivity of a certain kind of art audience.

The Friedrich-Wöhler-Siedlung Visitors often asked me how the project was received by the residents of the housing complex. I am certainly the last person who could answer that question! It seems obvious that an answer would involve a value judgment. That would mean that if the project was received well it was a success and if not, then it was a failure. The *Bataille Monument* project was not a matter of acceptance or rejection and it was not about 'functionability'. It was an assertion. This assertion first had to be endured before it is possible for any conclusions to be drawn. The *Bataille Monument* was built as an experience; but the experience has to be made.

I was confronted with people who live at the outskirts of a mid-sized German city. In many discussions I experienced the incredible strength of questioning through art. In the Friedrich-Wöhler-Siedlung I perceived the importance of art, philosophy, and poetry; even its necessity as something existential and fundamental. With respect to the *Bataille Monument*, I noticed that the tolerance, acceptance, confrontation, and exchange grew with each day of the exhibition. One conviction for me grew stronger in everyday practice in the housing complex; the conviction that art can fight for and assert a space. It is the conviction that art can create a mental space, that it can penetrate the brain. I was encouraged by this.

I paid the workers for their assistance, but nevertheless the whole money issue remains unresolved for me with respect to this project. Of course, for all workers it was first and foremost a way to earn money. There is nothing wrong with that; that is reality. But the problem and unresolved issue is that as soon as payment is involved, inevitably the working hours and achievement of the co-workers are observed. A 'working relationship' develops. The paid labour has the disadvantage that the question of giving (how much effort, how much work will I invest?) is weighed against the question of taking (how much do

I earn; how much profit will I have?). This led to many unproductive, non-beautiful situations. I was overwhelmed each Monday when new groups were formed and work was divided-up and I had to accept these egotistical comparisons among the participants.

Media response The *Bataille Monument* received what I considered a surprising amount of attention from the media. I have no complaints about that–we needed it; but I was also surprised at the superficial level of the reporting. The *Bataille Monument* with all the questions it raised was hardly reflected in its problematic complexity. I noticed in the reporting and through some discussions with journalists how great the time pressure and sales pressure was with respect to 'reader-friendly' writing and topic selection. This is why I also realise that the great media response had nothing to do with the artistic value of the project. I was well aware that this was a matter of quantity, of media presence, and not refined analysis. Right at the beginning of the project I decided to accept all requests for interviews and all possible meetings with journalists. Without exception I planned to answer all questions posed by the media and to provide information about the *Bataille Monument*. I did it deliberately for the project. I did this for the housing complex, the workers and all the helpers. I assumed that not every *Documenta* visitor could come to the *Bataille Monument* because of time constraints. Therefore I thought it would be important to take advantage of all possible channels of the media to talk about our project. I deliberately attempted to weigh the geographical disadvantage and balance it out through media presence. In any case this media presence was assessed positively in the housing complex and I cannot imagine how the *Bataille Monument* would have lasted in the Friedrich-Wöhler housing complex if there was no media coverage, no radio or TV reports, and no articles on it, and if fewer visitors had come.

Taking down I wanted to be present when the project was taken apart, I did not want to leave the residents of the housing complex with the job of dismantling the project. What I did not foresee, however, was that it would only take three days to take down or rather be torn down.

I understood the actual process of dismantling or tearing down the project as a ritual. In no time at all, virtually all usable materials–the Plexiglas panes, wooden posts, boards, strings of light, chairs, lamps–everything that was at all reusable was torn down and put in small storage piles at all the building's entrances. Everything was then taken inside by the residents and put in the basement or elsewhere. It all went so fast that I had the impression it was all prepared in advance or was a ritual in which taking away and transferring the materials marked the appropriation (or reclamation) of something. Of course it could also be assumed that many of the families living in the Friedrich-Wöhler housing complex were forced by their economic situation to reuse materials and not to let things go to waste. Nevertheless I remember those final days as moments

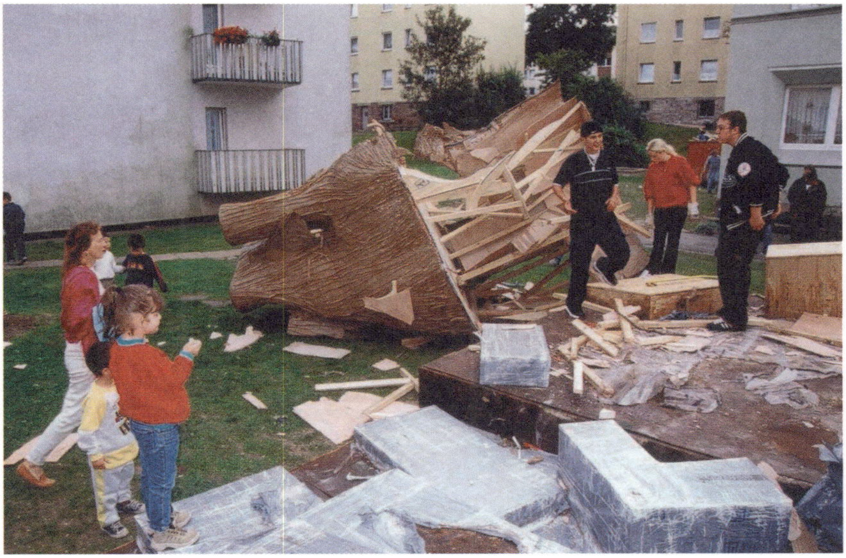

of frenetic reclamation according to unspoken rules. Was reclaiming materials thus reclaiming the space used including the housing complex and their values? All of this happened without sadness or aggression. I wanted to leave the space as it was when I arrived, for the sake of the residents but also for the sake of the *Bataille Monument*, because I think that the memories of the residents, visitors and workers, as well as my memories of the joint experience we had, is an essential part of the project through the notion of 'monument' to the notion of 'memory'.

The only things that were kept and brought back to storage or put in the *Documenta* archives in Kassel were the books and the texts and videos that were produced during the course of the exhibition. All hi-fi and video equipment, tools and vehicles used by the shuttle service were raffled off in a tombola to the participants, so everyone could take something home with them. It was a method of distributing the materials without regard for the amount of work or time invested or the earnings of the individual workers, but instead as a matter of chance. This tombola was a transition back to the realities of daily life without nostalgia or sentimentality.

Thomas Hirschhorn
Bataille Monument
(Deinstallation)
Documenta 11,
Kassel, 2002

I am aware of the importance and strengths of the *Bataille Monument* and the fact that it set an example. But I am less sure whether, in order to carry through such a project, this requires a level of inconsistency from the artist focusing on the goal.

Adam Dant
Donald Parsnips
Daily Journal

Adam Dant first came to attention with *Donald Parsnips Daily Journal*, a quirky, knowing, comic-strip pamphlet which he distributed between 1995 and 1999. *Donald Parsnips* also appeared as a weekly column in *The Independent on Sunday*. Dant's characteristic drawings, plans, maps and narratives, provide a satirical response to art and life. Here the artist provides a brief introduction to the origins of Donald Parsnips and an insight into the project as process. This is an extract from Dant's lecture in Bristol, February 2004.

Donald Parsnips Daily Journal was a strategy to get my work out of the gallery and into a wider context. I produced an eight-page A5 pamphlet every day of the working week for five years. I had become aware that I was building up a backlog of work in the studio and just waiting for people to come and take it away–for them to act as mediators of this work. I'd been taught at the Royal College of Art that I wouldn't have any control over where my work went when it left the studio. Whereas a lot of my work was dealing with issues of communication and the place of the artist within the fabric of global communication networks (newspapers, the internet, information technology), an artist's work is very much dependent on the ego and the individual voice. So I combined those two things in this pamphlet to address the idea of the artist engaging with the issues involved in mediation. I was responsible for the mediation of my own artwork. It was a very simple strategy.

So this was my routine. I'd wake up every morning about 6.30am and however much time I had in the morning to write the journal conditioned how it appeared. Some times it was very scrappy, sometimes it was more considered. In the same way that an artist might enter their studio and approach a canvas that's been sitting there for a month, in a different fashion each day of the week. You could see the whole of *Donald Parsnips Daily Journal* as one canvas that took five years to complete. Having written that day's journal, I'd go to my local photocopy shop, make 100 copies, cut and fold it and walk from the East End of London (where I live and ran a gallery from 1995 to 2000, which is proximate to the City of London, the financial centre). I'd walk from there to a very old fashioned picture house gallery where I was working at the time and on the way I'd hand this 'newspaper' directly to strangers: the idea being that this was a form of mediation that didn't contain any mediation. It was direct and referenced the way that newspapers would have first been distributed. The birth of the press took place in the coffee houses of the City of London, which grew into the big insurance houses like Lloyds. News would come from the boats, from abroad, from the colonies, news of trade directly from one person to the other and it was all about direct communication, no mediation in between, there was nothing but a person who had news communicating it to someone else within a social environment. The proximity of the City of London for this project was very important to me in this sense.

I'd hand the 'newspaper' to strangers, so there was no strategy of identifying a particular audience as you might do in a gallery. It was completely random. I wanted it to echo the randomness of events in the City, the street life of London, much the same as anything else that might happen to you in the course of your day in London, this newspaper would be a part of that. It was unexpected and was supposed to touch individuals in an unexpected way. Eventually, because I was proposing the project as an approach to being a artist, I was invited to various museums to show the work. So ironically the work began to have two contexts, a museum and the street life of the City. I also made a series of woodcuts (the woodcut being the first form of graphic reproduction) to fund the whole project because of course the work didn't make any economic sense because all the journals were being given away.

The Donald Parsnips character could be seen as a way of de-centring my practice so that I was no longer the author of this piece, and his hat became a corporate identity in the same way that the Disney corporation have the three circles of Mickey Mouse's face and ears. The hat referred to the costumes of the people who would frequent the City's coffee houses in the early eighteenth

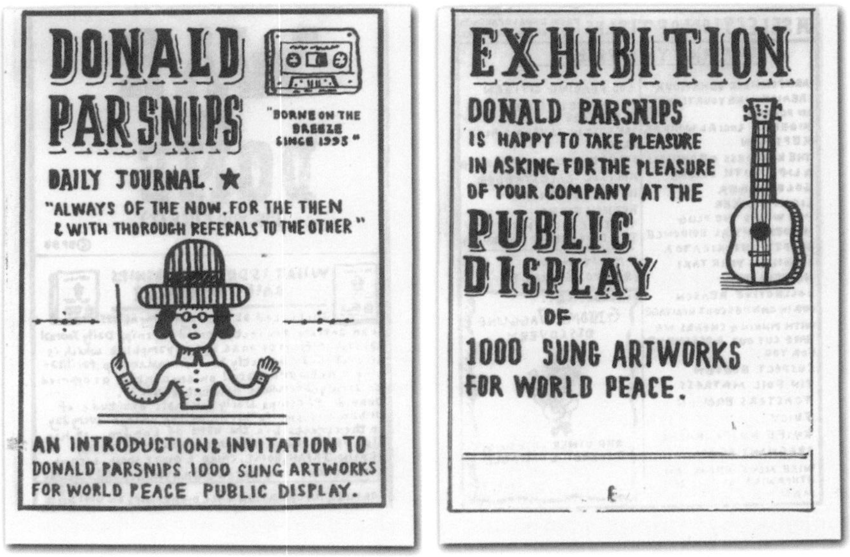

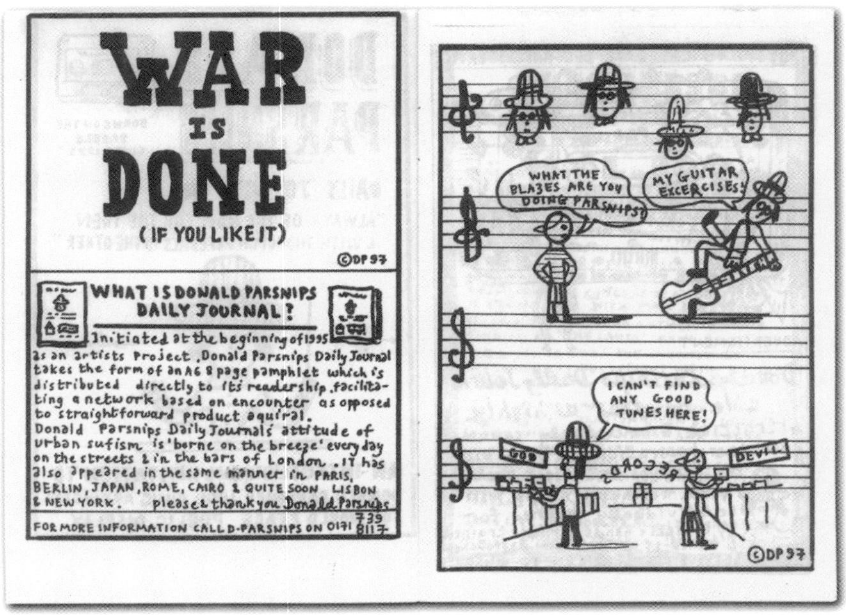

century. So I made a series of caricatures of Donald Parsnips with this Disney idea in mind and they became a very well honed and identifiable product–even when a series of monoprints turned this Parsnips character into a series of splodges, you knew it was him.

Parsnips was a very small figure, representing the idea of the artist as an individual trying to fill a very large void, the space of the every day in whichever city I happened to be in. The whole project was conceived as having a specific duration of five years, after which I contacted most of the newspapers in Britain asking them to mark the new millennium by printing a blank editiion of their paper, just with the banner headline of the newspaper, which none of them did of course because that was the day that they wanted to fill the newspaper with more news than ever. But I printed an image of Parsnips with an X across the figure, signalling an end and a breathing space, it was millennial and eschatological and utopian in that sense.

The Independent on Sunday's response to my proposal was to approach me to write a newspaper column for them, so Donald Parsnips became a fictional voice commenting on real events in the world of culture. He would review various exhibitions, dance and music events as a fictional correspondent, placing real events within a fictional context. For example, there was a Dan Graham exhibition at the Serpentine Gallery in London, but Parsnips chose to represent the gallery as the Nutwood Arts Centre in a leafy glade. The Dan Graham work was like the magical phenomena that appear in Rupert Bear stories. I don't think the Serpentine curators minded that I changed them into badgers and hedgehogs but then again my role as an artist was given a great deal of liberty by having this de-centred practice. I could say things without being responsible for saying them because it was done through the guise of fiction. That's how I came to lose my job at *The Independent on Sunday*, having compared the singer Madonna to a pig, presenting a prize called 'The Trotty Prize'. It was a comic strip called pig school about some little pigs who go to the Tate Gallery to see this Trotty Prize exhibition and are more interested in the celebrity who's presenting the prize than the prize itself. *The Independent on Sunday* was Madonna's newspaper of choice.

De-centred practice not only enabled me to have a role outside of my ego as an artist, but it also provided the readership and the viewer with a magical fictionalised realm which they could enter, where the familiar of their everyday life became formalised in a fictional realm. In that way it referred back to the works of Hogarth and Swift and the historical tradition of satire.

All images: Adam Dant, *Donald Parsnips Daily Journal, "Donald Parsnips Sings 1000 Songs for World Peace"* 1999. Collection Musée d'Art Contemporain, Lyon

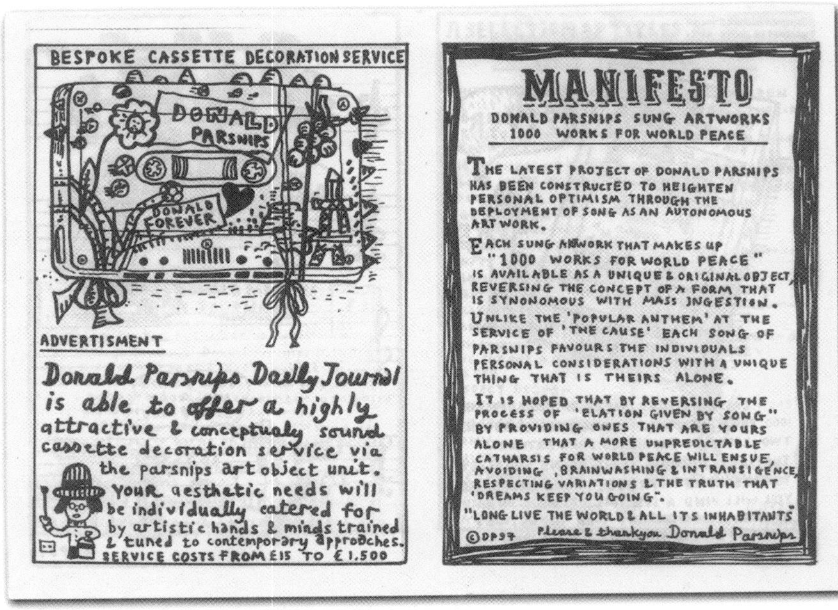

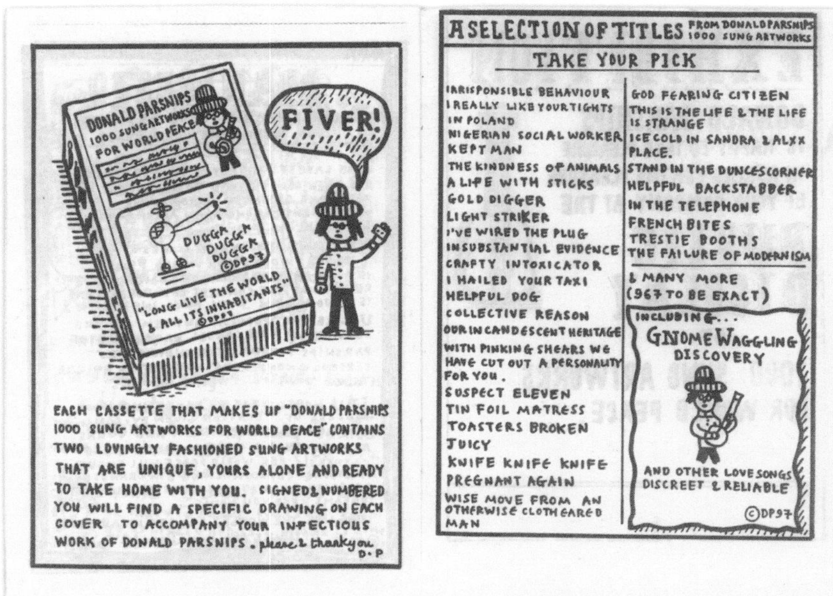

Cuauhtémoc Medina

Mejor Vida Corp.

Minerva Cuevas created Mejor Vida Corp. (Better Life Corporation): a multinational and non-profit company. The activities of MVC include the free distribution of public transport tickets, student identity cards, lottery tickets, or barcode stickers that reduce prices on supermarket food. Regarded as actions and interventions there is a concentrated subversion in Cuevas' work that aims to question the capitalist system. In the following text, Medina sets out the context in which MVC was initiated and the dilemmas it may face within a global art context. This is an edited extract of his text "Recent Political Forms: Radical Pursuits in Mexico" published in *TRANS>8 Magazine*, 2000, which also discussed the work of artists Francis Alÿs and Santiago Sierra.

Cuauhtémoc Medina

Mejor Vida Corp.

In 1998 the artist Minerva Cuevas launched an ingenious and complex ongoing economic fiction as a means of exploring the politics of contemporary hope: *Mejor Vida Corp.* (Better Life Corporation). According to Cuevas, the project started more or less spontaneously around 1997, and derived from her interest in defying the strictures of the art market by anonymously distributing small-scale art objects in public spaces.

Later on, in the winter of 1997 to 1998 while traveling in the New York City subway system, Cuevas saw a poster produced by the train administration bearing the slogan "Awake is Aware", warning the passengers against the dangers of falling sleep while travelling. To prevent passengers from having a 'rude awakening', Cuevas started leaving small bags with caffeine doses attached to the posters located in the cars, as if the subway administration were distributing them in the guise of 'safety pills'. The more or less classical intention of defying the status of art as a commodity was replaced with the more radical intention of playing with the goal of achieving public good by means of art practice. The project was refined by the invention of a corporative identity. The company would experiment with an unheard of modality of aesthetic and political intervention involving systematic acts of generosity purportedly fulfilling urgent demands from the public. According to the corporation's motto, MVC works "for a human interface".

Further mocking the structure of a private corporation, Cuevas rented an office on the fourteenth floor of the tallest skyscraper in Mexico City. From this local 1950s modernist icon, Cuevas designed a website that is part of the irational.org group, which also has contributors in England and Spain, and set out to establish a whole range of products and services to be given away for free on request and with no obligation to reciprocate. MVC's catalogue is a small compilation of contemporary dreams and antidotes to frustration.

Cuevas leaves random 'magic' seeds (very much in the tradition of Ben Vautier's unlabelled cans of 'mystery food') next to ATMs, suggesting to the customer an agrarian turn to make money. She has tested people's reaction to unexplained gifts by giving away subway tickets at rush hour in the Mexico City underground, saving travellers the long morning queues. On occasion she has discreetly volunteered to clean public buildings (including subway stations), to write letters for the illiterate, or to support small campaigns through disinterested voluntary work. Some of MVC's products reflect the fears of the population, for instance providing tear gas for personal protection. Other products are more related to wishful thinking in general: MVC does not distribute money as such, but can provide the customer with lottery tickets. Finally, there are those services which, despite seeming rather simple and cheap parasites of public or private services, entail quasi-criminal activity: MVC distributes pre-stamped envelopes, accepting full responsibility for their contents. Cuevas produces customised, *trompe l'oeil* bar code stickers (or

Mejor Vida Corp.
Risk Management,
Advertisement, 2003

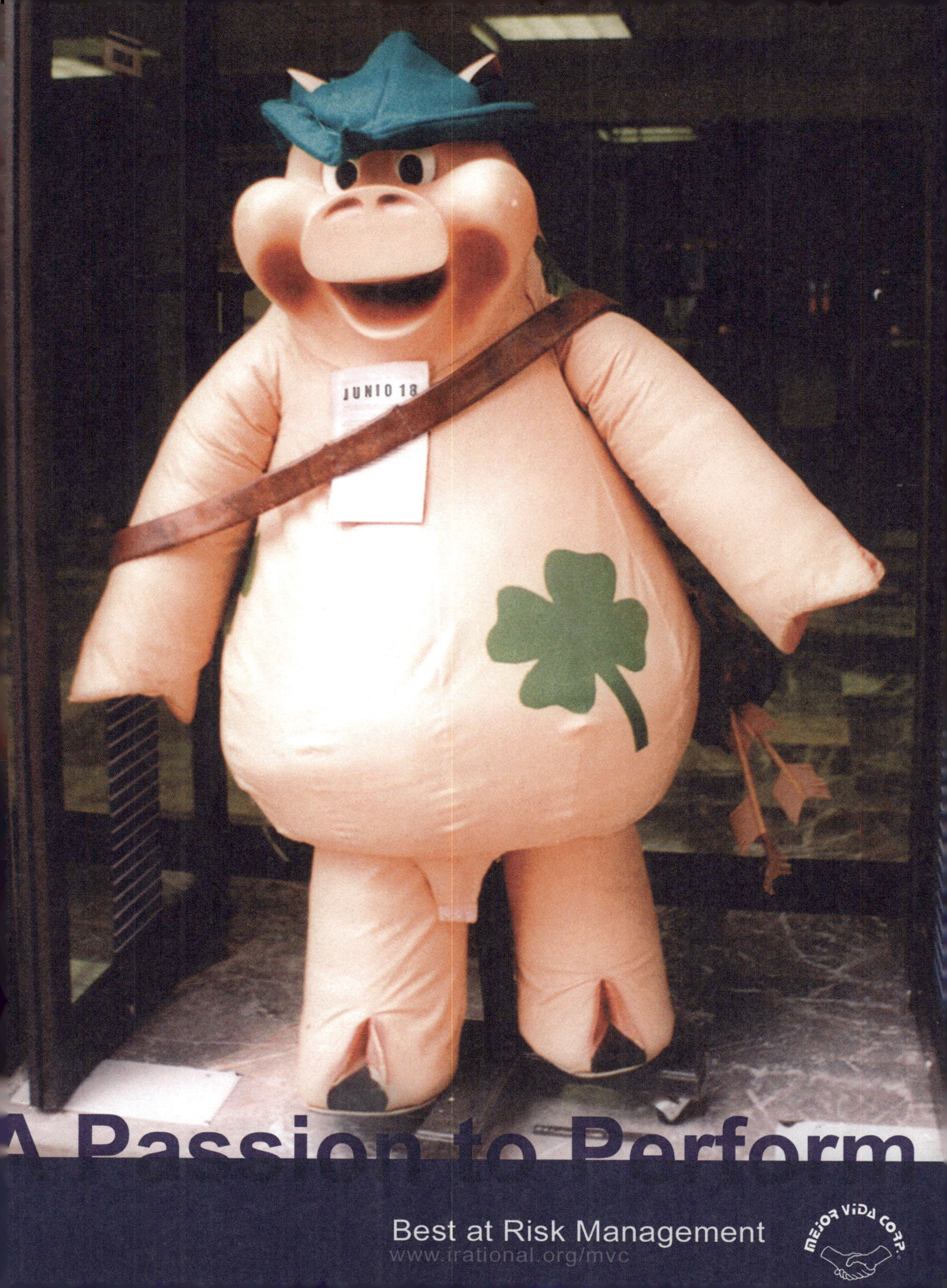
JUNIO 18
A Passion to Perform
Best at Risk Management
www.irational.org/mvc
MEJOR VIDA CORP.

"trompe l'scanner" as the artist says) to reduce prices of articles in the supermarket. So far the most successful and iconic of the MVC projects has involved the issuance of student ID cards that allow one to get the international student identity card and apply for discounts.

An experience like MVC might be analysed in several ways, from discussing its importance in terms of the gift economy and the anticapitalist hopes post-modernity attributed to symbolic exchange, to an analysis of the construction of corporative identity. This single woman charitable company somehow plays a double role: on the one hand, it provides a service based on goodwill, that momentarily brings aid or relief, or at least seems to provide it. But as any anthropologist would understand, this form of micro-potlach also implies an acquisition of prestige, power and rank that mocks a structure of clientelism. Mejor Vida Corp. evidently copies the contemporary structure of the transnational corporation, but radically inverts its economic rationale. The office, web page, distribution, packaging, and public relations of the corporation have so far been entirely performed by Cuevas alone. Part of the conceptual structure of the project is, in fact, to deal with the necessary bureaucratisation and productivity crisis of the corporation. Since MVC can't by definition grow, its success is at the same time its decadence. The more customers the company draws, the more likely it will be to end up leaving them unsatisfied and, eventually, even close down.

Working on the basis of one person's budget, donations from members of the public, or institutions that might want to endorse it, MVC's economies are always leading to built-in bankruptcy. Anti-capitalist in spirit, the corporation is

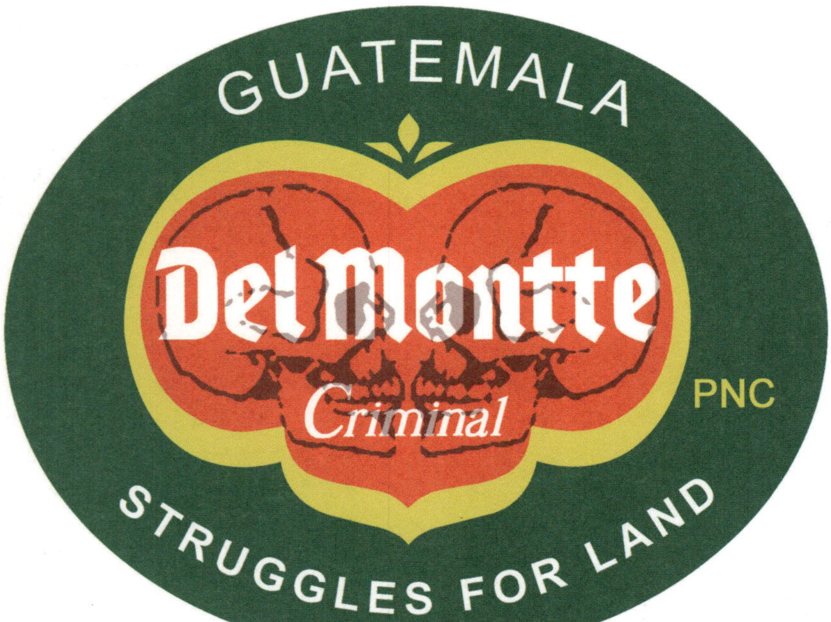

Mejor Vida Corp., *Del Montte* International Media Campaign 2002, fruit sticker

a test tube in which to examine the plausibility of non-capitalist interpersonal relationships. For the artist, a certain exchange is involved in the whole of MVC's operations: she spends money and time fulfilling people's needs, but her 'customers pay her back' with the questions and commentary. In part, MVC suggests an active critique of the current Left, the paucity of its discourse and its inability to transform people's lives. MVC substitutes for a missing form of activism: it directly participated in the anti-WTO demonstrations in Mexico City in 1999, and many other global political actions since then, and through its website it has tried to develop awareness on different issues around the process of integration of the Third World in the global capitalist economy. More recently, in fact, the corporation has turned its attention to providing organisational skills and support, and means of propaganda to social movements of any kind.

Cuevas herself frequently insists that MVC has no ideological leanings, and that its activities, despite being focused on issues of equality and freedom, are set apart not only from political parties, but also from left or right wing traditions. This post-political status is in part a result of its corporative identity, but is also related to the fact that MVC actions do not question political parties or call for social mobilization. In a way, MVC adopts an administrative attitude toward its work. MVC's radicalism consists of testing non-capitalist forms of human interaction rather than becoming the mouthpiece of established ideologies.

MVC's profile as an economy of promises also suggests the mourning for a local political history. This company of monetary losses and critical gadgets seems quite logical in a context like Mexico, not only because of the immense need that poverty and underdevelopment imply, but also because of the ideological importance that apparent generous gestures has for the image of the state. This is a country where among other things constitutional law includes the promise of good health, and where presidential tours are awaited with the same sense of expectation that children attribute to the visits of Santa. When global capitalism and the advance of electoral democracy is about to erase the last remnants of the old paternalistic state, MVC somehow has built a dialectical image of it. This is a corporation that recuperates the hopes of a population that has been equally betrayed by the promises of the former social structure of political clientelism and the untenable dreams of world-class development. Despite its mocking of corporate culture and the radical and anarchist leanings of its creator, one can credit MVC with having replicated the unconscious structure of this fake version of the welfare state. Cuevas' work, in that sense, is a timely counter-monument for a cunning postrevolutionary populist regime that seems on the way to vanishing entirely, eroded by the democratic struggles of its population and the unstoppable advance of global capitalism.

Kathrin Böhm
public works

Working as part of an art/architecture team, public works, with Andreas Lang, Stefan Saffer and Studio 3, Kathrin Böhm is interested in the existing dynamics between formal and informal structures that are imminent to our everyday life. Recent and current projects undertaken by public works are placed between the users and the governing bodies of public sites, trying to create new overlaps between different and differing interests and expectations. The wish to apply their practice to concrete situations meets an interest in generating new spaces for engagement and development.

Mobile Porch In November 1999 Kathrin Böhm and Stefan Saffer were invited by the North Kensington Amenity Trust (NKAT) to propose a temporary project for the Trust land underneath the Westway flyover in North London. Architect Andreas Lang became involved just a month later to create a stronger link between an art project, architectural and urban issues. The project received an Art for Architecture Award from the Royal Society of Architects and a Year of the Artist Award from the London Arts Board. The resulting project, *Mobile Porch*, developed into a prototype for public sites. It was designed in order to create an appropriate object for a public sphere that was multi-functional in its use and flexible in its purpose. *Mobile Porch* can be a shed, a reception desk, a stage, a bench, a lamp, a screen, a workshop, a vehicle, etc.. It is both a physical structure but also a social one. During the two-month residency at NKAT, *Mobile Porch* was used by a large number of people to create short-term activities, to organise social events or to drop ideas for further projects on site. The desire to communicate art outside its institutional context remains an important motivation for this artist and architect team.

On being commissioned by NKAT, it became immediately clear to us that we didn't want to do anything that was permanent or would attempt to compete with the Westway as a structure in any sense, but that we wanted to construct something that was mobile, a platform that could roam underneath the flyover. We made a list of things we wanted this project to be: it should be a logo for itself; it should be a place for workshops, for receptions, for dinners, for music events, for publishing material and for lectures. We started with a list of functions we wanted this object to fulfil and then we designed it. It looks like a wine barrel and runs on two large bearing wheels and it unfolds and opens up and becomes multi-functional. You can take the lid off and turn it into a table. You can take most elements off and disperse them, which claims quite enough area within a public setting to become physical space, not just a small intervention. The concept behind the design is that it is an aluminium structure, so it's extremely sturdy and durable. It's clad in plywood with the idea that if it gets damaged or vandalised we can replace the cladding. Our intention was to create a very mobile and flexible platform for people who use that public space to articulate or express or publish ideas. This concept seemed to be difficult for people to understand at first, and we seemed to spend the first two weeks explaining that it was a public platform, that it was non-commercial and that everybody could use it.

During the two months' stay of the *Mobile Porch* under the Westway, we had about 40 small-scale events, and a long list of ideas about what could, should and should not happen in public space. We set out to trigger ideas or discussion about how public space is used and whether there is a need or urge or desire for using it. *Mobile Porch* was also listed in *Time Out*, after a number of arguments around the fact that the *Mobile Porch* did not have an address, but in the end the fact that it had a mobile phone number permitted it to be listed. The

Mobile Porch was used for poetry readings and performances–it was marked by an infamous local graffiti artist and it hosted workshops with children, who turned it into a UFO and clad it in aluminium foil so that it wouldn't burn when it came close to the sun. We used it at night. We had 'happy hours' where we gave cocktails away for free, which was always a success of course, but we weren't just trying to be popular, we wanted to set up situations where people

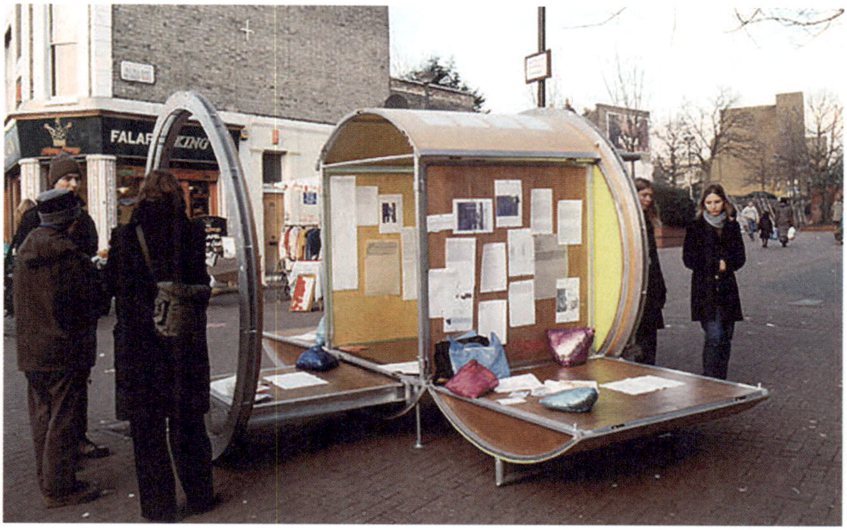

with different interests might meet, very informally and on a very low-key level. We created social situations which would not normally be encountered within public space. Eventually the *Mobile Porch* was burnt, which wasn't a problem as we could reclad it. This vandalism was sad but had a positive outcome. As a result, people came forward, talking about the way they had looked at it and walked past it for two months and what they thought it had done to their immediate environment. NKAT regarded the *Mobile Porch* as a successful tool to maintain and form a relationship with the users of their public space. Even though there was an intention to make it an annual event, this wasn't feasible due to insurance reasons caused by the fire. The *Mobile Porch* has since travelled to a number of places where it has been used in similar ways, including Munich and West Bromwich. We talk about it as an 'urban toy', as a way of suggesting a more playful and spontaneous and less programmed approach to public space. In West Bromwich, Jubilee Arts used it as a tool for publishing some of their ideas, for being active, to be one-to-one on the street. There was a funny incident with their PR department: they were forced to use the *Mobile Porch* for a day, and it was scary for them to 'meet the public' and actually 'talk' to people, but I think that's exactly what the *Mobile Porch* is about, testing and appreciating one-to-one encounters in public space.

Mobile Porch, London, 2000
Ideal Space Survey
with Brigid McLear
Courtesy public works

Fitting was a six-month communication and design project at a firestation in Munich in 2002 in which Böhm and her team negotiated the daily needs of the users of the building with the formal and aesthetic vision of the architecture, leading to a number of long term implementations.

During our stay in Messestadt Riem, Munich with the *Mobile Porch*, we were approached by the fire fighters who have a new firestation in this new garden city. They were experiencing problems with the concept and practicality of their new building and were looking for an artist to work with them to improve it. I think they were expecting us to paint the concrete walls or hang some pictures. We were more interested in the disparity between the intention of the architect and the everyday reality of the fire fighters–why the building wasn't working and what could be changed. There was quite a dilemma between the modernist design of the building and the fire fighters' attempts to contribute their own designs: they built a shed in the garden, they put their collection of fire extinguishers up in the main hall and plastered the exposed concrete, all of which had led to a major argument between them and the architect.

It was important that we came in as artists. In all our projects we are interested in what the position of an artist means and how you use it. As an artist you're non-threatening because no one expects you to have power–you're not representing something that's familiar. You're not representing the architect, you're not representing the council, and you're not representing any of the

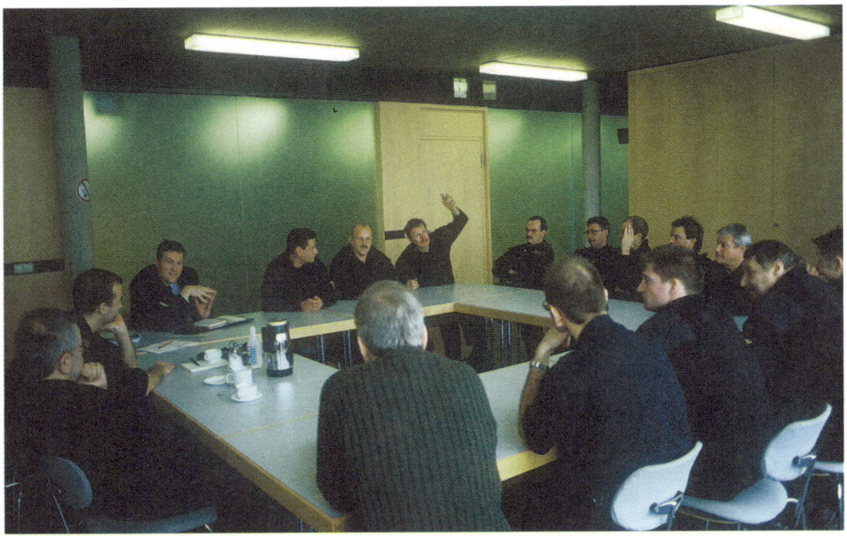

powers they have to deal with on a daily basis. At the same time, for the architect we represent someone who can talk about aesthetics and we understand a specific history and language of architecture. So in the beginning we invited everyone back to the table: the architect, the fire fighters and the people who commissioned the building, to make them talk about the intentions

Both images:
Fitting Firestation 10,
Messestadt Riem,
Munich, 2002-2003
Courtesy public works

behind the building, the reasons for commissioning it, for designing it, but also all to reveal why it didn't work on an everyday basis.

There was an amazing moment when the architect explained the beauty of exposed concrete in regards to a certain architectural history. This was crucial because, until then, the fire fighters had thought it was purely cynical that they had been left with exposed concrete all over the building. Those conversations didn't resolve the basic issue, but at least led to an understanding of the criticisms and dilemmas between the different groups. At the beginning of the

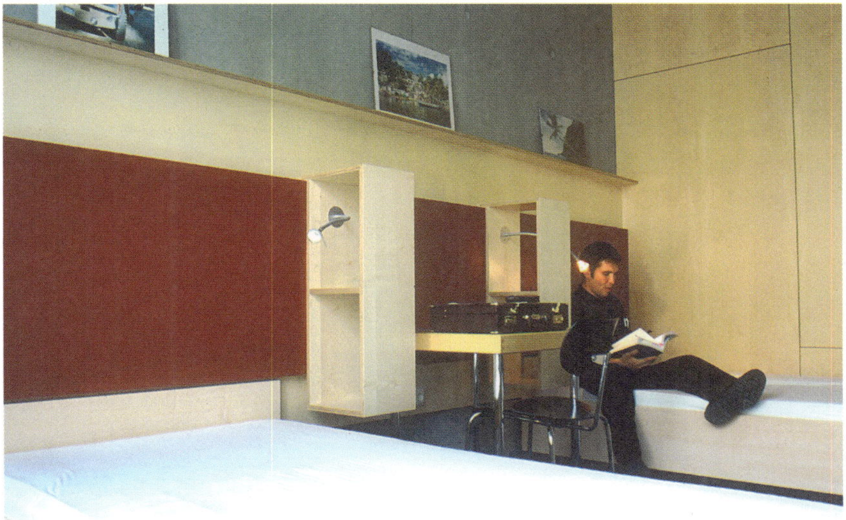

project we installed a shelf in the canteen which acted as an information board and interface between us and the fire station but also between the different shifts. After the first roundtables we asked everyone to come up with ideas for change and to write down what they thought were the main issues, what they wanted to see discussed in the longer run. So the billboard became a publishing tool within the building. We stressed from the beginning that the project wasn't about taste, but rather about the criteria that make and change architecture. It was about some of the professional needs of the fire fighters, to which the building hadn't responded, i.e. the need to relax during working hours.

There were three major issues which came out of this initial two-month exchange and brainstorm period: they were very unhappy about the fact that the building wasn't recognised as a firestation: it looked like any other office building and they had a real wish to change this. Another issue was that after 5pm in the afternoon, during standby (the shift is 7am to 7am) they wanted to have somewhere cosy, as all that was provided was one type of office chair. Initially we thought, "Easy, we'll buy a sofa", but of course it took us two months to understand that they didn't mean a sofa at all. Every other firestation in Munich had this L-shaped bench, a very traditional piece of furniture in

Bavaria and that's what they wanted. This was the kind of information that we didn't get out of those formal meetings, but rather when we were having lunch together. It's those informal encounters and the informal communication that reveals the essential information about how things work, which are crucial to our practice. The third issue was with their sleeping or resting rooms. They had three walls of concrete, a big window and another concrete wall in front of it and they didn't feel that they could relax. During those 24 hours and especially after very heavy call outs, there's a real need for them to relax. They had no space for putting up anything private, photos of their family or just small personal items.

After about three months into the project, it became clear that we had talked enough, and so we suggested three changes: paneling for the bedrooms, a mural for the façade and the L-shaped bench for the canteen. At this point in the project the fire fighters also offered to construct and install all the changes themselves. The success of the project was that the fire fighters are thinking of change as something possible within the rather strict hierarchy of their profession but also within the hierarchy between architecture and its users. After the official hand-over they have taken it upon themselves to negotiate and make changes when and where necessary, respecting the intention of the architecture.

Layout was a consultation and market research project for Gasworks Gallery, London. It took place on site at Gasworks during July and August 2002 and resulted in a catalogue of proposals that showed various strategies for the development of the organisation in the short, medium and longer term. The first phase development is currently underway.

The project was quite a mix between one-to-one activities and architectural planning. Quite literally we opened up the façade and placed a set of furniture in the street, and we hung out. We were on site for three months, three days a week and it was a mix between set-up meetings with other local initiatives or the local Council, discussions with other colleagues and conversations with passers-by. The existing façade just didn't indicate what Gasworks did. Our starting point was not to attempt to interest people in the gallery or in art, but that a public building needs to be recognisable as such and what it does and what it provides to the public should be transparent within the urban pattern. First of all, we used the façade as a billboard, just pasting things we were doing and other things that were going on–ideas and proposals. Because most of our projects are informal, we face the problem that anecdotes are crucial to the understanding of the nature of projects, but might at times obscure the conceptual intentions. For Gasworks we developed software, together with e2, that allowed us to archive and store all encounters on site. It's an existing online database, where we recorded encounters and published our proposals, providing a link between on-site research and subsequent planning stages.

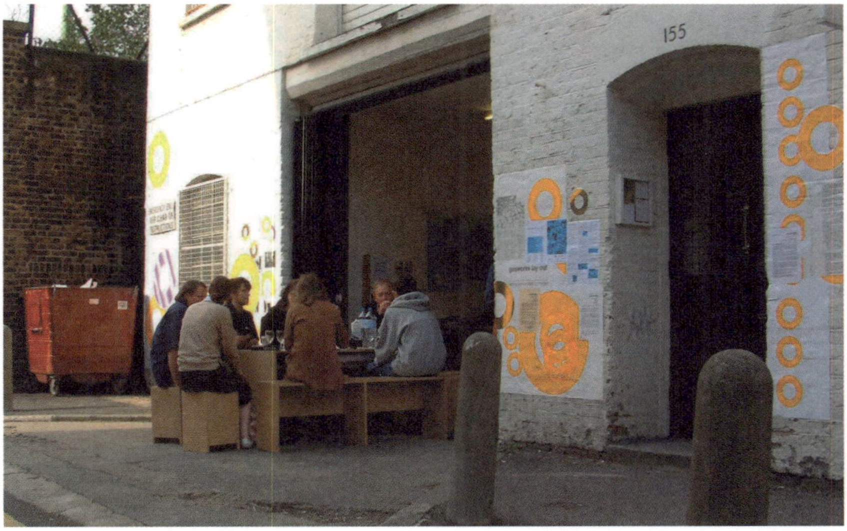

Layout (open office),
Gasworks, London, 2002
Courtesy public works

One of the starting points in our practice is that each encounter potentially holds a proposal, so whoever you encounter and whatever your conversation, it might be about a potential change or proposal. What emerged was that not only the official formal meetings, but also those chats in the street, revealed some kind of proposal, so in the end our plans were based on the observation of overlaps–for instance, how the gallery's plans overlap with the neighbouring estate. The Director, Fiona Boundy, used the proposals to gain funding to redesign and restructure the ground floor and the façade of Gasworks. We are doing the follow-up design, which is based on our research and which will create a social space or junction where all the different activities in the building come together, creating quite a transparent interface with the street.

This project developed from an artist-led research project to an architectural project where we have planning permissions, building control and fire exit issues to deal with. For me, there's a distinction between the first phase–the art project where there is quite a lot of freedom to argue about what you're doing, and now that it's this formalised architectural project, roles and responsibilities are much more prescribed. All of a sudden, I might get asked if it's difficult to move the toilets and it's now funny once the label of a project changes, the perception of you being involved in it immediately changes.

We argue for art to be involved in non-art processes as a way to develop criteria for decisions which don't have to be based on functional, commercial or efficiency basis. The appliance doesn't lie within a functionalisation of art but in linking the experience and knowledge gained through it, to other processes.

Becky Shaw
Twelve Museums

Becky Shaw explores the relationship between the artist and public, the individual and the group and the individual and wider society. This ongoing project involves entering work, leisure, health and education contexts, finding live, written and visual ways to explore and create new situations. *Twelve Museums* is an architect's model of a museum, attempting to house one man's lifetime of studying and presenting artefacts for television. The project was a collaboration between Becky Shaw and Michael Gill, who now has dementia. Through the project the artist raises questions about the current interest in 'collaboration', and the representation of those who are considered disadvantaged.

Today, so many projects involve 'collaboration'. Obviously the term is common in the 'art world', but collaboration or 'partnership working' is also highly desirable in a range of other contexts now: private and public economic development agencies are expected to work in partnership and scientific research is expected to work across departments or to create 'clusters'. On the one hand, this is an intelligent way to maximise resources and create the conditions for inspirational ideas. On the other hand, it is curious why the state is so keen to see us all working together, perhaps it is to give some kind of community spirit which they have no power to create. In the context of an art 'world' there are a multitude of different types of collaboration: artists working with artists from different disciplines, artists working with specialists from other fields, and the one that interests me here, artists working with people considered disadvantaged in some way. These situations may present fascinating conditions to make new work, but to what extent they are 'collaborations' remains open to question.

In 2002 I was one of the artists in Age Concern Kensington and Chelsea's "Dementia Arts Project". The project involved two visual artists, myself and Eric Fong, working with five people with dementia, over an eight-month period. This text focuses on this project to explore what constitutes a collaboration and whether it supports or negates the artist or person with dementia. The project was initiated by artist David Clegg as an exploratory process, investigating whether it could be possible for two people, one with dementia and one a contemporary artist, to share a common visual language. Age Concern were responsible for the project so there was an expectation that the activities should be beneficial to those involved with dementia. Clegg continually emphasised 'process' and the development of artistic thinking as methods relevant to the needs of the person with dementia. It was made clear that the process might lead to no visual product or no product of quality. At the same time, however, it was anticipated that there should be a final exhibition. This was partly to give a context in which the process might be called 'art', actualising the work through contact with a conventional audience.

The exhibition might motivate people to be involved and to make work, and it would also promote the work of the Dementia Arts Project and therefore Age Concern. The addition of an exhibition seemed strange, but activated an interesting tension between the value of process and product which would not otherwise have existed. This tension, the play between individual and 'collaborator', private experience and public presentation, and expectations of the health profession and art audience, was at once the most uncomfortable and most interesting aspects of the project. One of the three people with whom I worked over three months was Michael Gill. Michael Gill was responsible for directing and co-producing, amongst many other broadcasts, Kenneth Clark's seminal TV series, *Civilisation,* in the 1970s. Over 18 meetings, Michael described his own vision of the historic development of civilisation. With a muscular intellect, Michael sought to put forward his ideas, but his illness interfered with the ordering, communication and sustaining of these, causing repetition and sentences that lost their goal and changed direction midway. At times Michael was concerned about the lack of structure of our conversations. I responded to this need by suggesting that his ideas had their own architecture and that we might literally build a house, or museum for them.

When we tried to make decisions directly about the form of this building it became impossible to visualise. Rather than placing pressure on Michael (and all of us), we chose a method which, it was hoped, would reflect the reality of the situation. I recorded our conversations and after each session they were transcribed, creating large complex diagrams. To begin with I sought a rational concept in making these drawings, so that particular spoken movements and certain types of change in direction etc. were always recorded in the same way. This proved impossible so the conversations were recorded diagramatically but with intuition and the space of the paper deciding on the form. These diagrams would go on to represent literally the shape of Michael's thought.

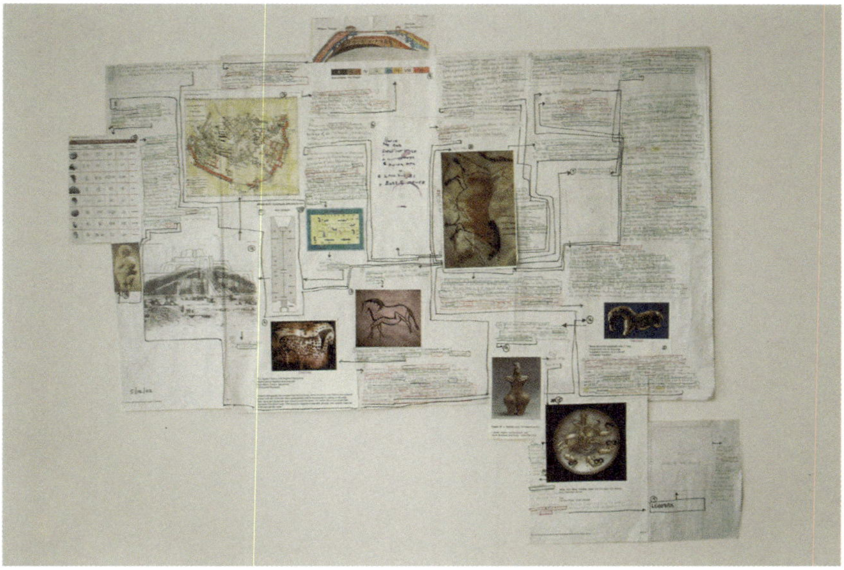

The daily working process involved developing structures, sometimes like games, so that distractions or tangents could be avoided and Michael could make decisions about the intention of, and appearance of the work. For example, we continually experimented with developing categorisation systems for the museum. In the end it wasn't possible to decide on one, so fragments of several are overlaid in the floors, for example, "Men, Women, Horses" coexists with, "Communication, Art, Architecture, Community, Women and Men, Language, War, Animals, Horses, Gods". Other methods included asking Michael to choose definitive objects from his own collections of objects and books. Whether these methods represent a manipulation of choice should

Becky Shaw and Michael Gill
Twelve Museums
(diagrams), 2002

always be questioned, and remains difficult to answer as without such methods no decisions from Michael could have shaped the work.

The exact visual shape of the diagrams were traced on acetate, forming 12 floor plans. The plans have dead-ends and false corridors, rooms that double back on themselves and rooms too small to have anything in them. Yet they perhaps correspond more to my representation of Michael's thoughts than they do to his own thoughts. It is interesting to consider whether they actually represent the manifestation of dementia, as a conversation with someone without dementia, recorded in the same way, might actually look the same. But then there wouldn't be the same purpose or desire to repeat the process with someone who is 'well'. This opens up two issues, one is that the meaning of the plans lies in the need to make them, to try to reconstruct or catch rescued fragments. The other issue is that we have to acknowledge that there is a cultural currency to illness, we crave to see or represent the 'authentic' experiences of the infirm.

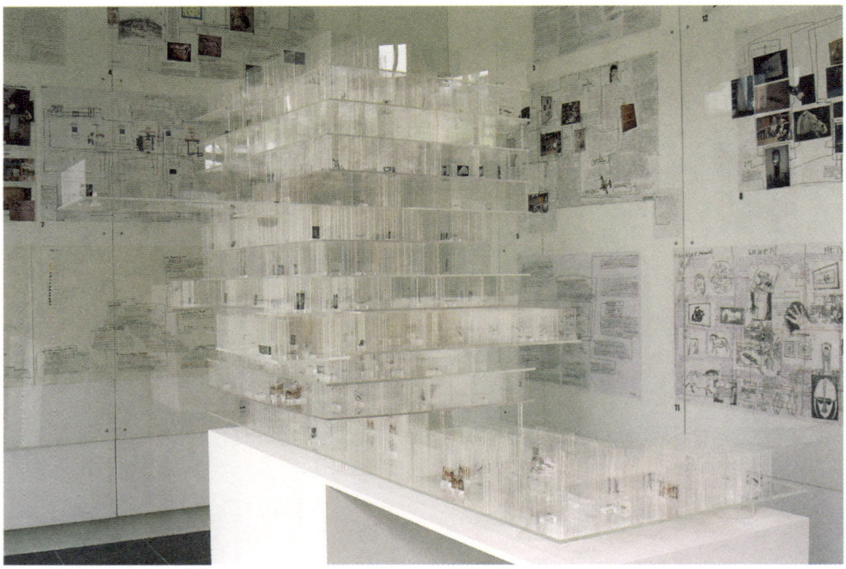

We commissioned Mark Fleming, a professional architect's model-maker, *Staticmodels*, to build the floors in a transparent acrylic. The 12 storeys of the museum took over a month to build, a pain-staking investment of time. I made tiny acetate images of the objects Michael referenced and installed them in the exact place they occurred in the diagrams. Where an object had been referred to, but we hadn't the image with us as we worked, we used the word, such as "Assyrian Gods". When the museums are viewed, the same object appears many times and on many floors, internal reflections making some objects and words appear upside down and doubled-up, texts appearing in front of images that are not connected. When the work was exhibited it was presented with all the diagrams and a guide so that visitors could read our thought processes.

Becky Shaw and Michael Gill
Twelve Museums, 2002
Serpentine Gallery,
exhibition view

Michael was preoccupied with whether humanity can move onwards and build a future, whilst conflict in Iraq continues. He was deeply interested in Iraq, understanding it as the seat of humanity and the home of the earliest human language. Michael was also fascinated by the representation of the horse in historic art, seeing the horse as both emblem of warfare, community and masculinity. In addition, Michael has written extensively about the representation of the female form, particularly in his book, *Image of the Body*, and this expertise also became visible.[1] He was intrigued by the depiction of gods, and the striving to represent the unknown. It is possible to relate Michael's interest in virile and vigorous emblems to his sense of physical decline, and an interest in gods to his own living experience of the 'unknown' in the 'absences' experienced by people with dementia. However, these sit within the larger metaphor of investigating fragments of memory and history, with Michael perhaps connecting his individual situation with the fall of empires and what he perceived as the end of civilisation. While Michael's health changed rapidly, fluctuating from visit to visit there were many moments when his insight into the process was sharp and revealing. He said, more than once, that the role of the artist was to provide "structure" and to "take him back to the beginning",

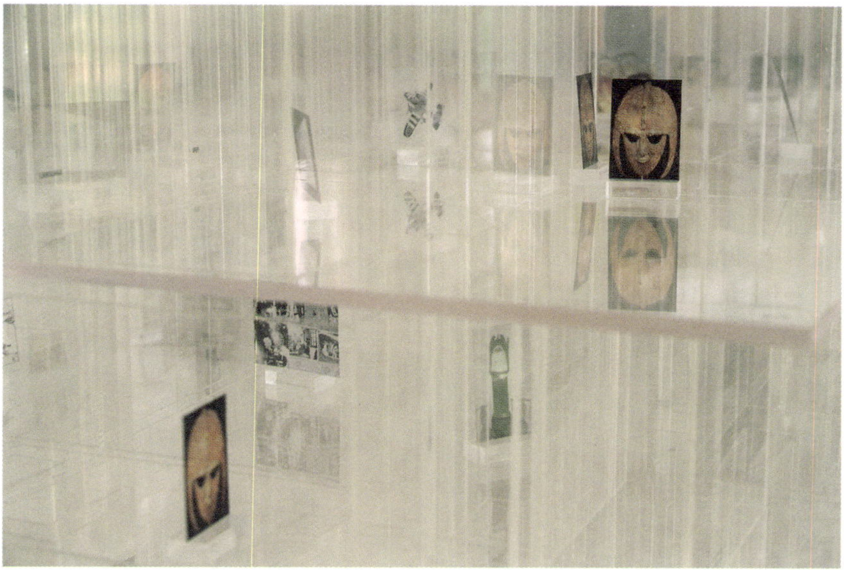

seeing the process as an archaeological excavation of his knowledge rather than a building above ground. When writing about the project, AA Gill, Michael's son, described the artist, me, as Michael's "amanuensis".[2] Gill saw the collaboration as a meeting between thinker and scribe, with Michael generating the content that I wrote down. While an attractive metaphor, this is, to some extent, wishful thinking as I believe the process of drawing 'content' from Michael to have been far more proactive, more 'producing' than simply recording.

Becky Shaw and Michael Gill
Twelve Museums
(detail), 2002

The work was presented within the exhibition, *Remembering the Present* at the Sackler Centre for Arts Education, Serpentine Gallery, London, April 2003. The audience responded positively, the spectacular appearance of the model and the apparent intellectual weight of the diagrams were instantly impressive. It seemed that this degree of aesthetic spectacle was essential to convey something of the high status activity in which Michael had been involved. However, some care professionals who came to the exhibition were disappointed and angered by the work, wanting to see the genuine 'brush-strokes' of someone with dementia. It seemed they wanted the project to "expand Michael's creativity" and did not find this in what they saw. To 'discover the creativity' of someone who has spent a lifetime producing television and radio broadcasts would seem rather pointless, and also, I suspect, would not have been entertained by Michael or his family.

In the case of *Twelve Museums*, the exhibition context was appropriate. Michael has spent many hours in museums and galleries, so fully understood the process of viewing objects and also the status of a show at the Serpentine. In addition, the product, a model of a museum, was appropriate for a formal exhibition. After the project ended Michael was unable to recall much of the activity. However, the positive responses of others to the work appeared to give him, and obviously all of us involved, great satisfaction. Michael's intellect and insight into his illness meant that decisions could be made together so some kind of collaborative process was possible. However, the issue of the relationship between artist and collaborator remains. Did I shape or create Michael's material? Is this work a joint communication or a work that I made about Michael, with his input? These questions remain open, though it is also interesting to assess the worth of the questions themselves. If Michael believes it to be an equal collaboration then does it matter what really happened? And then to think about the 'integrity' of the artist's vision: this work would not have been made without Michael so it is worthless to debate whether collaboration dilutes vision.

Finally, at one stage AA Gill suggested he might like to buy *Twelve Museums*. This simple, potentially financial transaction complicated the work further. How could a work which contained something of one person be sold to his son, and at what price?

[1] Michael Gill, *Image of the Body: Aspects of the Nude*, New York: Doubleday, 1989.

[2] AA Gill, "Mind Games", *Sunday Times Magazine*, 2 March 2003.

 Becky Shaw and Michael Gill, *Twelve Museums* (detail), 2002

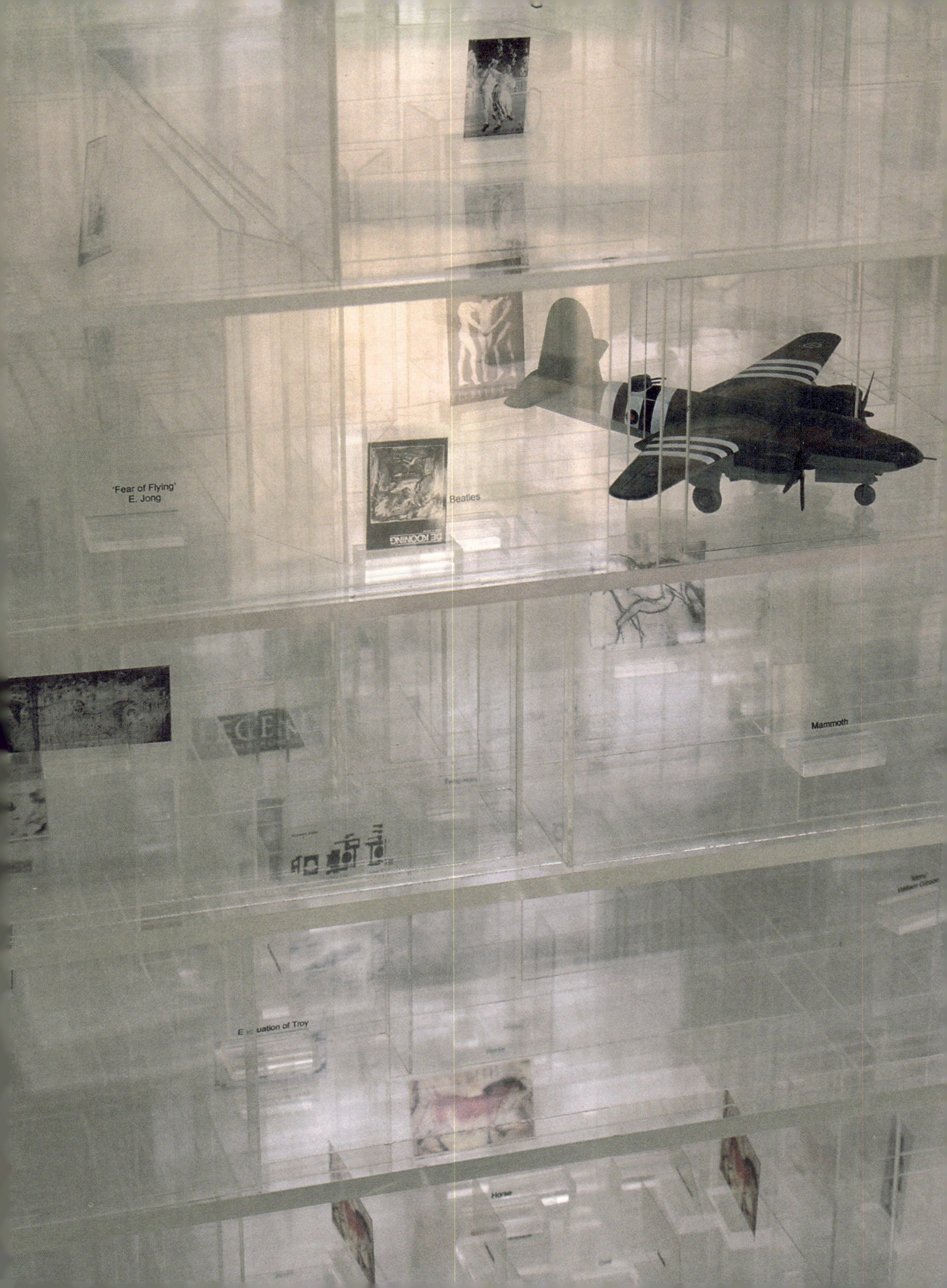

'Fear of Flying'
E. Jong
Beatles
DE KOONING
Mammoth
Evacuation of Troy
Horse

Jimmie Durham
Situations

In the early 1960s Jimmie Durham became active in theatre, performance, and literature in the US Civil Rights Movement. In 1969, Durham moved to Geneva, Switzerland, returning to the US in 1973. Durham was a political organiser in the American Indian Movement from 1973-1980 and director of the International Indian Treaty Council and representative at the United Nations. In 1986 he moved to Mexico, returning to Europe in 1994. For the past ten years Durham has been working against the European traditions of architecture and monumentality. What follows is a transcript of a lecture delivered by Durham at The School of Chemistry in Bristol as part of the *Situations* lecture series in 2004.

It's funny to be in the Chemistry Building. Chemists are marvellously strange people. It's already strange to take petroleum from the ground and to think then to distil it and get gasoline to run your engine, but then how do you think, "What if I put lead in it, wouldn't that make the engine run better?" How would you think something like that? I think I might say, "What if I put some soap in it?". I don't think I would ever choose lead, but it worked for a long time and now it turns out to be not so good.

When I have the idea to talk about my situation, it's as if you prepare by saying, "I'm going to take stock of my situation," and then you have to think, "Well in that case, what is my situation?" I'm getting older, I work too hard and I don't have enough money–that's my basic situation. And then as soon as I think that's my basic situation, I think when you make a report on your situation you're making a complaint and then I think, "Well, I am making a complaint but who am I complaining to? Who am I making the complaint to?" And I'm not complaining *to* you, because nothing would happen, so I hope that I'm complaining *with* you and then I can be a little more specific in my complaints.

It's a little strange to be an American Indian because everyone knows all about us. We're over-defined as a group of people, but the knowledge is completely false. Everyone is more sure of it, after all of these years of stupid conversations and stupid questions, I no longer have the courage to make corrections and these days everyone is easily bored and no one has time to listen to corrections, so my first complaint, my first position is: I belong to a group of people very visible and very invisible; very known and not the least bit known. It's not exactly a complaint because it allows freedom of movement.

I've been back in Europe since 1994. People often think that I am in exile in Europe but that eventually I'll go back. Actually, I don't really say "I'm in Europe," I say that I live in Eurasia because there is no continent called Europe. Europe is just a little fat peninsula on the Eurasian continent. If it weren't for bandits, I could walk from Brussels to Peking. If I had the time. So people say I'm in exile in Eurasia, that's what I meant to say. I was born in exile. I was born under the State of Arkansas, I'm not from the US. The US is my enemy. I'm in a much less exiled position in Europe than I am in the US.

I've lived in Berlin since 1998 and I was just talking recently about what a funny place Berlin is, such a nice place to live. It's not very German and it never has been very German. It doesn't have this German agenda that other German cities have. They don't care about Germany "The State". It started out a military barracks a few hundred years ago, from a fishing village, so the local people are basically working class without a national agenda. When Berlin became the capital again two years ago, Berliners didn't say that they were now the capital, they said "Bonn is coming", they think Bonn is the capital and Bonn is coming to Berlin. It's quite charming and 'low rent cosmopolitan' in a nice way.

I can live in Berlin in a way that I could not in Rome or Paris and I think not in London. There's no agenda at all, there is just–I don't know how to put this–it is cosmopolitan with very many artists. There's less and less money but the city is quite cheap and that makes it a nice place to live, in a sense of how I might address the city, address the world, address people–address the public I might say. To take away my complaint about being poor, in Berlin I'm quite rich. In my life now I never dreamt I would be so rich and have such a nice life. The city of Berlin has given me a studio that's a great giant studio made by Hitler for his favourite sculptor. I'm only the third person to have this studio and it's quite cheap. It's sat in the Grünewald Forest and I can listen to Wagner while I'm sculpting away.

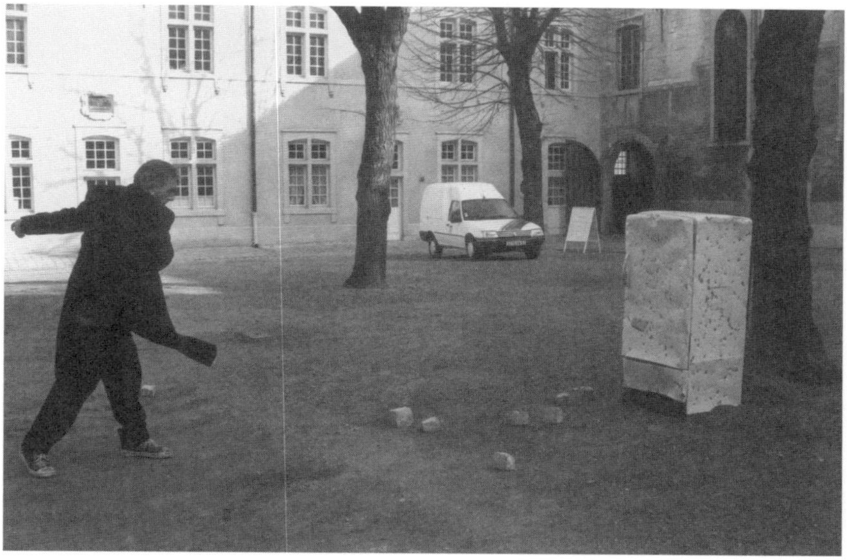

In my family I am extremely rich now. I think I don't have enough money and I have money worries like we all do. In the world, I am incredibly rich. In my neighbourhood in Moabit, there are very many black people from Africa, quite a few Turks and Arabs from other places, but the Africans are like me, they feel their lives are quite rich in Berlin. But this brings up something quite strange about what is my real situation in the world. There are countries in Africa like Ethiopia, the Sudan, maybe even countries that are not so known to be desperate that have practically no GNP and yet the World Bank has loaned them money and they have to pay everything they make on the interest of this money. Now where did the World Bank get this money to loan them? It got it from the Third World. That's where all the money came from, ripping off the Third World of practically everything, making them poor and then loaning them the money to develop themselves. But they have to pay the interest on the loan. That makes all of us rich. We get money from starving Ethiopians. That's a funny situation isn't it?

Jimmie Durham
Stoning the St. Frigo, 1996

I teach in Malmö in Sweden and I was there a few weeks ago with a guy from the Congo, a very nice guy, and his field of expertise and his problem is the same, something called *combilene tantalon*–isn't that a nice name? It's a stone, it's a mineral and it only comes from the Congo. Oh no, I ask him if it only comes from the Congo, he said, "No, no of course it doesn't only come from the Congo, there's also some in Congo-Brazzaville". It only comes from this area in other words. It's in mobile phones, you can't have a mobile phone without this mineral. His problem is not that they sell it for $3 a lb and the middle man sells it for $300 a lb, his problem is how to keep these desperately poor people who have been subsistence farmers all these years from destroying their own land as they're doing, they're stopping farming, because they've never had any cash before. Now they can dig up the land, find a piece of combilene tantalon and get $3–so they're no longer doing cattle, they're no longer doing gardens, they're just looking for this stone and looking to get a little bit of money. His job is to put governmental control on his own people to keep them poor in a certain way so they aren't made poorer by a double rip off. I didn't meet him in the Congo. I didn't go to the Congo to meet him, I met him in Europe. This is my Berlin situation.

When I look at the audience here, and especially when I walk along the corridors of the Chemistry Building, I can see something that's quite clear and quite celebratory I think. We're not who we think we are. England is not the England that it thinks it is. We live now in a world where everyone is some sort of immigrant, everyone is moving. The world is changing so rapidly that we only know it as a problem, thinking, "Oh, too many foreigners coming into Great Britain," or we think too many foreigners coming into Europe or something. I see it very strongly in Berlin because we have quite silly neo-Nazis who don't have a job and don't want a job. Not much money, but still there are jobs that only immigrants are willing to do and we need the immigrant workers as Germany always has, as Great Britain also does.

Instead of seeing the phenomenon as a human phenomenon, everyone sees it as a problem. If it's a problem, then I'm part of the problem. I don't want to be German. I don't want to be a Berliner even, my real ambition is to be a homeless orphan, but I want to be a homeless orphan who has the opportunity to address the world and we're in a moment when it looks like, for the first time in history, humanity wants to address humanity. At the same time we want to kill each other but we always had that, that's not a new thing. What's new is we have a strange population problem, we're more deadly than we ever have been, we're more cruel than we ever have been, more blood thirsty and we intend to be nicer at the same moment. We're trying to be enlightened at the same moment. Humanity is trying to address humanity, we're trying to talk to ourselves for the first time and so much we're trying to do it with art. I think most of the things that humanity does, we do it cynically and stupidly, I know we do it stupidly but I think we also do it cynically.

When humanity first got bronze tools, for example, there were tribes that were the same as guilds and they had their secret bronze technology and they travelled from India to Russia to all over Europe trading their bronze tools to people who only had stone tools at that moment. They were getting quite rich and they were protecting their secret, but at the same time they were spreading technology. We can say they were using their primitive capitalism as an excuse to talk to each other, just like we do now when we go to the shopping mall. Of course we're alienated, of course we're desperate, of course we're being sold a bunch of stupid lies about the shopping mall and what it will do for us, but I think we're also trying to connect, we're trying to join in when we go to the shopping mall and the only way we can do it is buy a shirt or buy some new sandals or something, because nothing else is presented to us as a way to do it, so we buy some Nike shoes and we feel like we're part of the "Nike generation" or something. The impulse is a nice human impulse I think. So to go back to what I was saying about the arts. I think the *Gwangju Biennale* for example is just to bring in tourist money for the Korean Government. I think it's a cynical biennale. I think they care nothing about art and they care nothing about the discourse of art, they just want some tourist money and some art money, but I don't care so much, because not everyone in Gwangju and not everyone in Korea is infected, so maybe I'm going to agree to be in the *Gwangju Biennale* this year (I never have before) because maybe something different will happen.

I want to go back in time now and tell another story. I was in New York as an artist in the early 1980s and I was part of a group that I fell in with quite accidentally, a group of maybe 50 people and we were Puerto Rican, American black, Chinese American, Indians–all the minorities–and we didn't have any galleries, we only had one space where we could regularly show, run by a black couple. Almost everything we did was in Harlem or in Brooklyn or in the lower part of the Lower East Side and we did a lot of shows in the lower part of the Lower East Side at the very same moment that there were already extremely famous and successful alternative galleries on the Lower East Side. These places, these successful places only showed white artists of course, but they didn't think they were doing that, they didn't think they were racist, they didn't think they were exclusionary. They were showing what they thought was interesting, contemporary art and they wouldn't show any of us because we weren't interesting, we were a minority art of some sort and these places got so rich they would bring buses of German collectors into the Lower East Side so that they wouldn't get mugged. It was a marketing scheme to make them feel like they were transgressing–it worked quite well.

Quite a few artists in these places got very famous very quickly (I left New York in 1987) and I suppose we did a show practically every two months during that time from 1984 through 1987. Everybody just creating and finding whatever place, having great fun, completely invisible except to ourselves and our

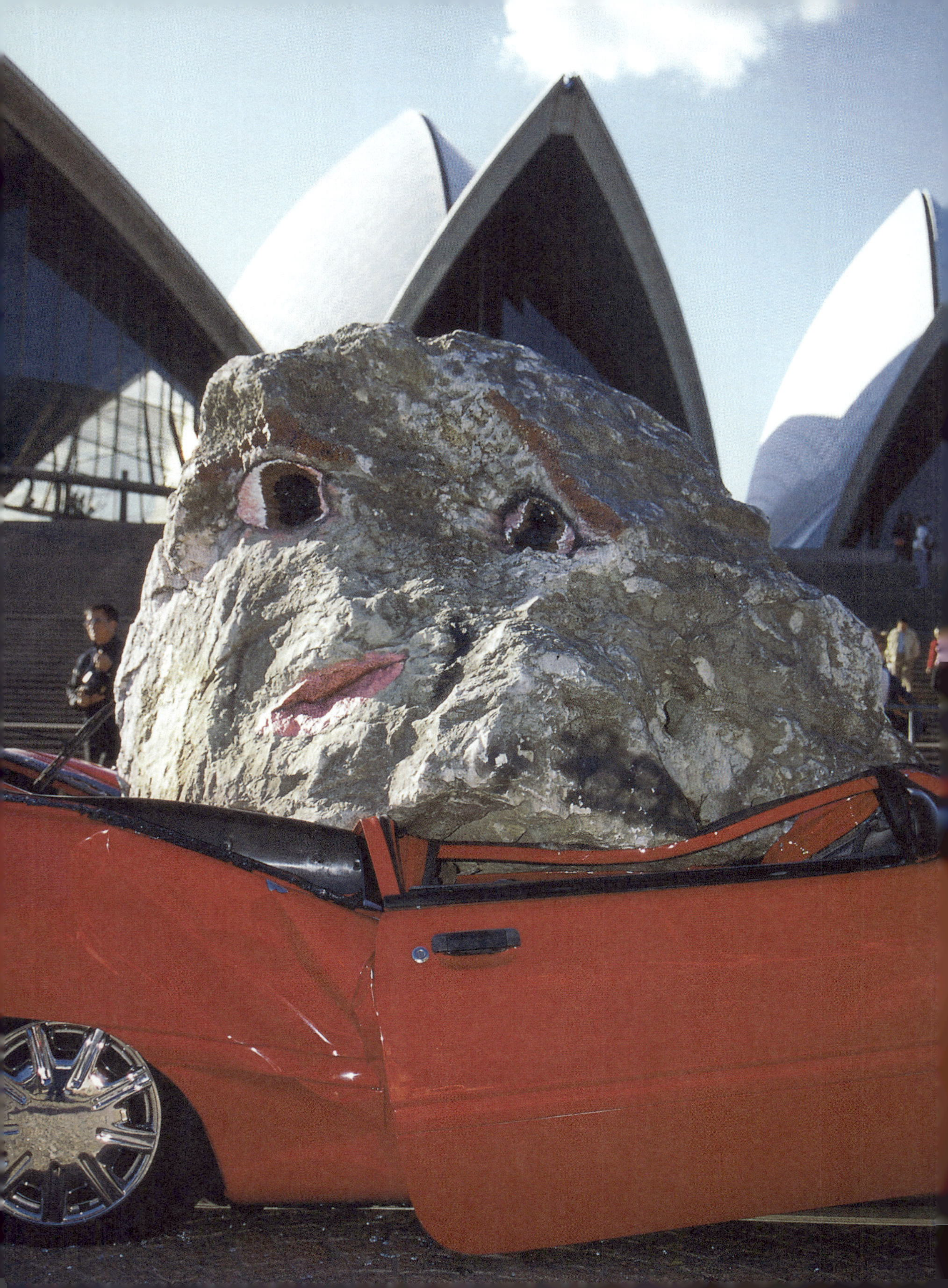

communities. Quite a few of us from that time are now well known in some way or other, and I don't mean at all that this is proof of success or anything, I don't know what success might be except to be of some good influence, that's success. Nevertheless, quite a few of us are now more well known than the white artists who were so well known in the 1980s that they got bus loads of German collectors coming to visit them.

The situation we were in was not the situation that other people thought we were in, because the other people didn't even think about us, they looked at their situation and now we have, still I think in Europe–maybe especially in London–all of us have an idea that post-colonialism or Third World arts or minority arts or anything that's not 'mainstream' is at the mercy of the mainstream and for the edification and delectation of the mainstream. However living in Berlin it's easy to see this is just a naïve mistake, the mainstream doesn't exist and it hasn't for a long time. You're not the white people, you're not the English people, there's not this separation that we thought there probably was, so there are still quite a few of us minority artists who make an attack one way or another and I think that's excellent, I'm not against us making an attack, but we are not the outsiders talking to the insiders, that's not the situation. I think I'm personally quite lucky because I'm not an outsider or an insider and I still have the great privilege to talk.

I don't live in Germany, I live in Berlin, a cosmopolitan city. I don't live in Europe, I live in Eurasia. I'm not here as a stranger, I'm not here to attack and I'm not here to join up either. My situation surely is the ideal situation, that we should all see ourselves in, and I think we do personally, don't we? I think when you go home, you don't say, "Well here I am, I'm a nice English student", you think maybe the opposite, you think, "I want to tell these people something", not to attack, but, it's you who wants to participate, your individual self who wants to participate and be of influence in the world and not be part of the football team or something, not be part of the 'defined group'. This is the good part of art, this is where art gives us knowledge and energy at the same time.

Jimmie Durham, *Still Life with Stone and Car, Biennale of Sydney*, 2004

General reading list and sources

Books

Marc Augé, *Non-Places: Introduction to an Anthropology of Supermodernity*, London and New York: Verso, 1995

David Blamey, ed., *Here, There, Elsewhere: Dialogues on Location and Mobility*, London: Open Editions, 2002

John Carson and Susannah Stewart, eds., *Out of the bubble: approaches to contextual practice within fine art education*, London: London Institute, 1999

Alex Coles, ed., *Site-Specificity: The Ethnographic Turn*, London: Black Dog Publishing, 2000

Douglas Crimp, "The Art of Exhibition" and "Redefining Site Specificity", *On the Museum's Ruins*, Cambridge, MA: MIT Press, 1993

Michel de Certeau, *The Practice of Everyday Life*, trans. Steven Rendall, Los Angeles: University of California Press, 1984

Rosalyn Deutsche, *Evictions: Art and Spatial Politics*, Cambridge, MA: MIT Press, 1996

Barnaby Drabble, Dorothee Richter and Eva Schmidt, *Curating degree zero, an international curating symposium*, Nürnberg: Verlag für moderne Kunst, 1999

Hal Foster, "The Artist as Ethnographer", *The Return of the Real: The Avant-Garde at the End of the Century*, Cambridge, MA: MIT Press, 1996

Renée Green, ed., *Negotiations in the Contact Zone*, Lisbon: Assírio and Alvim, 2003

Anna Harding, ed., *Curating: the contemporary art museum and beyond*, London: Academy Group, 1997

David Harding, ed., with Pavel Buchler, *Decadent: Public Art, Contentious Term + Contentious Practice*, Glasgow: Glasgow School of Art, 1997

Susan Hiller and Sarah Martin, eds., *The Producers: Contemporary Curators in Conversation 1, 2, 3*, Gateshead: BALTIC, 2000-2001

Miwon Kwon, *One Place After Another: Site-specific Art and Locational Identity*, Cambridge, MA: MIT Press, 2002

Lucy Lippard, *The Lure of the Local: Sense of Place in a Multicultural Society*, New York: New Press, 1997

Paula Marincola, *Curating Now: Imaginative Practice / Public Responsibility*, Philadelphia, PA: Philadelphia Exhibitions Initiative, 2001

Sarah Martin and Sune Nordgren, eds., *Artists at Work*, Gateshead: BALTIC, 2001

John Durham Peters, "Exile, Nomadism and Diaspora: the Stakes of Mobility in the Western Canon", in Hamid Naficy, ed., *Home, Exile, Homeland: Film, Media and the Politics of Place*, London: Routledge, 1998

Irit Rogoff, *Terra Infirma: Geography's Visual Culture*, London: Routledge, 2000

Julian Stallabrass et. al. eds., *Locus Solus: site, identity, technology in contemporary art*, London: Black Dog Publishing, 2000

Erika Suderburg, ed., *Space, Site, Intervention: Situating Installation Art*, Minneapolis: University of Minnesota Press, 2000

Gerrie van Noord, *Off-Limits: 40 Artangel Projects*, London: Artangel and Merrel, 2002

Gavin Wade, *Curating in the 21st Century*, Walsall: New Art Gallery, Walsall and Wolverhampton: University of the Wolverhampton, 2000

Articles

Penelope Curtis, "Old Places for New Art", *AN Magazine*, February 2003, p. 22

Thierry De Duve, "Ex Situ", in Andrew Benjamin, ed., *Installation Art: Art & Design*, vol. 8, no. 5/6, May-June 1993

Tim Griffin, "Global Tendencies: Globalism and the Large-Scale Exhibition", *Artforum*, November 2003, pp. 152-163, 206, 212

Grant Kester, "Dialogical Aesthetics: A Critical Framework for Littoral Art" at www.variant.ndtilda.co.uk/9texts/KesterSupplement.html

Exhibition catalogues

Time and Tide: The Tyne International Exhibition of Contemporary Art, London: Academy Group, 1993

Nick Barley, ed., *Leaving Tracks: Arttranspennine98*, London: August Media, 1999

Mark Beasley, "Democracy", *Democracy: socially engaged art practice*, London: Royal College of Art, 2000

Klaus Bussmann, Kasper König and Florian Matzner, *Sculpture Projects in Münster 1997*, Ruit: Hatje Cantz Verlag, 1997

Claire Doherty, Deborah Kermode, Michael Prior and Jonathan Watkins, *as it is*, Birmingham: Ikon Gallery, 2000

Mary Jane Jacob, ed., *Places with a Past: New Site-Specific Art at Charleston's Spoleto Festival*, New York: Rizzoli, 1991

Mary Jane Jacob and Michael Brenson, *Conversations at the Castle: changing audiences and contemporary art*, Cambridge, MA: MIT Press, 1998

Nigel Prince and Gavin Wade, eds., *In the midst of things*, London: August Media, 2000

Websites

www.situations.org.uk
www.arnolfini.org.uk
www.bristollegiblecity.info

Biographies and further reading

Kathrin Böhm, Andreas Lang and Stefan Saffer form a team of artists and architects, public works, who are interested in the dynamics between formal and informal structures that are imminent to our everyday lives. An integral part of their work is the collaboration with the users of public space and the governing institutions. In order to articulate and address issues within the public sphere, they have developed different tools and strategies to initiate links between different interests: between the formal and the informal, between the temporary and the permanent and between the public and the private

Recent projects by public works include: *Fitting,* 2002, *Layout,* 2002, *Mobile Porch,* 2000 and on-going, and *Park Products,* 2004, a participative one-year design and exchange project in Kensington Gardens for the Serpentine Gallery, London, which makes use of the existing cultural and natural resources of the park. Böhm is currently also involved on *Spacemakers,* a public-space design project with a group of young people in Hartcliffe, Bristol.

www.mobileporch.net
www.layout-gasworks.net

Aleksandra Mir, ed., *Corporate Mentality,* New York: Lukas & Sternberg Inc., 2003

Parasite Paradise, exh. cat.,The Netherlands: Nai Publishers and SKOR, 2003

Shadow Cabinets in a Bright Country, exh. cat., Kassel: Kunsthalle Fridericianum, 2002

Alex Coles, "Kathrin Böhm: On the Move", *Art Monthly,* issue 247, June 2001

Nigel Prince and Gavin Wade, eds., *In the Midst of Things,* London: August, 1999

Nicolas Bourriaud is co-director with Jerome Sans of the newly created Palais de Tokyo Contemporary Art Centre in Paris. He was Founder and Director of the magazine *Documents,* 1992-2000 and the Paris correspondent for *Flash Art,* 1987-1995.
His exhibitions include: *Aperto, Venice Biennale,* 1993; *Commerce,* Espace St Nicolas, Paris, 1994; *Traffic,* CAPC Musée d'Art Contemporain, Bordeaux, 1996; *Joint Ventures*, Basilico Gallery, New York, 1996; *Contacts,* Kunsthalle Fri-Art, Fribourg, Switzerland, 2000; *Touch,* San Francisco Art Institute, 2002; *GNS,* Palais de Tokyo, 2003 and *Playlist,* Palais de Tokyo, 2004.

www.palaisdetokyo.com

Nicolas Bourriaud, *Esthetique Relationnelle / Relational Aesthetics*, Paris: Presses du reel, 1998 / 2002

Nicolas Bourriaud, *Postproduction*, New York: Lukas & Sternberg, 2001

Bennett Simpson, "Public Relations: an interview with Nicolas Bourriaud", *Artforum,* April 2001

Daniel Buren, from 1965, chose to use non-traditional art methods, opting for the use of striped fabric vertical stripes alternating between white and colour with a width of 8.7cm which has continued to form the basis of his work. Towards the end of 1966 Buren became associated with Olivier Mosset, Michel Parmentier and Niele Toroni. The four artists defied artistic practice through a series of works challenging how exhibition spaces are used, thus highlighting the system of 'exhibiting and showing' as obsolete. Daniel Buren continued this reflection through a period of work on space and context called *Élargissement du Champ Visual.* By applying the paint to the fabric in a minimalist way, Buren achieved an expression called absolute zero–"degré zero". He believed the painting to liberate itself from all its aesthetical contexts such as expression, composition, harmony of colour etc. allowing the focus to fall upon its surrounding space rather than on the actual painting itself.

In November 1967, he began to paste posters which were based on his work with striped fabric, directly onto the walls of buildings in Paris. The paintings, created *in situ,* consequently eliminated the object with nothing remaining but a visual sign which took the form of its space and context. He has since participated in the *Venice Biennale* winning a prestigious Golden Lion award and his work has been exhibited at the Museum of Modern Art, New York, the Art Institute of Chicago and Tokyo Museum of Contemporary Art. His work can be found in the permanent collections of Museo di Capodimonte, Naples, and Castello di Rivoli Museo d'Arte Contemporanea, Italy.

Parkett, no. 66, January 2003 (Texts by Robert Hobbs, Jeremy Millar, Hans Ulrich Obrist and a conversation with Daniel Buren)

Daniel Buren, *In situ*, Turin: Bruno Corà, Testo & Immagine, 2003

Mot à mot, Paris: Editions Centre Pompidou / Editions de la Martinière / Editions Xavier Barral, 2002

Guy Lelong, *Daniel Buren*, Paris: Flammarion, 2002

Daniel Buren, "Can art get down from its pedestal and rise to street level?", in Klaus Busmann, Kasper Koenig and Florian Matzner, eds., *Skulpture Projects in Münster*, Ruit: Hatje Cantz Verlag, 1997

Nathan Coley's work is based around an interest in the urban environment and the public space within it. This often means addressing issues such as the meaning and relevance of contemporary monuments and the social value of architecture. Notable solo projects include: an exhibition at The Fruitmarket Gallery, Edinburgh, 2004; *Show Home*, North Shields, Newcastle-Upon-Tyne, 2003; *The Black Maria* at the Physics Room, Christchurch New Zealand as part of the 2002 *Art and Industry Urban Biennial; The Land Marked*, Centro Cultural de Belém, Lisbon 2001, and *Urban Sanctuary*, a publication for the Stills Gallery in Edinburgh, 1996. Coley has contributed work to a number of group exhibitions including: *On Reason and Emotion:*

14th *Biennale of Sydney*, 2004; *Days Like These, Tate Triennial of Contemporary British Art*, Tate Britain, 2003; *Here and Now*, Dundee Contemporary Arts, 2001; *What If, Art on the Verge of Architecture and Design*, Moderna Museet, Stockholm, 2000; *as it is*, Ikon Gallery, Birmingham, 2000 and *artranspennine98*, Tate Gallery Liverpool, 1998. In 2000, as part of the Scotland's Year of the Artist initiative, Coley made himself the unofficial artist-in-residence at Kamp van Zeist, site of the Lockerbie Trial in the Netherlands.

www.showhome.org.uk

Nathan Coley: There will be No Miracles Here, Edinburgh: Fruitmarket Gallery, Newcastle: Locus +, 2004

Days Like These, Tate Triennial of Contemporary British Art, exh. cat., London: Tate, 2003

as it is, exh. cat., Birmingham: Ikon Gallery, 2000

What if, Art on the Verge of Architecture and Design, exh. cat., Stockholm: Moderna Museet, 2000

Fourteen Churches of Münster, exh. cat., Münster: Westfälischer Kunstverein, 2000

Urban Sanctuary, Edinburgh: Stills, 1997

Adam Dant is probably best known as the creator of *Donald Parsnips Daily Journal*, a comic-strip pamphlet he drew, photocopied and handed out to passers-by in London or wherever he travelled between 1995-1999. *Donald Parsnips* also appeared as a weekly column in *The Independent on Sunday*. He also created *The Anecdotal Plan of Tate Britain* for Tate Magazine in 2001 and won the Jerwood Drawing Prize in 2002.

His works, particularly the recent series of vignettes, *The People Who Live on the Plank*, are heir to William Hogarth's popular satirical prints of the eighteenth century, in which all manner of folly and vice was paraded before viewers for their amusement and supposed moral edification.

www.drawingroom.org.uk/Projects_Past_AdamDant.htm

Tom Morton, "Adam Dant", *Frieze*, September 2003

Sarah S. King, "Adam Dant at Almine Rech", *Art in America*, January 2002

Catherine David has worked since 2002 as director of the Witte de With Centre for Contemporary Art in Rotterdam. She worked during the 1980s as a curator at the National Museum of Modern Art, Centre Georges Pompidou, Paris. Her exhibitions since the 1990s have in the most part examined art practice in relation to contemporary socio-political issues. This approach was made highly visible by her direction of *Documenta X* in 1997, and more recently in her exhibitions at the Witte de With. Her recent projects include *Ulrike Ottinger: Bild Archive*, 2004; *Contemporary Arab Representations: Cairo/Egypt*, 2003; *based upon True Stories*, 2003 and *Contemporary Arab Representations: Beirut/Lebanon*, 2002.

www.wdw.nl

Catherine David, ed., *Politics: Documenta X The Book*, Ruit: Hatje Cantz Verlag, 1997

Catherine David, ed., *Tamass: Contemporary Arab Representations: 1 Beirut/Lebanon*, Barcelona: Fondaçio Antoni Tapies, 2002; *2 Cairo/Egypt*, Rotterdam: Witte de With, 2003

Jeremy Deller's work involves collaboration with individuals and groups of people. *Acid Brass* was a series of concerts and a recording by the Williams Fairey Band playing brass band interpretations of classic acid house anthems, and *The Uses of Literacy* was an exhibition of writing and artwork made by fans of the rock band The Manic Street Preachers. Deller and artist Alan Kane have recently initiated *Folk Archive*, an ongoing project that aims to investigate the state of contemporary folk art in the United Kingdom. The *Folk Archive* was first exhibited at Tate Britain in summer 2002.

The Battle of Orgreave was a spectacular re-enactment of one of the most violent confrontations of the miners' strike in 1984. Orchestrated by Howard Giles, historical re-enactment expert and former director of English Heritage's event programme, *The Battle of Orgreave* was filmed under the direction of Mike Figgis for Artangel Media and Channel 4, and was aired on Sunday 20 October 2002. In 2004, Deller was shortlisted for the Turner Prize, for *Memory Bucket*, a mixed-media installation at ArtPace, San Antonio, documenting his travels through the state of Texas.

www.artangel.org

John Slyce, "Jeremy Deller, fables of the reconstruction", *Flash Art*, no. 228, January-February 2003

Tom Morton, "Mining for Gold", *Frieze*, issue 72, January-February 2003

Kate Bush, "Jeremy Deller, *The Battle of Orgreave*", *Artforum*, December 2001

Alex Farquharson, "Jeremy Deller, *The Battle of Orgreave*", *Frieze*, issue 61, September 2001

Books by Jeremy Deller

After The Gold Rush, San Francisco: Éditions CCAC, 2002

The English Civil War Part II, Personal accounts of the 1984-85 miners' strike, Book and CD, London: Artangel, 2004

Rod Dickinson's work explores ideas of belief and social control. Using interventions into social groups, and detailed research into moments of the past and present, he has made a series of meticulously re-enacted events that represent both the mechanisms that enable belief, and the social systems that make belief systems function. In 2002 he recreated Dr. Stanley

Milgram's infamous 1961 social psychology experiment *Obedience to Authority* at the Centre for Contemporary Art in Glasgow. Other recent work has included a re-enactment of 1974 political, anti-American, anti-capitalist sermon and miracle healing given by Jim Jones, leader of the People's Temple religious movement infamous for their mass death in their self-built "Marxist utopia" in Jonestown in Guyana in 1978. Prior to this, Dickinson's practice has also included making and documenting many of the crop circle interventions in the English countryside throughout the 1990s.

www.milgramreenactment.org
ww.jonestownreenactment.org.uk
www.circlemakers.org

Neil Mullholland, "All You Need To Know", *Frieze*, March 2003

Steve Rushton, ed., *The Milgram Re-enactment: An Anthology of Essays*, The Netherlands: Jan Van Eyck Academie, 2003

Steve Rushton, "Rights and Responsibilities", *Metropolis M*, no. 4, September 2003

Sean O'Hagan, "It's Simply Shocking", *The Observer*, 10 February 2002

Claire Doherty leads the *Situations* project as Research Fellow in Fine Art at the University of the West of England and edits this publication. From 1995-2000, she was Curator at Ikon Gallery, Birmingham and from 2000-2001 established a new programme of projects and residencies at Spike Island, Bristol. She has worked extensively as a curator and writer, as Associate Curator for FACT Foundation of Art and Creative Technology from 2001-2004 and as Associate Curator for the new visual arts facility–firstsite newsite–in Colchester.

Committed to the relationship between contemporary art, its place and publics, she has contributed essays and articles to a broad range of exhibition catalogues and art magazines. She launched *Situations* in October 2003, a programme of projects, commissions, talks, publications and events, which investigate the significance of context in the commissioning and production of contemporary art. In 2005, she will curate the eight new public art commissions for Bristol City Council.

www.situations.org.uk

Articles and books by Claire Doherty

"I Never Meant to Stay", *Art Monthly*, November 2004

"The institution is dead! Long live the institution! Contemporary Art and New Institutionalism", *Engage 15*, 2004

"social work / social sculpture", *Supermanual: The Incomplete Guide to the Superchannel*, exh. cat., Liverpool: FACT, 2000

"Out of Here: Curating Beyond the Edifice", in Gavin Wade, ed., *Curating in the 21st Century*, New Art Gallery Walsall, and University of Wolverhampton, 2000

"Soft Cities", *Contemporary Visual Arts Magazine*, November 2000

as it is, exh. cat., Birmingham: Ikon Gallery, 2000

Paul Domela is Deputy Chief Executive of *Liverpool Biennial* where he is responsible for the *International* exhibition and the Learning and Inclusion programme. In 2004 he also co-curated the Liverpool/Manchester section of *Shrinking Cities*, Berlin. In collaboration with International Foundation Manifesta, he initiated *Coffee Break*, a series of discussions around visual art and contemporary cultural practice in a changing Europe. A publication is forthcoming in spring 2005.

www.biennial.org.uk

Jimmie Durham became active in the early 1960s in theatre, performance, and literature in the US Civil Rights Movement. Durham's first solo art exhibit was in Austin, Texas in 1965. In 1969, Durham moved to Geneva, Switzerland, returning to the US in 1973. Durham was a political organiser in the American Indian Movement from 1973-1980 and director of the International Indian Treaty Council and representative at the United Nations. From 1981-1983, he became the director of the Foundation for the Community of Artists (FCA) in New York City. Three years later he moved to Mexico, returning to Europe in 1994.

His poetry has been published in *Harper's Anthology of Twentieth Century Native American Poetry* and various small magazines. His book of poems, *Columbus Day* was published in 1983 by West End Press, Minneapolis. His essays and articles have been published in *The Los Angeles Times*, *Art Forum*, *Black Scholar*, and *Third Text* among others. Durham has exhibited in Museum van Hedendaagse Kunst, Gent; Palais des Beaux Arts, Brussels; Institute of Contemporary Art, London; *Documenta*, Kassel; *Whitney Biennial*; Kunstverein München and the *Venice Biennale*.

Jimmie Durham, London: Phaidon Press, 1995

Books by Jimmie Durham

Stoneheart, Kitakyushyu: CCA, 2001

Between the Furniture and the Building, Cologne: Walter König, 1998

Der Verfuhrer und der Steinerne Gast, Vienna: Springer, 1996

A Certain Lack of Coherence, London: Kala Press, 1994

The East London Coelecanth, London: Bookworks, 1992

FURTHER Up in the Air is a long-term project, spanning half a decade, developed and run by artist/curators Leo Fitzmaurice and Neville Gabie. Evolving from an earlier project, *Up in the Air*, this project expanded the vision with nationally and internationally recognised artists and writers responding to the same Sheil Park site in North Liverpool. For *FURTHER*, Linosa Close, the last tower block on the site, was the focus of 18 artists and writers from a broad spectrum of disciplines who worked in three phases of residencies.

www.furtherafield.org.uk

FURTHER Up in the Air, Liverpool: Further a Field, 2003

Ian Hunt, "161 Live Writer", *Art & Architechture*, no. 58, 2003

Allesandra Paudice, "A Block of Art Flats", *Casa Vogue*, no. 16, June 2003

Danny Louise, "Road Map", *AN Magazine*, June 2003

Graham Parker, "Further up in The Air", *Art Monthly*, November 2002

Hadley Freeman, "Self Denial of a Literary Sort", *The Guardian*, 26 September 2002

Henrietta Thompson, "High Art", *Blueprint*, September 2002

Charlie Gere is Reader in New Media Research in the Institute of Cultural Research, Lancaster University, Chair of Computers and the History of Art (CHArt) and the director of Computer Arts, Contexts, Histories, etc. (CACHe), an Arts and Humanities Research Board funded project looking at the history of early British computer art. He is the author of *Digital Culture* (Reaktion Books, 2002) and is currently undertaking research into the relation between art and speed from the early nineteenth century up to the present day, to be published as a book, *Art, Time and Technology: Histories of the Disappearing Body*, by Berg in 2005.

Charlie Gere and Cathy Gere, eds., special isuue "The Brain in a Vat", *Studies in History and Philosophy of Science Part C: Studies in History and Philosophy of Biological and Biomedical Sciences*, vol. 35, issue 2, June 2004

Thomas Hirschhorn is best known for his constructions of foil, plastic, cardboard and packing tape that appear both in art institutions and in public places. They gather together references to philosophy and popular culture, economics and poetry, artists and fashion designers, in a bombardment of information and imagery.

The initial effect is overwhelming, but close attention reveals careful explorations of the contemporary socio-cultural climate, and of the work of various left-leaning intellectuals including Gilles Deleuze and Georges Bataille. Hirschhorn's *Bataille Monument* was part of *Documenta 11*, 2002 and he recently took part in *Common Wealth* at Tate Modern, 2003, contributing *Hotel Democracy*, which assembled and housed different manifestations of the democratic spirit.

www.bataillemonument.de

Bataille Maschine, en deux volumes, Berlin: Merve Verlag, 2003

Documenta 11; Platform 5, exh. cat., Ruit: Hatje Cantz Verlag, 2002

Dan Fox, "Documenta XI", *Frieze*, September 2002

Linda Nochlin, "Platform muse, Documented Success", *Artforum*, September 2002

Jan Estep, "Reading Hirschhorn: A problem of his knowledge, or Weakness as a virtue", *Afterall*, no. 9, 2004

Miwon Kwon is Associate Professor in the Department of Art History at University of California, Los Angeles and is residence faculty in the MFA in Visual Art Program at Vermont College. Her research and writings engage several disciplines including contemporary art, architecture, public art and urban studies. She is a founding editor and publisher of *Documents*, a journal of art, culture, and criticism, and serves on the advisory board of *October* magazine. She is the author of *One Place after Another: Site-Specific Art and Locational Identity*, MIT Press, 2002.

Maria Lind was the director of Kunstverein München from 2002-2004 where she, together with a curatorial team–consisting at different times of Sören Grammel, Katharina Schlieben, Tessa Praun, Ana Paula Cohen and Judith Schwarzbartran–ran a programme which involved artists such as Deimantas Narkevicius, Oda Projesi, Bojan Sarcevic, Philippe Parreno and Marion von Osten. The format of a retrospective, or survey, was explored in a year long retrospective with Christine Borland 2002-2003, only ever showing one piece at a time and a retrospective project in the form of a seven-day long workshop with Rirkrit Tiravanija. The group project *Totally motivated: A sociocultural maneouvre* was a collaboration between five curators and ten artists looking at the relationship between 'amateur' and 'professional' art and culture. From 1997-2001 she was curator at Moderna Museet in Stockholm and, in 1998, co-curator of *Manifesta 2*, Europe's biennale of contemporary art.

Responsible for Moderna Museet Projekt, Lind worked with artists on a series of 29 commissions that took place in a temporary project-space, within or beyond the Museum in Stockholm. There she also curated *What if: Art on the Verge of Architecture and Design*, filtered by Liam Gillick. Lind was one of 10 contributing curators to Phaidon's *Fresh Cream* book, and she has contributed widely to magazines including *Index* and *Site*, as well as to *Frieze*, *Art Monthly* and *Parkett*.

www.kunstverein-muenchen.de

Articles and books by Maria Lind

"Models of Criticality", in *Contextualize*, exh. cat., Hamburg: Kunstverein, 2002

"Exchange and Transformation" in *Critical Interventions/Biennale of Sydney*, 2002, Sydney: Artspace Visual Arts Centre Ld., Woolloomooloo, 2002

"Selected Nodes in a Network of Thoughts on Curating", in Carin Kuoni, et al, *Words of Wisdom: A Curator's Vade Mecum on Contemporary Art*, New York: Independent Curators International, 2001

"Learning from Art and Artists", in Gavin Wade, ed., *Curating in the 21st Century*, Walsall: The New Art Gallery, 2000

"Spatial facsimiles and ambient spaces: some reflections on site-specificity in contemporary art", *Parkett, no. 54*, 1998-1999

James Lingwood has been Co-Director, with Michael Morris, of Artangel, since 1991, and Artangel Media, since 2000. He has commissioned and produced a range of projects for Artangel from Rachel Whiteread's *House*, 1993, to Tony Oursler's *The Influence Machine*, 2000, Michael Landy's *Break Down*, 2001, and film and television projects such as Matthew Barney's *Cremaster 4*, 1995, Douglas Gordon's *Feature Film*, 1999, and Steve McQueen's *Caribs' Leap / Western Deep*, 2002. Lingwood also curates exhibitions and projects for museums in Europe and North America–most recently retrospectives of the work of Thomas Schütte, Vija Celmins and Julião Sarmento, *Bernd & Hilla Becher/Robert Smithson–Field Trips*, Juan Muñoz's *Double Bind* at Tate Modern 2001 and a survey of Susan Hiller's work at Baltic, Gateshead, 2004.

www.artangel.org

Gerrie van Noord, *Off-Limits: 40 Artangel Projects*, London: Artangel and Merrel, 2002

Cuauhtémoc Medina is an art critic, curator and historian. He is researcher at the Instituto de Investigaciones Estéticas at the National University of Mexico and Associate Curator of Latin American Art Collections at Tate, London. He is also member of Teratoma, a group of curators, critics and anthropologists based in Mexico City. In 2002 he organised Francis Alÿs' action *When Faith Moves Mountains*, curated the exhibition *20 million Mexicans Can´t be Wrong* at the South London Gallery, 2002, and was one of the researchers for the *International* exhibition at the *Liverpool Biennial* 2004.

www.geocities.com/cmedin/

Mejor Vida Corp. was initiated by artist Minerva Cuevas. Her practice is focused around public intervention and corporate critique, which are integrated with her art through the subversive visual and socio-political messages her works convey, and the inclusive participatory elements of endeavours in urban civic and virtual space. Cuevas uses images, objects and actions as a means of stimulating reflection, asking members of the local and global public to reconsider their relation to their everyday environment. Principally, this venture has focused on economic and social activities–namely those of governments and trans-national corporations–and the ways in which the mass media is implicated in these activities as a powerful mediating element.

www.irational.org/minerva
www.minervacuevas.org

Cuauhtémoc Medina, "Recent Political Forms, Radical Pursuits in Mexico"and Hans Ulrich Obrist, "Conversation with Minerva Cuevas" both at above web links.

14th Biennale of Sydney: Emotion and Reason , exh. cat., Sydney: Biennale of Sydney, 2004

Aleksandra Mir, *Corporate Mentality*, New York: Lukas & Sternberg Inc., 2003

Aleksandra Mir's practice focuses on collaborations with a wide variety of institutions, the public and the academic realms, science, media and business. For each new work, a new model of production is developed. Mir has collaborated with various art institutions in the United Kingdom: Centre for Contemporary Art, Transmission Gallery, The Modern Institute, Glasgow; Fruitmarket Gallery, Edinburgh; Waygood Gallery, Newcastle; Barbican Centre, Cubitt, Serpentine Gallery and Institute of Contemporary Art; London. She also held a residency at Delfina studios in the spring of 2001, where her work on *Plane Landing* and relationship with Compton Verney began.

Aleksandra Mir's works often take the form of social processes. The work of art is an exercise that operates in everyday life; a humanistic and playful organism with a large social appetite. The work's course of events is often started by Mir in relation to both specific events and the work's location. From this starting point the discussion is extended to more general conditions like traditions, norms and categorization.

www.aleksandramir.info

Aleksandra Mir, *Corporate Mentality*, ed., New York: Lukas & Sternberg Inc., 2003

Will Bradley, "Life and Times", *Frieze*, issue 75, 2003

Gilda Williams, "Aleksandra Mir from A to Z", *Art Monthly*, no. 266, 2003

13th Biennale of Sydney: (The World May Be) Fantastic, exh. cat., Sydney: Biennale of Sydney, 2002

Ralph Rugoff, ed., *How Extraordinary that the World Exists!*, San Francisco: CCAC Wattis Institute, 2002

Emma Mahoney, *Democracy!*, exh. cat., London: Royal College of Art, 2000

Oda Projesi began their work in 1997 in Galata, an old neighbourhood in Istanbul. The project is still based in Istanbul, now with ties to other locations worldwide. The Oda Projesi team is composed of Özge Acikkol, Gunes Savas and Secil Yersel. The main aim of the project is to draw on aspects of everyday life–social gatherings, meal-times, discussions–to expand the possibilities for a social sculpture.

Oda Projesi have extended their practice by initiating process-based and participatory projects at the Istanbul Museum of

Contemporary Art: Project 4L, the *Fourth Gwangju Biennial* in South Korea, Kunstverein München and Kunstprojekte_Riem in Germany, and most recently the *Istanbul Biennial*, 2003 and the *Venice Biennale*, 2003.

www.odaprojesi.com

Irit Rogoff is Chair of Art History and Visual Culture at Goldsmith's College, London. Rogoff writes extensively on the conjunctions of contemporary art with critical theory with particular reference to issues of colonialism, cultural difference and performativity. She is author of *Terra Infirma: Geography's Visual Culture*, 2000; editor of *The Divided Heritage: Themes and Problems in German Modernism*, 1991 and co-editor, with Daniel Sherman, of *Museum Culture: Histories, Theories, Spectacles*, 1994. Rogoff is director of an international Arts and Humanities Research Board project "Translating the Image: Cross-cultural Contemporary Arts" housed at Goldsmith's College. Her current research project investigates audience participation in contemporary art spaces.

Articles and books by Irit Rogoff

"Looking Away: Participations in Visual Culture" in Gavin Butt, ed., *Art After Criticism*, Oxford: Blackwell, 2004

"We–Mutualities, Collectivities, Participations", *I Promise It's Political*, Cologne: Museum Ludwig, 2002

"Not There Of", *ARS 2001*, Helsinki: Kiasma Museum of Contemporary Art, 2001

Terra Infirma: Geography's Visual Culture, London and New York: Routledge, 2000

Becky Shaw looks for new ways to understand and explore the relationship between the artist and public, individual and group and the individual and wider society. This ongoing project involves entering work, leisure, health and education contexts, finding live, written and visual ways to explore and create situations. Following a practical and theoretical doctorate in 1998, projects have included *The Generosity Project*, a critical exploration of the artist's role as 'do-er of good', for Kunstprijs Amstelveen, a re-production of an ultramarine factory using leisure activity as opposed to hard labour for Grizedale Arts, and a harnessing of exerciser's energy to power a commercial cappuccino bar in Stratford Gallery and Visitors Centre.

A recent response to a residency in the Department of Social and Policy Sciences, University of Bath, involved Shaw becoming her own receptionist. Often frustrated by the circumstances of artistic practice, Shaw creates structures of distribution through *Static*, an organisation dedicated to building discursive and critical activity in Liverpool and beyond. She co-edits *Static*'s online *Pamphlet* with co-director and architect, Paul Sullivan.

www.static-ops.org
www.occasionaltrade.com

Alan Dunn, "So Near", *Static Pamphlet 1*, 25 May, 2003

Becky Shaw, Mark Ramsden, "Stazione di Topolo: Changing the World or Escaping it?", *Third Text*, Spring, 2003

Becky Shaw, "The Architecture of Collaboration", *The Journal of Dementia Care*, vol. 11, no. 6, 2003

Richard Wentworth is a sculptor and photographer, an urban explorer, walker and talker. He has lived in King's Cross for some 25 years. Wentworth's work is an ongoing conversation with his native habitat, fuelled by daily walks down the Caledonian Road and expeditions into the hinterlands of King's Cross. He has played a leading role in New British Sculpture since the end of the 1970s. His work, exploring the notion of objects and their use as part of our day-to-day experiences, has altered the traditional definition of sculpture. This post-dadaist approach was also present in *Thinking Aloud*, the National Touring Exhibition, curated by Wentworth, which gathered together disparate uncanny items as well as works of art.

He is Master of Drawing at the Ruskin School of Drawing and Fine Art, University of Oxford. His works have been shown in various institutions such as the Serpentine Gallery, Whitechapel Art Gallery, Hayward Gallery, London, and Arnolfini, Bristol, the Israel Museum, Jerusalem, Institute of Contemporary Art, Philadelphia, Irish Museum of Modern Art, Dublin, Museum Moderner Kunst Stiftung Ludwig, Vienna and Musée d'Art Moderne de la Ville de Paris.

www.artangel.org.uk

Jonathan Jones, "Richard Wentworth", *The Guardian*, 19 September 2002

Gerrie van Noord, *Off-Limits: 40 Artangel Projects*, London: Artangel and Merrel, 2002

Richard Wentworth, Thinking Aloud, exh. cat., London: Hayward Gallery, 1998